PERFECT ENEMIES

PERFECT ENEMIES

The Religious Right, the Gay Movement, and the Politics of the 1990s

John Gallagher

and

Chris Bull

CROWN PUBLISHERS, INC.

New York

Published by Crown Publishers, Inc., 201 East 50th Street, New
York, New York 10022. Member of the Crown Publishing Group.
Random House, Inc. New York, Toronto,
London, Sydney, Auckland
http://www.randomhouse.com/
CROWN is a trademark of Crown Publishers, Inc.

Printed in the United States of America

Design by Deborah Kerner

Library of Congress Cataloging-in-Publication Data
is available upon request.

ISBN 0-517-70198-7

10 9 8 7 6 5 4 3 2 1

First Edition

To Mom, Dad and Hans

C.B.

To Michael

J.G.

Contents

Acknowledgments

T HIS BOOK WOULD NOT HAVE BEEN written without the support of our editor at Crown, Michael Denneny. Not only did he help shape the very structure of the book, but he brilliantly shepherded it through the difficult writing process, especially when we were unsure of our direction. We also wish to thank our agent, Gail Ross, who was willing to take a chance on us as novice book writers and who, with savvy and good humor, guided us through the daunting process of finding a home for the book.

This book is the result of years of reporting on and writing about gay politics and the religious right. Along the way, we have gained valuable insights that helped form the basis for our ideas from hundreds of activists, academics, policy makers, and journalists. They are too numerous to name here, but they all helped make this book possible.

By reading various drafts and chapters of the book, several people were particularly helpful to the editorial process by providing their unique insights. Among them were Tom Mallon, David Kirp, Ann Imbrie, Ed Alwood, Janice Castro, Andrea Sachs, and Cathy Kudlick. Hans Johnson, whose detailed knowledge of the subject matter is unparalleled, provided crucial editorial comments to every chapter.

Our editors at *The Advocate* generously provided us with the time to complete the book. Christine Lenschow, Mary Conway, Erik Piepenburg, and Carol Keys at People for the American Way's library, an invaluable resource for information on the religious right, graciously gave of their time in the research stage of the book. Michael Denneny's assistant, John Clark, was unfailingly polite, patient, and efficient. James M. Drozdale of Sullivan and Cromwell went out of his way to dig up critical military documents for us. Robin Miller provided voluminous background information about Colorado's antigay initiative. Donna Red Wing supplied crucial information about the campaigns in Oregon. Human Rights Campaign's sharp communications director, David Smith, found several years of fund-raising letters. Jeremy Riva's computer expertise saved the book from potential disasters.

⁓ In addition, Chris Bull would like to thank a number of people who provided perhaps the most important element of all, friendship. Ed Alwood, Paul Amato, Andy Blauvelt, Michael Bronski, Jerry Cabrera, Jeffrey Escoffier, Marc Geller, Richard Laermer, Matthew Lore, Ann Imbrie, Eric Lee, Tom Mallon, Neil Miller, Fred Morris, Wickie Stamps, and Eric Yesson gave me personal support and intellectual inspiration, as did my family. John Gallagher, whose writing and analytical skills never cease to amaze me, is the best collaborator and friend I could have.

⁓ John Gallagher would like to thank his friends for their encouragement from the time the book was conceived through the research and the writing. First and foremost, I am blessed to have Michael Bitterman as a partner. His love and support sustained me throughout the entire process. Sabi Inderkum, Laureen Asato, Helen Cooluris, Jean-Clare Plebani, Kathleen Oshiro, and Melissa Rubinsky helped in more ways than I could ever describe, and I am lucky to count them among my friends. Finally, my gratitude to Chris Bull, whose idea this book was. His friendship made the arduous task of writing a book a pleasure, and even fun; his tenacity and attention to detail enrich the final product beyond measure.

Introduction

THERE IS A GREAT BATTLE RAGING in America today. The cause of the hostility is one the nation's founders could never have imagined: gay rights. On one side of the battlefield are religious conservatives who believe they are taking a last stand against moral decline; on the other, gays and lesbians who believe that they are fighting for the basic civil liberties guaranteed by the Constitution. After years of skirmishes, two groups that had been largely unknown to the public and unnoticed by the press seem suddenly to be everywhere, locked in combat. That combat promises to be part of the political landscape for years to come.

This book chronicles the emergence of gay rights as *the* social issue—and perhaps the most divisive political issue—of the 1990s. Starting from the waning days of the Bush administration through the presidential campaign of 1996, the status of gay people in society has become a matter of increasingly heated debate. Some of the most intense controversies have taken place at the highest levels of government, most notably in the showdown over gays in the military. Other battles have been local, such as the antigay ballot measures in

Oregon, Colorado, and Idaho. Each of the local fights is part of one enormous war over the place of gays in American society.

The most fervent opponents of gay rights are conservative Christians who have been dubbed the religious right. As a group, they are more diverse dogmatically than that title makes them out to be. Evangelicals, who constitute the largest segment of the religious right, emphasize salvation through faith in God's grace. Among their allies, fundamentalists believe in a literal interpretation of Scripture, and charismatics rely on direct inspiration from God in the form of healing powers and speaking in tongues. Moreover, the ranks of the religious right include a smattering from other Christian traditions, particularly conservative Roman Catholics, to whom leaders of the right are making a strong outreach effort. They are all concerned, with reason, about the torn moral fabric of the nation. They are upset that their faith sometimes appears to others to be an embarrassment or, worse, a flaw. Drawing from biblical condemnations of homosexuality, they see gay rights as the embodiment of everything they deplore about modern life. But the religious right is not a monolith. Some prominent evangelical leaders refuse to see homosexuality as the direst threat to the nation, but rather view it as another in a long line of sins. Even among leaders of the religious right who do not shrink from blasting homosexuality, there is a wide divergence. For some, gay rights is just part, though a key part, of their overall complaint against secular society. Others are fixed monomaniacally on homosexuality as the source of all evil in society. Some rely on a traditional view of religious morality to condemn gays and lesbians; others concoct wild allegations and statistics to deny the validity of gay rights. However, they are united on one point: the fierceness of their rhetoric never diminishes.

The gay movement is just as diverse. Although gay rights has been considered a liberal cause, a significant number of gays and lesbians identify themselves as conservative. While some see themselves in the vanguard of redefining society and its institutions, many others—perhaps a majority—want nothing more than to become equal members of contemporary culture. Like conservative Christians, gays and lesbians do not speak with one voice, except on one matter—their right to live their lives free from discrimination and fear.

Equally important, individuals on both sides share many of the same values, of hard work, family, volunteerism, and even church. Yet in the ongoing debate about gay rights, "values" is the property to which the religious right lays sole claim. The way religious conservatives view the phrase *family values* in the political arena, virtue has become a partisan commodity. They have managed to shape the debate over gay rights and have in many ways defined the gay community, however falsely. Much of the battle over gay rights is a refutation of charges made by conservative Christians against gays and lesbians. Constantly on the defensive, gay activists find themselves responding to an agenda that has been laid out for them, not one that they would choose for themselves.

This battle over gay rights comes at a time when gays and lesbians are attaining unprecedented acceptance in our society. After years of purveying the worst stereotypes of gay life, mass entertainment has begun to portray gays and lesbians as normal, even admirable people. The national press regularly provides favorable, even sympathetic, coverage to gay issues. More and more businesses are happy to sanction gay employee groups, and some have gone so far as to extend benefits to the partners of their gay workers just as they have done to spouses of their heterosexual workers. The gay community, and especially gay culture, has flowered, extending its influence far beyond its own borders. It is impossible to overestimate the enormity of the strides that gays and lesbians have made toward acceptance over the past decade.

Inevitably, these gains had to meet with a backlash. With their growing ability to organize and mobilize Christian voters, leaders of the religious right such as Pat Robertson reacted not in the cultural arena, where their relative absence put them at a disadvantage, but rather in the political arena. The effort toward broad acceptance of gays and lesbians was narrowed down to the law and the ballot box. Unable to stop the pro-gay trend any other way, conservative Christians have tried to legislate a change in people's minds. Just beginning to flex their own political muscle, gays and lesbians have often been on the defensive, trying to keep to a minimum the erosion of their gains.

This culture war, as it has been dubbed, is a replay of the battles of the 1960s, as conservatives strive to undo the changes they believe the counterculture wrought on society, chief among them the relaxing of sexual codes and the birth of gay liberation. To that fight, they have brought the fund-raising strategies of the 1970s, which found that the proper combination of databases, slick mailings, and heated rhetoric could produce an unimagined financial bonanza. Gay rights quickly emerged as one of the hottest issues, guaranteed to generate a substantial return for evangelical leaders, and has remained a favorite target ever since. In a more modest way, gay organizations have responded in kind, painting the threat of the religious right to gays, and society as a whole, in the darkest possible terms.

Yet, in many ways, these two groups are remarkably alike in their tactics and their place in the political system. Both are true believers in the righteousness of their cause, setting up ideological clashes that electoral politics seldom see. Both have a limited base of natural supporters and have to devise ways of broadening their appeal. Both work best when they have a threat to work against. Both have captured significant power within their respective political parties and are scrambling to expand their leverage from beyond their peripheral positions. And both groups are hardly the favorites of the majority of Americans, who have long viewed them with suspicion and ignorance.

The participation of both groups in the political debate should be cause for celebration. Both the gay community and conservative Christians have for too long felt alienated from the system, and their willingness to engage it is a positive contribution. Unfortunately, the bitterness of the fight has done little to shed light on either side. Underlying the debate are competing values of private sexual behavior and public religious standards. But the heat of the rhetoric obscures those arguments. Slanderous, unsupported charges, especially from the religious right, and characterizations have come to replace civil discourse. The battle over gay rights shows in a nutshell why Americans currently have such a low opinion of politics. The emphasis is on scoring points, on winning at all costs, without respect for the other side or even for the truth. It is, as one leader of the religious right unhappily concluded, easier to nauseate than educate. As some leaders on both sides have discovered, it is easiest to raise money when your opponent is demonized out of all recognition.

Religious conservatives and gay activists have become perfect enemies, propelling each other's movement and affecting the politics of the country as a whole. This book is meant to educate readers about both the gay community and the religious right, their similarities and their differences, their flaws and their strengths. As journalists, we have tried to be as evenhanded as possible, assessing not only the successes and failures, but the implications of their struggles for American politics. Most of all, we have tried to show the pitfalls in the debate as it now stands.

PERFECT ENEMIES

CHAPTER 1

The Battle Lines Are Drawn

THE ORIGINS OF THE TWO POLITICAL movements at the heart of America's culture war are as humble as they are contemporary. The cultural ferment of the 1960s stands as the prelude to the battle to come. The first rousings of the modern gay movement date back to a sultry summer night in June 1969 when a ragtag group of drag queens and teenage hustlers rebelled against police harassment outside the Stonewall Inn, a Greenwich Village gay bar. The gays and lesbians who led the disturbance had little more to rely on than their anger. In a time when police raids on gay bars were the norm, they were largely at the mercy of hostile city officials. Routinely described as freaks and perverts in the press (one newspaper mockingly described the protesters as "Queen Bees"), they had little political organization to speak of, were characterized as mentally ill by the mainstream of the medical profession, and were generally banished from jobs and families if their sexuality was discovered. The political weakness and precarious social position of gays and lesbians at the time of Stonewall remains a fact that the religious right, intent on painting them as privileged and pathological, has been loath to accept.

The founding of the Christian evangelical movement was equally inauspicious. While gays and lesbians were rioting in New York City, Pat Robertson and Jerry Falwell, who would one day come to serve as a potent one-two antigay punch, were preaching in obscurity with little following, profoundly ambivalent about entering the political realm. Robertson had refused to aid his own father's senatorial reelection campaign on the grounds that to do so would be to participate in an evil political system, while Falwell inveighed against the clergy's participation in and support of the civil rights movement.

Even in Republican circles, evangelical Christians were still widely considered part of the crackpot fringe for their extreme politics and faith in the inerrancy of the Bible. In a time when liberal politics and cultural experimentation were at an apex, Robertson, Falwell, and the fledgling evangelical political movement seemed like a throwback to a bygone era. Much like gays and lesbians, evangelicals had yet to see themselves as a self-contained political force. Moreover, evangelicals lacked a galvanizing event like Stonewall from which all progress could henceforth be measured.

⮑ Less than twenty-five years later, during the 1992 presidential campaign, both movements had burst into the center of America's cultural wars, pitted against each other, often in unfair and damaging ways, as diametrically opposed voting blocks. With Robertson, who had by then eclipsed Falwell as the most powerful evangelical voice in the country, as its lead general, the religious right had become the most powerful special interest group in America. By the 1996 election, every serious Republican presidential candidate would have to come to the religious right on bended knee.

Though their financial resources and number of supporters were dwarfed by those of the religious right, gay activists had become darlings of the media, routinely garnering positive coverage for the first time in the movement's history. Gays and lesbians had become a central, though still controversial, constituency within the Democratic Party. For the gay movement and the religious right, the obscurity of the late 1960s and early 1970s found their recompense in the visibility of the 1990s. Gay activists and religious conservatives have long had the unmistakable feel of smoldering archenemies. But how did these two mortal foes go from the margins to the mainstream of American politics in such a relatively short time?

The explanation lies in the unique politics of both movements and in the media coverage of them. In the 1960s and 1970s, the leaderships largely eschewed electoral politics. Derided by mainstream America, they were, with ample justification, deeply suspicious of the mainstream political process. Both saw politics as essentially corrupting, but for different reasons. The religious right wanted to remove itself from this world, while left-leaning gays wanted to restructure the world radically. Yet, both were largely content to organize underneath the general public's radar.

The media contributed to the movements' marginalization by failing to depart from newly coined, but still stereotyped, images and myths in their depictions of both groups. Only when journalists realized that the growth of these two movements was creating clashes that would make good copy did they step up—and improve—their coverage. Yet the media, by and large, still failed to move beyond conflict to create more complex portraits of the two movements or to assess the potential impact of their respective aims, thus leaving each group to characterize each other's objectives (and often to distort them in the midst of heated political battles).

During much of the last quarter century, both sides were busy establishing their own independent communications systems, press, political organizations, fund-raising apparatuses, and political strategies—the bread and butter of political movements. Thus it was almost inevitable that, given the right circumstances, they would burst onto the national scene as well-armed foes fighting incendiary battles that the general public—those who were in neither camp—viewed with bewilderment. For many Americans, it was like being deluged with competing theories of advanced physics without first having mastered basic math.

The newness of the two movements, alone, does not explain their parallel growth. From the ERA battles of the 1970s to the

AIDS wars of the 1980s, from the elections of Jimmy Carter to George Bush, each has used the other as fodder for the growth of its own movement. Seeking hot buttons to win converts to its cause, each could alternatively invoke the "gay threat" to American families or the "radical right" threat to the health and happiness of gays and lesbians. The tactic was financially lucrative, especially for the television ministries of the religious right. It made up for in success what it lacked in fairness.

⌐⌐ The histories of the religious right and the gay movement, of course, predate the 1960s, when tumultuous politics and rapid social change helped create cohesive and easily recognizable political movements with discernible agendas. Gay and lesbian communities first began to appear after the demobilization of World War II, usually around military installations in major American ports. The earliest official gay group, the Mattachine Society, which was founded by Communist organizer Harry Hay in 1950, served primarily as a self-help group for gays and lesbians coming to terms with their sexual identity, and only secondarily as an advocacy group. Led by activists Franklin Kameny and Jack Nichols, one of the earliest Mattachine demonstrations to receive press coverage took place in front of the White House in May of 1965. (The respectable suit-and-tie attire of the marchers would give way to tie-dye and beads just a few years later.) Since Mattachine was composed primarily of men, the Daughters of Bilitis was founded in 1955 to provide much the same function for lesbians.

Though urban gay enclaves have thrived for decades—with their own cultural scene, night life, and community—many gays and lesbians were cut off from mainstream society with virtually no political representation, locally or nationally. Many felt compelled by social and economic pressure to settle down and marry an opposite-sex partner. It was not until the late 1960s and early 1970s that significant numbers of gays and lesbians felt comfortable enough to leave or forgo heterosexual unions, migrate to big cities, and lead openly gay lives. That migration, in turn, contributed to the birth of gay liberation, especially in the aftermath of Stonewall.

By contrast, conservative evangelicals have played a more visible role in American history since its founding, which dates back to New England Puritanism. According to the religious historian George Marsden, evangelicalism did not metamorphose into a conservative rebellion against secular liberalism until the 1920s, in the revolt against growing support for evolutionary theory. Under the banner of fundamentalism, orthodoxies that cut across traditionally strict Protestant denominational boundaries were united for the first time, notes Marsden, "by their strict opposition to attempts to bring Christianity into line with modern thought." In 1925, the American Civil Liberties Union sued the state of Tennessee over a law forbidding public schools from teaching evolution in biology classes, claiming it lacked the authority to enforce such a law. Sarcastically dubbed the "monkey trial" by journalist H. L. Mencken, the "Scopes" case would prefigure many of the empty debates over sexual politics starting in the 1960s. The law in question was never intended to be enforced, and evolution was only obliquely mentioned in school textbooks.

The trial had the effect of causing evangelicals to retreat noticeably from the political stage, as William Jennings Bryan, a prominent evangelical social reformer and three-time Democratic presidential candidate, was thoroughly embarrassed by Clarence Darrow, the ACLU's silver-tongued attorney, when Bryan took the stand to defend his strict biblical views. Mencken took great glee in ridiculing the devout Bryan, who died a week after the trial concluded, as a know-nothing Bible-thumper. As historian Garry Wills has pointed out, Bryan merely wanted to make the point that evolutionary theory had the potential to give rise to a mean-spirited "survival of the fittest" attitude among young people. Bryan was hardly the contemporary religious right's idea of a true-blue conservative. In fact, he was far more politically liberal than Mencken: he supported women's suffrage, Mencken did not. Nor did Bryan espouse overtly anti-Semitic views, as Mencken did.

Darrow and Mencken saw the Scopes trial as the death knell of fundamentalism in America. But like the critics of the religious right to come, they severely underestimated the movement's tenacity and staying power. In fact, historian Martin Marty traces *the origin* of modern fundamentalism to the trial. While chastened religious conservatives did retreat from the political world for a time, they hardly died away, as the throngs of followers whom Father Charles Coughlin attracted just a few years later demonstrated. Activists adept at blending revivalist rhetoric with right-wing politics continued to preach, found colleges, publish magazines, and write books. Under their influence, schools quietly went about exorcising evolution from textbooks until the 1960s, when science began to make a comeback. The misunderstandings of that famous trial established the tone for the battles that would resurface decades later. From then on, it was not enough to win; both sides seemed intent on portraying the other as, in Mencken's words, "the forces of darkness."

The ideological forerunners of what has come to be known as the religious right are a long line of religious crusaders who share what historian Richard Hofstadter termed the "paranoid style." Though the politics and techniques of the preachers vary widely, they share a vision of America dominated by the forces of good and evil, both from inside and outside its borders, leaving little room for political accommodation. Coughlin, a Catholic radio preacher who achieved a huge following in the 1930s and 1940s, cloaked fascist politics in Christian garb. Like the televangelists who would burst onto the scene later in the century, Coughlin understood that right-wing antiestablishment views and savvy exploitation of the media were the keys to building a political empire. Coughlin's career was cut short when a paramilitary strike on the nation's capital, which he had encouraged to overthrow the Roosevelt administration, was foiled by the FBI. (The plot, in which members of the American Legion, with a number of corporate supporters, hoped to recruit several thousand fascist-style militia members to take over the federal government, ended when several of its leaders, including Coughlin, were interrogated by federal agents.)

Twenty years later, Billy James Hargis came closer to translating a fundamentalist worldview into mainstream politics. The segregationist and anticommunist leader of the Christian Crusade,

Hargis made headlines in the 1950s for floating millions of balloons bearing Scriptures over the Iron Curtain from West Germany to Czechoslovakia. Hargis and Carl McIntire, leader of the Twentieth Century Reformation, charged that the Federal Council of Churches was an outpost for Marxism.

While the early Christian right groups were motivated primarily by anti-Semitism, anticommunism, and the defense of racial segregation, they also expressed fear about changes in the nuclear family and the relationship between the sexes. By the 1970s, when open espousals of anti-Semitism and racism were no longer socially acceptable, blacks and Jews were largely replaced by gays and feminists. But until the arrival of Robertson and Falwell, Billy Graham, a political and theological moderate who boasted of drawing opposition from "extreme fundamentalists of the right and extreme liberals of the left," represented the public face of evangelicalism in America.

Any comparison of the rise of the evangelical political and gay rights movements must take into account the huge built-in advantage that conservative Christians bring to contemporary politics. Not only can the religious right draw upon the millions of Americans who consider themselves "born-again Christians" in their appeals for support, but upon a religious and moral tradition that dates back centuries and condemns any nonmarital sexuality. While the gay liberation movement and the broader sexual liberationist movements of the 1960s remain extremely potent and visionary forces in American politics, they are no match as yet for two millennia of heavily accreted Christian teachings classifying homosexuality as immoral. Fundamentalism, of course, is hardly the only brand of Christian theology. But many liberal denominations, still uncomfortable with homosexuality, have largely shied away from direct challenges to the religious right's increasingly strident and self-confident claims to representing *the* Christian position on crucial issues and candidacies.

⁓ Much of the contemporary religious right's political motivation can be seen as revolt against the 1960s. The liberal Warren Supreme Court dealt a series of devastating blows to conservative evangelicals throughout the decade. In a 1968 ruling that would have made William Jennings Bryan turn in his grave, the high court struck down an Arkansas ban on the teaching of evolution in public schools as a violation of the constitutional separation of church and state. In *Engel v. Vitale,* the court struck down state-sponsored prayer recitations in the schools. And in the 1971 ruling *Lemon v. Kurtzman,* the court ruled that state support for teacher salaries at parochial schools, even when the subject was secular, represented "excessive entanglement" between church and state.

Much like the modernism of the 1920s, the 1960s presented a plethora of changes, from the proliferation of divorce and pornography to the repeal of state sodomy laws to the removal of religion from the public schools, that these religious leaders attributed to secular humanism. But it was the various liberation movements of the 1960s that caused right-wing evangelicals finally to overcome their distrust of the political system.

Though religious conservatives were largely unaware of the disturbance at the time, by spawning a more confrontational generation of gay activists Stonewall unleashed a torrent of demands for social change that conservative Christians found profoundly threatening. The Gay Liberation Front, formed shortly before the riots, sought to form alliances with left-wing groups like the Black Panthers. The group's statement of purpose described it as a "revolutionary group of men and women formed with the realization that complete sexual liberation for all people cannot come about unless existing social institutions are abolished. We reject society's attempt to impose sexual roles and definitions of our nature. We are stepping outside these roles and simplistic myths. We are going to be who we are. At the same time, we are creating new social forms and relations, that is, relations based upon brotherhood, cooperation, human love, and uninhibited sexuality." Though the Gay Liberation Front was quickly superseded by the more mainstream Gay Activists Alliance, its guiding philosophy would influence many gay and lesbian activists for decades to come. The Alliance, in turn, quickly earned a reputation for col-

orful street theater to draw attention to the movement's largely
overlooked claims.

From the beginning, the gay movement was deeply influenced by the left-wing and antiwar movements and the hippie
counterculture of the 1960s. Despite widespread antigay views on
the left, many early gay activists first saw the opportunity for their
own movement in the incipient political awareness of other minority groups. As a result, these activists were deeply influenced
by the left's emphasis on class consciousness, connections among
disenfranchised minority groups, and liberation from traditional
gender and sexuality constraints. For these early pioneers, being
gay was about more than just same-sex attraction; it was about
changing the world for the better.

Early gay politics were rarely about achieving specific goals;
gay rights legislation was unpracticable until the mid-1970s in most
American cities. The point was more to draw attention to the very
existence of gay people. The tactic succeeded in increasing the visibility of homosexuality, but the transition from the anarchistic, liberationist movements of the 1960s to an institutionalized gay rights
movement, which demanded the formalization of organizational
structures, was marked by bitter ideological clashes.

Jean O'Leary personified the tumultuous politics. In 1972,
O'Leary organized a lesbian-feminist revolt against the Gay Activists Alliance that resulted in the formation of Lesbian Feminist
Liberation. The combative O'Leary then would lead another
fight, this time to ban transvestite entertainers from the 1973 gay
pride rally in New York City. O'Leary saw drag queens as gay men
ridiculing women, a position she quickly recanted. O'Leary's ability to weather such clashes and draw lessons from them made her
one of the few gay activists to maintain a leadership position in the
movement over several decades. Like many lesbians of her generation, O'Leary, who became a nun as a young woman in part to
avoid her sexual feelings, never imagined until 1969 that she
could live her life as a lesbian. The discovery of the movement,
and the freedom it allowed her to develop her own identity, motivated her to dedicate much of her adult life to its advancement. In

1972, O'Leary became one of the first directors of the National Gay Task Force, which was established to mold the burgeoning, but often random, gay activism across the country into a cohesive political force. From that post, O'Leary would go on to lead National Gay Rights Advocates, a national legal group based in San Francisco, from 1979 until its spectacular collapse in 1991. In 1976, O'Leary served as the first openly lesbian delegate to a Democratic National Convention.

Formed in 1972, the National Gay Task Force, the first national gay political group, served as a clearinghouse for the growing, but unorganized, gay movement. The organization functioned primarily as an advisor to local groups pursuing antidiscrimination ordinances or the repeal of state sodomy laws. Howard Brown, the former New York City health services administrator who came out on the front page of the *New York Times* in 1973, lent early legitimacy to the group. In 1985, the group moved to Washington, D.C., where it became the National Lesbian and Gay Task Force and added lobbying Congress to its mission.

⌁ One of the first major confrontations between the left-wing liberation movements of the 1960s and the emerging religious right was not specifically about homosexuality. Passed by Congress in 1972, the Equal Rights Amendment guaranteed "equality of rights" for women, but did not specify how they would be achieved. After an initial surge of support, the amendment died in 1982, falling three states shy of the thirty-eight required for the adoption of a constitutional amendment. The responsibility for the turnaround can be attributed in large part to one person: Phyllis Schlafly. By putting a female face on antifeminist politics, Schlafly was the ideal spokesperson for the anti-ERA forces.

At the time, Schlafly was the little-known president of the Eagle Forum, a tiny Illinois-based political group that catered to conservative homemakers. Schlafly had her start in right-wing politics as the author of *A Choice, Not an Echo,* a glowing chronicle of Barry Goldwater's 1964 presidential campaign. As a Catholic, Schlafly was an unlikely choice to lead the evangelical revolt against feminism. Some of her Protestant counterparts, including Falwell, had equated the papacy with the "whore of Babylon," cited in the book of Revelation in the New Testament. But Schlafly's hostility to the feminist values she saw exemplified in the ERA far outweighed her distrust of evangelicals. As she saw it, the ERA was a no-holds-barred attack on the traditional role of women. Whereas many feminists saw that role as restrictive or even demeaning, Schlafly, a housewife who considered her massive political involvement to be little more than dabbling, believed that it provided women with special status. Loosening the role, she thought, would abolish husbands' responsibility to care for their wives, tear apart families, and throw women into the increasingly competitive job market. If women had actual complaints of discrimination, they would "take their case to God," rather than the government, she declared in 1973.

The ERA fight was a harbinger of future battles. In her attacks on the ERA, Schlafly established the tone for the wildly exaggerated charges and scare tactics—many of them involving homosexuality—that would come to be employed by antigay activists for years to come. Throughout her ten-year battle, Schlafly erroneously claimed that the ERA would lead to the conscription of women for military service on a par with men, force the sharing of public bathrooms by both genders, and mandate state-funded abortions. In one particularly incendiary advertisement, the Eagle Forum claimed that the ERA, or Amendment Six, was not just about the "sex you are, male or female," but the "sex you engage in, homosexual, bisexual, heterosexual," or even "sex with children." Over a photo depicting two stereotypical-appearing gay men from a New York City gay parade, the headline announced, "Who Hid the Sex in Six?"

One of Schlafly's most potent charges was that the amendment would result in the legalization of gay marriage, even though its Senate sponsor, Democrat Birch Bayh, had made sure that the legislative record specified that it would not. With a series of far-ranging liberal court decisions culminating in the 1972 ruling *Roe v. Wade,* which legalized first- and second-trimester abortions, Schlafly could suggest with some credibility that the courts were likely to interpret the amendment more broadly than even its supporters suggested. As outlandish as it sounded at the time, Schlafly may not have been so far off on the last point. In 1993, the Hawaii Supreme Court ruled that the state's ban on same-sex marriage amounted to gender discrimination under the Hawaii constitution.

The debate quickly sank into a morass of increasingly pointless charges and countercharges that had little to do with the actual language of the ERA. As soon as Schlafly and her colleagues on the right were able to divert the debate's focus from discrimination against women to the "radical feminist agenda" and the supposed homosexual threat to the "American way of life," they had gained the upper hand in the debate. That in 1972 the fledgling gay rights movement was confined almost exclusively to obscure left-wing political circles in New York City, Los Angeles, and San Francisco hardly seemed to matter.

For Schlafly, the injection of the gay issue into the ERA debate had the added benefit of dividing the amendment's supporters. After the lesbian and socialist banners that dotted pro-ERA demonstrations became staples of the opposition's depictions of them, the National Organization for Women banned them from their demonstrations. The lesbian purges threatened to tear apart the feminist movement. In one infamous episode Betty Friedan, author of *The Feminine Mystique* and cofounder of NOW, called the presence of lesbians among the pro-ERA forces the "lavender menace," eliciting an outcry from lesbian activists both inside and outside the organization.

NOW and other women's groups engaged in their own distortions of the opposition and their cause. Plagued by internal divisions, the groups painted a black-and-white picture of inequality for women to help recruit volunteers and fire up the ranks. Exaggerating the probable effect of the ERA, feminist activists claimed that adoption of the amendment could mean federally funded abortions, equal access to combat roles in the military, and the overthrow of the patriarchal family structure. Like the gay groups who would later face down the barrel of high-caliber attacks from the religious right, they lacked the self-correcting mechanisms that would allow them to align their rhetoric with political reality.

Feminist leadership, while benefiting from sympathy for the concept of greater equalization, tended to overestimate their resonance and grew out of sync with the more pragmatic rank and file of women activists, who, faced with everyday problems, had little patience for the overblown rhetoric of self-appointed leaders invoking the specter of radical social change.

⟿ At the same time, another development would contribute to the hostility of the political battle and pave the way for the cultural wars of the 1980s. Campaign financing reforms, passed in the wake of the 1972 Watergate scandal, limiting political contributions for federal elections to $1,000 catapulted direct-mail fund-raising to the center stage of national electoral politics. To be effective, direct-mail campaigns relied upon incendiary political charges of the sort concocted by Schlafly hurled at political opponents who could be identified as a threat to basic values and the American way of life. The point of the fund-raising letters was to stir up hostilities toward an identifiable target. The "shriller you are," admitted Terry Dolan, the founder of the National Conservative Political Action Committee, in 1982, "the easier it is to raise money." With little understanding or support, the emerging gay rights movement would make the perfect fodder for the right's fund-raising endeavors.

The conservative who first exploited the opportunities for astute insurgent interest groups with the redrawing of the political landscape was Richard Viguerie. As the de facto leader of a younger generation of angry conservatives who were known collectively as the "new right," Viguerie got his start in fund-raising in the early 1960s as an assistant to Marvin Liebman, a conservative political operative who was one of the founders of Young Americans for Freedom. Viguerie compiled the first of his legendary computerized mailing lists by copying Liebman's Barry Goldwater for President mailing list, which was stored on index cards in Liebman's Manhattan office. Computerized, this list would later expand into the millions, securing Viguerie's standing as a sought-after Republican campaign consultant and forming the basis for the political ascent of the candidates of Viguerie's choice. Viguerie was one of the first conservative fund-raisers to realize the value of playing on the reflexively antigay feelings of the right-wing rank and file of America. In his 1983 book, *The Establishment vs. the People: Is a New Populist Revolt on the Way?* Viguerie anticipated the "special rights" argument the religious right would rely upon to overturn bans on antigay discrimination, beginning nearly a decade later: " 'Gay' life as promoted by homosexual radicals is not an alternative life style," he wrote. "It is a defiant denial of the basic human instinct of procreation and the central tenets of our Judeo-Christian Faith. I feel we should have the right not to hire, work with, rent to, or live next to a homosexual, or an adulterer, or a sexually promiscuous heterosexual, if we so choose."

Such rhetoric would later cause Liebman to wish he had never hired Viguerie. Realizing that gays and lesbians had become one of the chief targets of his former associate's fund-raising missives and public pronouncements, Liebman announced in a 1992 letter to the conservative magazine the *National Review* that he was gay. Liebman's pangs of conscience came too late to help rein in the antigay attack dogs his brilliant organizing had unleashed. But he may have given them at least some reason to reflect. Though Liebman was shunned by many of his former colleagues on the right, Viguerie demonstrated his loyalty to his mentor by making an appearance at Liebman's seventieth birthday party at the National Press Club in Washington, D.C., where he listened politely as several young gay men gave testimonials to Liebman's positive influence on them. By coming out, Liebman saved himself from the unhappy fate of Terry Dolan. Like Liebman, Dolan was a closeted gay man whose work contributed mightily to antigay causes. But unlike Liebman, Dolan never fully came to grips with the duplicity of his past. In 1986, still deeply in the closet, he died of AIDS.

By allowing him to appeal directly to right-wing donors, Viguerie's fund-raising skills paved the way for the conservative movement's transition from the "old right," dominated by Eastern conservative establishment figures like William F. Buckley Jr., to a harsher, more radical, turn-back-the-clock breed of activists. "Direct mail has allowed conservatives to bypass the liberal media, and go directly into the homes of conservatives in this country," Viguerie bragged in Alan Crawford's *Thunder on the Right,* published in 1982. "There really is a silent majority in this country and the new right has learned how to identify them and communicate with them and mobilize them."

The "silent majority," Viguerie determined, was as motivated by a constellation of family issues, exemplified by gay rights and abortion, as the old conservative standard, anticommunism. The transition was a relatively smooth one. The old right had couched its anticommunism in the rhetoric of family values long before it was fashionable. Even though communism both in the United States and abroad was notoriously homophobic, the old right viewed it as weakening the Christian fabric of the nation, which would enable homosexuals to gain a stronger foothold. Homosexuals were often lampooned as limp-wristed "pinkos," and perhaps the staunchest anticommunist of all, J. Edgar Hoover, took to attacking both homosexuals and communists in identical terms. Faced with the reality that communism was a dying ideology even before the decline of the Soviet Union, the new right and the religious right came to depict homosexuals as one of the chief evils of the modern world. It was the homosexual movement, particularly by gaining admission to the U.S. armed services, that would destroy America from within and make it vulnerable to foreign armies. Furthermore, by infiltrating the schools, homosexuals, like communists, had an insidious influence on the nation's most vulnerable commodity, its children. The new emphasis would leave the new right well stocked with new enemies closer to home after the fall of the "Evil Empire" in the mid-1980s.

Viguerie knew that to be successful the new right required a massive, well-funded organizational structure at its disposal and a constantly expanding base of members and activists. Joined by Paul Weyrich, and Howard Phillips of the Conservative Caucus, Viguerie began the laborious process of identifying the foot soldiers necessary to swell the grass roots. Viguerie had watched conservative groups like the John Birch Society, with its open expressions of racism and anti-Semitism, fizzle after tapping out their base and reaching overambitiously for power. The most logical candidates, he understood, were evangelical churches, which had the potential to surpass organized labor as the most powerful interest group in American politics. According to polls, an estimated 30 to 50 million Americans were born-again Christians. Add to the holy mix conservative Catholics and orthodox Jews, and a political force was born.

At first, the results of Viguerie's efforts were mixed. Schlafly and her fifty thousand-member Eagle Forum, for instance, retained their independence by refusing to allow their mailing list to be bought or rented. Many of Viguerie's earliest clients, including Citizens for Decent Literature, financier Charles Keating's Cincinnati group that later became Citizens for Decency Through Law, and Conservative Books for Christian Leaders, made little impact. More successful was Robert C. Grant's Christian Voice. According to one of Grant's fund-raising letters, the gay rights movement was "just a fraction of a master plan to destroy everything that is good and moral here in America." Grant, of course, never identified the author or authors of the "master plan," but for his Viguerie-generated audience of unreconstructed Birchers weaned on conspiracy theories of one-world government and Jewish manipulation of media and finance, mere allusion was sufficient. For the new right and its allies among religious conservatives, the best was yet to come.

⚬ Until the late 1970s, occasional antigay appeals from the right had been like valuable ores left unrefined. But the new right struck pure gold in Anita Bryant. A mother, celebrity singer, former Miss America, and spokeswoman for the Florida Citrus Growers ("A day without orange juice is like a day without sunshine"), the chirpy Bryant was the ideal model for its antigay crusade. She could safely emphasize the supposed danger the homosexual movement posed to families without appearing mean-spirited. In a 1977 fund-raising letter filled with passages underlined in red, she wrote: "Dear friend: I don't hate the homosexuals! But as a mother, I must protect my children from their evil influence. When the homosexuals burn the holy Bible in public, how can I stand by silently?" Like those of a host of her antigay successors, Bryant's fund-raising appeals would fail to identify which gays had burned a Bible or where, much less acknowledge any anger gays might justifiably harbor at what they took as her appropriating Scriptures for her own partisan political purposes.

Building on her friend Phyllis Schlafly's anti-ERA campaign, Bryant founded an antigay group, Save Our Children, Inc., which would establish the tone of the gay rights battles long after Bryant, whose well-publicized divorce cut into her credibility, had dropped out of politics. In response to passage of a 1977 Dade County, Florida, ordinance protecting gays and lesbians from discrimination, Bryant launched an initiative drive to overturn it. After her ballot initiative passed by a large margin, Bryant, who also described herself as a fundamentalist Christian, traveled the country promoting similar initiatives in other municipalities. From 1977 to 1980, voters overturned gay rights bills in St. Paul, Minnesota; Wichita, Kansas; and Eugene, Oregon; but retained them in Seattle.

Across the country, gay activists reacted to Bryant's attacks by stepping up lobbying for inclusion in ordinances that banned discrimination in housing, employment, and public accommodations. Across the country gays and lesbians held spirited anti-Bryant protests, including a celebrated incident in Des Moines, Iowa, where Bryant suffered a cream pie in the face. Tens of thousands of gays and lesbians participated in the 1979 gay and lesbian march on Washington, D.C. The White House, too, became a focus for the first time. Midge Costanza, one of then-president Jimmy Carter's top aides, held two White House meetings with gay activists in which they discussed, among other things, the need for federal antidiscrimination protections to circumvent Bryant-inspired measures on the local level. It was around this time that gay lobbyists, realizing that the grass roots of American politics were hostile to their cause, began to concentrate their efforts on Congress and the White House, further widening the gulf with mainstream America that the religious right would come to exploit.

For many religious conservatives, the news that a born-again president—who did not attend either meeting and who had previously admitted on national television that he was "confused" by homosexuality—would allow gays and lesbians even to step inside the White House was the last straw. They turned on the president who just two years earlier had enthusiastically encouraged their participation in electoral politics and vigorously courted their vote. Wrote John Donovan, Pat Robertson's official biographer, in 1988: "The disappointment of Carter as an unabashed liberal served to forge the Republican Christian alliance of which Robertson rides the crest."

The most bitter showdown came in California in 1978, when state senator and gubernatorial candidate John Briggs of Fullerton, armed with Bryant's contributor list, launched a drive to ban open homosexuals, or anyone advocating the "gay lifestyle," from teaching in public schools. Largely as a result of unexpected opposition from then-governor Ronald Reagan and other prominent conservatives, the Briggs initiative lost by more than one million votes, 3.9 million to 2.8 million. Under intense lobbying from gay activists including David Mixner, who would go on to become a key adviser to President Clinton, Reagan refused to endorse the initiative on libertarian grounds, which should have tipped off his religious right supporters that he was not to be their messiah. The initiative "is not needed to protect our children—we have that legal protection now," Reagan said. "It has the potential of real mischief. . . . What if an overwrought youngster, disappointed by bad grades, imagined it was the teacher's fault and struck out by accusing the teacher of advocating homosexuality. Innocent lives could be ruined."

Embittered by the unexpected defeat, Briggs, who once described gay men as "women trapped in men's bodies," called San Francisco the "moral garbage dump of homosexuality in this country." The Briggs battle coincided—indeed, helped propel— the first stirrings of urban gay political power. In San Francisco, Harvey Milk was elected to the Board of Supervisors in 1977.

In Milk, antigay crusaders like Bryant and Briggs had met their match. The product of a middle-class Jewish family in Woodmere, New York, Milk supported Barry Goldwater's right-wing presidential campaign in 1964. Caught up in the radicalism of the 1960s, Milk grew a ponytail, traded in his suit for bell-bottoms, and headed off to San Francisco, where he opened a camera shop on Castro Street. By 1973, Milk was already blazing gay political trails, finishing tenth in a field of thirty-two candidates for the Board of Supervisors, despite the gay establishment's warning that it was too soon for an openly gay candidate to seek elected office.

Milk was not alone in his trailblazing. In 1974, Elaine Noble was elected to the Massachusetts House of Representatives as an open lesbian. By 1978, Noble had retired from politics, citing the overwhelming expectations that came along with being the gay community's representative. "The gay community expected me to be on call twenty-four hours a day," she told the gay magazine *The Advocate*. "It was like they felt they owned me." Milk had no such qualms about assuming the community's leadership. By the time he was elected to the San Francisco Board of Supervisors, the Castro district had become America's gay mecca, with homosexuals from across the nation migrating there by the thousands. Milk forged coalitions with African-Americans, Chicanos, and labor unions and whipped up support among the growing gay and lesbian population, emphasizing the threat to their freedom posed by the Anita Bryant–inspired antigay backlash sweeping the country. In what became known as the "give 'em hope" speech, delivered to gay audiences across the country, Milk was fast becoming the gay movement's Martin Luther King Jr.

After suffering a string of Bryant-inspired losses at the ballot box, the National Gay and Lesbian Task Force announced in a 1979 report on the state of gay politics that "failure could be seen as a form of victory in terms of overall movement development." But constant turnover, staff burnout at the Task Force and the Human Rights Campaign Fund, which was founded in the late 1970s as a political action committee, and the early-1980s onset of the AIDS epidemic meant that during the next spate of antigay initiatives in the late 1980s and early 1990s the crucial lessons of the earlier defeats were all but forgotten. The gay movement's dearth of visionary leadership—exacerbated by Milk's assassination in 1978—was not just about high turnover: it was built into the structure of the gay movement.

For the religious right, the issue of leadership cut both ways. The hierarchical organizational structure of the independent churches led by political preachers like Falwell and Robertson was both a blessing and a curse. While it allowed leaders like Falwell free rein to develop massive multimedia empires, it also left the television ministries wholly dependent on charismatic leaders and vulnerable to their often huge egos and glaring eccentricities. By contrast, the gay groups, which grew out of the collectivist philosophy of the 1960s left, tended to be inherently skeptical of formal structure and unitary leadership. While gay activists' deep-seated faith in the democratic processes led them to seek input from and remain responsive to a greater number of activists, it made them resistant to charismatic leaders. In fact, activists with egos big enough to become forceful leaders were often viewed with great suspicion. As a result, the gay movement never developed leaders with Falwell's or Robertson's following or stature.

⌖ In 1979, after extensive consultations with new right leaders like Viguerie, Falwell, pastor of the Thomas Road Baptist Church in Lynchburg, Virginia, and host of the *Old-Time Gospel Hour,* founded the Moral Majority. Though religious conservative groups had existed for decades, the Moral Majority marked the religious right's official entrance into interest-group politics. As Viguerie had hoped, the organization—and a plethora of imitators—would go on to play an important role in the mobilization of evangelical voters for Ronald Reagan's 1980 presidential campaign.

As testimony to the religious right's growing clout, Reagan addressed the 1980 convention of the National Association of Religious Broadcasters, which Falwell was hosting in Lynchburg. Like many evangelicals, Falwell had initially supported Reagan's Republican rival John Connally, whom he believed to be more comfortable with religious conservatives. As a presidential candidate, Reagan had rejected Falwell's suggested running mate, Jesse Helms, in favor of George Bush, a moderate on the issues most dear to the religious right. As California governor, Reagan had kept religious conservatives at arm's length and, just two years earlier, had helped stymie the antigay Briggs initiative. For Falwell, Reagan's opposition to Briggs was the most serious obstacle to throwing his support behind Reagan. Homosexuals in the schools was one of the major themes of his sermons and of the Moral Majority's fund-raising missives. At the convention, however, Reagan laid Falwell's concerns to rest. While ducking the gay question, Reagan confided in his audience that he had grave doubts about evolutionary theory; declared that the Bible contained the answers to the country's social ills; and accused liberals of using the separation of church and state to keep conservative religious activists out of politics. For Falwell, the power of Reagan's overtures to the religious right overwhelmed any remaining qualms he might have had.

Once elected, Reagan steered clear of the treacherous waters of religion and politics. Instead, he made grand gestures. In 1981, for instance, he endorsed the Family Protection Act, a bill that in the name of stabilizing the family would have declared that no federal funds should be earmarked for "any organization that suggests that homosexuality can be an acceptable alternative lifestyle," knowing full well that the amendment would be deleted by the more Democratically aligned Congress. Reagan appointed Gary Bauer, a close associate of James Dobson, president of the powerful Christian conservative group Focus on the Family, as a domestic policy adviser. Bauer, though, had little actual influence over policy and spent much of his time in office plotting his return to lobbying.

Reagan's grandest gesture of all, the appointment of anti-abortion crusader C. Everett Koop as Surgeon General in 1981, turned out to be an unexpected black eye for the right. Despite his oft-stated view that homosexuality is a sin, Koop defended the need for federal funding of sexually explicit AIDS education in the schools and gay-positive educational material. "You cannot be an efficient health officer with integrity if you let other things get in the way of health messages," Koop told the *Village Voice*. For his principled stance, Koop was vilified by Falwell and the religious right.

Falwell's power in the GOP was a far cry from his humble origins, when he adhered to deeply held Baptist notions that true faith eschews temporal politics. Starting in 1956, Falwell's sermons to a small audience in a broken-down factory building focused primarily on damning other denominations for their biblical "misinterpretations" on the evils of drink and sexual promiscuity. In a now-famous 1965 speech titled "Ministers and Marchers," Falwell, who, despite his apolitical posture, supported segregation, maintained that mainline denominations had corrupted their faith by backing the civil rights movement. If ministers could support Southern blacks, he reasoned, they should fight alcoholism with equal fervor. There are as many "alcoholics as there are Negroes," he reasoned. In announcing the founding of the Moral Majority, Falwell explained that his earlier position on racial politics was the result of "false prophecy."

Falwell's political aspirations reflected the needs of his congregants. The world of the *Old-Time Gospel Hour* was one of Jesus as a "he-man," of clearly delineated right and wrong as determined by Falwell himself, and of boundless prosperity for all true believers. While Falwell's message about the future of America was often pessimistic, Falwell himself came across as upbeat about the potential for individual salvation. As Frances Fitz-Gerald pointed out in a 1981 profile of Falwell in *The New Yorker*, evangelical television shows provided Americans a "vast revival tent, offering immediate mass escape from eternal damnation." If viewers were seeking salvation, the televangelists had something far more material on their minds. The television revival tent offered them a golden opportunity to tap contributors through the use of telephone banks and fund-raising solicitations. In a style reminiscent of the Catholic Church's sale of indulgences half a millennium earlier, the implicit message of the shows was that viewers who contributed generously would find salvation easier to achieve.

What set Falwell apart from his more traditional predecessors was his remarkable marketing ability. His newfound interest in politics dovetailed with the introduction of sophisticated fund-raising techniques, many of which were modeled on Viguerie's campaigns. Depending on the political and biblical pet peeves of his audience, Falwell targeted fund-raising letters to decry the spread of pornography, or appeal to antigay sentiment. The slick packaging of *Old-Time Gospel Hour* was a far cry from the spit-and-baling-wire operations of the early days of the gay movement. Falwell's fund-raising pitches came with a full-color magazine, *Faith Aflame,* free Jesus pins, Bibles, his own books, and miniature American flags. Nor was Falwell above using scare tactics to raise extra cash. On several occasions, he threatened to close his ministry if viewers failed to dig still deeper into their wallets. By contrast, the Human Rights Campaign Fund, the country's wealthiest gay group, did not develop a magazine of its own until 1995. Even then, like most gay groups, it felt compelled to omit its name from the outside of its direct-mail envelopes to avoid exposing recipients as gay or lesbian or even supportive of their cause.

Both the gay movement and the left, which was slow to adopt the gay cause, lacked the equivalent means of communication, the comforting rhetoric in which to package their message, and the fund-raising ability so amply demonstrated by the religious right. When Falwell founded the Moral Majority in 1979, the National Gay Task Force still lacked a Washington office. Its budget was less than half a million dollars per year; the Campaign Fund was nothing but a gleam in the eye of its founders. Neither group had access to anything more than graveyard-shift public-access television, a problem that plagues the movement to this day. The mainstream media showed little interest in their cause until well into the AIDS epidemic. The gay press, edited almost exclusively for gays and lesbians, reached an audience a fraction of the size of Falwell's. This communications imbalance allowed religious conservatives like Falwell the freedom to frame the debate by depicting homosexuals in highly negative and inaccurate terms to a huge audience. It is an advantage that gay activists have fought against again and again as they have attempted to take their cause to the

nation. As the imbalance has persisted, the gay movement has become, in the face of so much countervailing rhetoric, increasingly
defensive and unable to articulate a compelling vision of its place
in American society.

Without the gay rights and the women's movements—and
the tragic advent of AIDS—Falwell's political ascendancy might
well have crashed and burned far earlier than it did. It was in
support of Phyllis Schlafly's anti-ERA campaign and Anita
Bryant's antigay crusade that Falwell's fund-raising campaigns
really caught fire. (Schlafly, in fact, would become the first
nonevangelical religious figure to address Falwell's church.) In
the mid-1970s, before other right-wing Christian activists like
Robertson and Jim Bakker had latched onto politics, *Old-Time
Gospel Hour* took on an increasingly political tone. Falwell began inviting conservative politicians to appear on the show and
held dozens of "I Love America" rallies across the country. In
1975, he sought to train a future generation of evangelical leaders by launching the fundamentalist Liberty Baptist College in
Lynchburg.

Inevitably, Falwell's rise led to skirmishes with the more
secular mainstream political establishment. In 1979, he came
under fire for regularly describing America as a "Christian nation"
and contending that "God does not answer the prayers of an
unredeemed gentile or Jew." In a defense against charges of anti-
Semitism that Robertson would mimic more than a decade
later, Falwell dug himself a deeper hole by saying that his support for the state of Israel immunized him from the charge. (He
later told a Christian audience that Jews "can make more money
accidentally than you can on purpose.") Eventually, Falwell was
forced to renounce an essential tenet of fundamentalism by
assuring his critics that God "hears the heart cry of any sincere
person who calls him," though it is unclear whether homosexuals—
let alone Jews—could ever attain the category of "sincere people"
and thus gain the deity's ear.

For Falwell and the religious right, the tension between adhering to a literal interpretation of the Bible and allowing the
compromise inherent in mainstream politics never fully eased. In

a pluralistic democracy, the voice of every participant has a priori equal standing. Yet with its insistence on the inerrancy of the Bible in public policy, the religious right raised the specter of theocracy. To deal with the competing demands—theological and political—Falwell, like Pat Robertson later in the 1980s, simply opted to adopt two contradictory positions, one intended for his core audience and one suited for public consumption, and hoped no one would notice. After backing Briggs's and Bryant's campaign to ban gays and lesbians from teaching positions in the public schools and repeatedly in sermons and fund-raising letters harping on the homosexual threat to children, Falwell told the *Washington Post,* "I have no objection to a homosexual teaching in the classroom as long as that homosexual is not flaunting his lifestyle or soliciting students."

Falwell generally escaped censure for such blatant contradictions because the press was often reluctant to take him to task. When his statements and motives were called into question, he has adhered to the premise that the best defense is a good offense. Instead of answering the substance of charges, Falwell would simply suggest darkly that his critics were part of a liberal conspiracy to repress the role of Christians in government. Responding to attacks on his political views in a 1976 sermon, Falwell said, "The idea that religion and politics don't mix was invented by the devil to keep Christians from running their own country."

⌣ While the outbreak of the mysterious and deadly disease in the early 1980s spurred many religiously motivated caregivers to new heights of compassion, Falwell used it to craft new fund-raising appeals. In AIDS, religious conservatives like Falwell found the punitive manifestation for homosexual behavior for which they had been searching. No longer, they reasoned, could homosexuals pretend that homosexuality was without consequences. AIDS and homosexuality would become virtually synonymous in the rhetoric of the religious right and in the nation's consciousness. Ignoring the inconvenient facts that many people with AIDS are not gay, that the vast majority of gay men would never contract HIV, and that lesbians are at extremely low risk,

Falwell and his colleagues on the right played AIDS as divine ret-
ribution for sodomy. In a 1987 fund-raising letter, for instance,
Falwell accused gay men of donating blood because "they know
they are going to die—and they are going to take as many people
with them as they can."

AIDS marked the birth of a cottage industry of antigay research led by Paul Cameron, director of the Institute for the Scientific Investigation of Sexuality in Lincoln, Nebraska. The
misnamed group, which later became the Colorado Springs,
Colorado–based Family Research Institute, which Cameron
described as "scientists defending traditional family values,"
produced a series of lurid pamphlets about the supposed social ills
associated with homosexuality. Gay sex, declared one Institute
flyer, was a "crime against humanity." Another pamphlet featured
a grainy photo of a young girl being threatened by an ax-wielding
man, presumably gay. It is hard to imagine a more discredited figure than Cameron. During a 1981 debate over a Lincoln gay
rights measure, Cameron publicly stated that a four-year-old boy
had been sexually mutilated in a mall rest room because of a "homosexual act." The Lincoln police were never able to locate the
boy in question and issued a statement that there was no evidence
for Cameron's charge.

Cameron has spent the better part of the AIDS epidemic devising studies to demonstrate that gay men brought AIDS on
themselves and the rest of the world. AIDS first became an epidemic, he insisted, because promiscuous American gay men went
on "worldwide sex tours," in which they engaged in "unsanitary"
practices. "Homosexuals have a different way of having sex," he
said. "You are mixing germs on an international basis." AIDS provided Cameron the medical justification he required to advocate
the forced segregation of homosexuals from society. Cameron's
solution to the epidemic was universal HIV testing and the quar-
antine of everyone who tests positive for virus antibodies.

Despite his shoddy research, Cameron's crackpot theories
found their way into mainstream conservative thought. Cameron's
1993 study indicating that the average life expectancy of gay men

is thirty-nine is a case in point. Culled from obituaries published in the gay press, the study was regularly cited by prominent conservatives from William Bennett to Pat Buchanan. Desperate for evidence for their antigay pronouncements, few on the right stopped to question the credentials of the discredited source or the basis for the study. That AIDS was killing gay men in their prime was undeniable; that being gay meant you were doomed to an early death, particularly in light of AIDS prevention efforts, was simply false. Cameron had no way of canvassing the death certificates of broad samples of gay men, since many were not identifiable as such in life, let alone in death. But to make political points Cameron ignored rudimentary scientific guidelines.

Cameron manufactured even worse statistics. It was he who "proved" that gays were ten to twenty times more likely to be child molesters than their peers, and five to twenty times more likely to commit bestiality. It was Cameron who claimed that a person was fifteen times more likely to be murdered by a homosexual than a heterosexual. It was Cameron who said that lesbians were twenty-nine times more likely to infect a sexual partner with a venereal disease on purpose. Some of the figures were of Cameron's own reckoning, based on a survey he conducted in 1983, which had a statistically insignificant sample of forty-one gay and twenty-four lesbian respondents. (Given the patent bias of the survey—reasons why the respondent became homosexual included "I was socially inept" and "I had a weak character [was lazy, immature, no moral strength]"—it seems entirely possible some of the gay respondents decided to treat the whole thing as a joke.) The statistic about renegade lesbians infecting their partners was based on a sample of seven.

Cameron also reinterpreted other studies as well, and it was here that he ran into trouble. "He misrepresents my findings and distorts them to advance his homophobic views," A. Nicholas Groth, director of the Sex Offender Program at Connecticut's Department of Correction, wrote to the Nebraska Board of Examiners of Psychologists in 1984. Groth studied pedophilia and had noted in his research that men in his sample who molested boys were either pedophiles by nature or heterosexual, but not homosexual. Cameron took a homosexual *act* to be a sign of homosexual *orientation* and concluded just the opposite.

For all its flaws, the religious right was dependent on Cameron's research to supplement its biblical arguments about the supposed deleterious social consequences of homosexuality. For all their boasts about the power of strict biblical interpretation, Falwell and other evangelical leaders had to know that in a society that values the scientific method as highly as religious convictions, theological arguments alone were not enough to win converts. The 1973 decision by the American Psychological Association to delete homosexuality from its list of mental illnesses, after a bitter internal fight, dealt a shocking blow to antigay forces by placing the mainstream of the medical profession on the side of gay rights advocates, effectively reducing antigay research to the level of eugenics and racially motivated intelligence theory.

Indeed, an accumulation of cooked statistics and questionable professional behavior led to Cameron's expulsion from the American Psychological Association on ethical charges in 1983. Cameron would later claim he had resigned or, alternatively, been drummed out by radical supporters of gay rights upset at his research. The group, however, does not allow resignations of members under investigation. Cameron was censured by a variety of other professional organizations as well. When he began to be identified in the press as a sociologist instead, the American Sociological Association, a professional group, passed a 1986 resolution asserting that "Paul Cameron is not a sociologist, and [this group] condemns his constant misrepresentation of sociological research."

AIDS would also play a paradoxical role in the gay movement's political rise. The epidemic took the lives of hundreds of the community's leaders, many before they had reached their prime. It diverted already limited resources away from politics. It threw large sections of the community into political paralysis. But at the same time, the movement was thrust into the national limelight for the first time in its short history. Gay celebrities, from

Rock Hudson to Liberace, were forced out of the closet by the disclosure that they had AIDS. A broad cross section of the general public saw gay men as real people—coworkers, neighbors, family members—suffering inexorable loss. Only the hardhearted could avoid feeling sympathy for the plight of gay men in America.

The gay and lesbian community itself rose to the occasion. In the early days of the epidemic, with the Reagan administration dragging its heels, the community took on AIDS by itself, setting up AIDS prevention campaigns to reach the uninfected, and service groups to care for the sick and dying. As a result of the prevention measures, new infections quickly dropped substantially, according to public health departments across the country. Although the infection rate began to rise again in the early 1990s, notably among young gay men, public health experts—Cameron notwithstanding—marveled at the unprecedented behavioral changes achieved by the community's intervention. Many of the early groups established to battle the epidemic, such as Gay Men's Health Crisis in New York, went on to serve as models for other communities' responses to the disease.

As impressive as the gay community's early response was, the massive scale of the epidemic was more than it could handle alone. Gay political groups, both nationally and locally, were forced to grapple with mainstream political institutions over the inevitable AIDS appropriations. Working with liberal members of Congress like Ted Kennedy in the Senate and Henry Waxman and the late Ted Weiss in the House, AIDS lobbyists were able to overpower the Reagan administration's recalcitrance. With the exception of funding for sexually explicit AIDS prevention measures, which were often blocked by congressional conservatives, the lobbyists coaxed large outlays of federal funding to combat the disease, especially in the 1987 Ryan White Care Act, which provided billions of dollars in aid to cities hard hit.

The AIDS epidemic also brought a renaissance of fiery street activism harkening back to the Stonewall era of the 1960s and early 1970s. In 1986, the AIDS Coalition to Unleash Power and its later spin-off, Queer Nation, adopted many of the tactics of the

Gay Liberation Front with its colorful street theater and "zaps" of antigay foes. The founder of ACT UP, Larry Kramer, argued that desperate times required desperate measures. Though the federal government was pouring money into the epidemic, Kramer believed that the country had failed to treat the epidemic with sufficient urgency because its primary victims were gay men. An accomplished screenwriter and novelist, Kramer, who was also one of the founders of Gay Men's Health Crisis, sounded an alarm about AIDS long before it had reached public consciousness. In the August 24, 1981, edition of the *New York Native,* a gay newspaper, Kramer warned that 120 gay men in the United States were suffering from a rare cancer known as Kaposi's sarcoma. "Many of the things we've taken over the past years may be all it takes for a cancer to grow from a tiny something-or-other that got in there who knows when from doing who knows what," he wrote. His 1983 essay "1,112 and Counting" sounded a similarly prescient note.

While some gay men tried to deny the relationship between HIV and unsafe sex, Kramer was in an ideal position to understand the profound ramifications of the fledgling epidemic. He had long been a critic of the wild sexual promiscuity of a small urban subset of gay men in the 1970s and early 1980s. Kramer's 1978 novel *Faggots* sparked a firestorm for its negative portrayal of gay bathhouse culture. When Kramer determined that Gay Men's Health Crisis's response to AIDS was insufficiently political, he founded ACT UP to establish a more confrontational tone.

The debate over gay sex in the age of AIDS, which often revolved around the bathhouses, threatened to set back the gay movement by dividing it. Those who stubbornly adhered to the liberationist perspective saw bathhouses as symbolic of the sexual freedom gays and lesbians had fought so hard to achieve. Others, like noted gay journalist Randy Shilts, author of the best-selling AIDS chronicle *And the Band Played On,* saw them as death traps for gay men. Exacerbating the emotional tone of the debate was the ever-present fear that the religious right would capitalize on the tragedy. "You have given the Moral Majority and the right wing the gasoline they have been waiting for to fuel the flames that will annihilate us," one gay activist screamed at an opponent during a public forum on the bathhouse closings. But the debate was over almost before it had begun. AIDS had obscured far larger trends in the gay community toward stable, monogamous relationships and even parenting. Though they were not necessarily mutually exclusive, sexual liberation was superseded by the gay version of family values.

Kramer, who was diagnosed with AIDS himself, was the charismatic leader the gay movement desperately lacked. The anger he imbued in ACT UP inspired an entire generation of activists who would play important roles in gay and AIDS activism long after the direct-action group had petered out in the early 1990s. But Kramer's hot temper and relentless personal attacks on his foes inside and outside the gay community eventually restricted his ability to lead the movement into the second decade of the AIDS epidemic, when the disease more closely resembled a permanent fact of life than it did a state of emergency.

⌐ At its apex in 1979, Falwell's *Old-Time Gospel Hour* raised $37 million on 2.5 million appeals, a sum unimaginable for a gay organization. Yet throughout the 1970s, the show was in and out of receivership. The pressure of mounting debt drove Falwell, whose penchant for overspending was as great as his gift for overstatement, to rely ever more heavily on solicitations stressing the alleged gay threat to American families. As Falwell's financial problems forced him to retreat from the public stage, the religious right's baton passed to the biblical reconstructionist Pat Robertson. Though he owed much to Falwell's trailblazing evangelism, Robertson, who practiced faith healing and speaking in tongues, would soon eclipse him as an entrepreneur and political preacher. Vowing not to repeat Falwell's mistakes, Robertson allowed the Christian Broadcasting Network to grow at a slow but steady rate. Until 1984, when he changed his party registration from Democratic to Republican, he largely abstained from Falwell's vituperative style of political activism.

After watching with dismay as President Reagan failed to deliver anything of substance to the religious right and the moderate

Bush surfaced as the heir apparent, Robertson took matters into his own hands by entering the 1988 presidential race. Launching his campaign on the front steps of an old brownstone in a predominantly poor, black section of Bedford-Stuyvesant in Brooklyn where he had worked as a young preacher, Robertson declared that the core of his campaign would be opposition to abortion and homosexuality. Robertson's announcement was greeted by an angry group of activists, many from ACT UP, which at the time was at its apex as a direct-action group. Robertson could not have prayed for a better greeting. In photos published across the country, the angry mob, toting ROBERTSON EQUALS DEATH posters, managed to make Robertson look reasonable by comparison or at least unfairly ambushed.

Even the fodder offered by ACT UP could not save the televangelist's campaign. After a series of early surprises, such as finishing second in Iowa in front of George Bush, Robertson floundered. Frustrated that the media had pigeonholed him as a religious candidate even though he had taken the largely symbolic step of resigning from his ministry, Robertson, like Falwell before him, was dogged by his own long history of intemperate remarks and a record of insensitivity to racial minorities. During the campaign, he made groundless claims about Russian missiles in Cuba and accused prominent Republican operative Lee Atwater of engineering the exposure of televangelist Jimmy Swaggart to taint all evangelical leaders. By the end of the primary season, Robertson was reduced to bargaining for a token appearance at the Republican National Convention.

But like the gay activists of a decade before, left battle-hardened by Anita Bryant, Robertson understood that defeat contained the seeds of victory. After his withdrawal from the campaign, Robertson vowed that religious conservatives would never again be dependent on the goodwill of a few ultraconservative politicians. The huge mailing list Robertson compiled during the campaign became the cornerstone of a new political cathedral of right-wing religious partisans, the Christian Coalition. By building the most powerful grassroots political organization in the country and controlling GOP machinery, the group would come to dictate the terms of the debate. Six years later, the organization would go a long way toward fulfilling Robertson's goal by spearheading the Republican congressional landslide of 1994.

⌐ For many gay and lesbian activists, Jesse Jackson played the role in 1988 that Pat Robertson did for religious conservatives. For the first time in the history of American politics, a presidential candidate taken seriously by the media openly and assiduously courted the gay vote. Jackson, whose oratorical gifts are a match for those of any evangelical preacher in the country, drew huge audiences of liberal gays and lesbians nationwide, who helped him achieve a series of stunning early finishes. By Jackson's own estimate, gays and lesbians accounted for nearly 50 percent of his support among white voters. By the end of the primary season, however, Jackson, like Robertson, was reduced to negotiating for a small voice in his party's platform. But unlike Robertson, Jackson failed to transform his campaign into something larger. Jackson's Chicago-based political organization, the Rainbow Coalition, never achieved the financial and organizational clout of the Christian Coalition. Jackson's influence on electoral politics would fade as fast as Robertson's would rise.

The Rainbow Coalition's failure to play a prominent role in "Beltway politics," as power-brokering in the nation's capital is called, reflects the ambivalence of many of its supporters about mainstream politics and its still-splintered loyalties, which Jackson's coalition of progressive activists could only temporarily recoup. Jackson supporter Urvashi Vaid, a brilliant activist who served as executive director of the National Gay and Lesbian Task Force from 1986 to 1992, is a case in point. Vaid, who got her start in gay politics as an editor at Boston's now defunct left-wing weekly newspaper *Gay Community News,* steered the organization to the left at the very time Robertson was taking the Christian Coalition mainstream. Under the peripatetic Vaid, the Task Force denounced the Persian Gulf War and took up a variety of causes reminiscent of the early liberationist days of the movement. In 1990, Vaid interrupted a rare AIDS speech by President Bush by shouting and holding aloft a sign reading TALK IS

CHEAP—AIDS FUNDING IS NOT. "I'm more comfortable behind a bullhorn than I am testifying at a Senate hearing, but I do both because I have to," Vaid told *Out* magazine in 1992, the year she left the Task Force to write a book about gay politics. Torn between the bullhorn and the Beltway, Vaid and the gay movement would do both with uneven gusto and neither to much avail.

The constant push and pull between liberationist and assimilationist impulses that Vaid embodied left the gay movement lacking in consistent direction and leadership. Robertson's smartest move, meanwhile, might have been in reducing his own highly unpopular profile as the head of the Christian Coalition by turning the day-to-day operation of the organization over to a seasoned political operative. In 1989, he convinced young Republican activist Ralph Reed to lead the fledgling organization as its first executive director. Reed, who holds a Ph.D. in history from Emory University, brought the credibility that Robertson, due to his years of extreme pronouncements, could never achieve. Reed followed the strategy outlined by onetime Robertson aide Thomas Atwood in a fall 1990 article published in the right-wing Heritage Foundation's *Policy Review*. The article, "Through a Glass Darkly: Is the Christian Right Overconfident It Knows God's Will?" argued that for the Christian right to reach its potential it had to follow the "basic rules of politics," including respect for opposing views and a willingness to compromise. For too long, Atwood argued, conservative Christians appeared "authoritarian, intolerant, and boastful, even to natural constituents."

With Robertson as his boss, Reed had his work cut out for him. Robertson's perch atop the religious right was a far cry from his troubled origins. By his early twenties, he had fallen far short of the lofty standards established by his father, Willis, a U.S. senator from Virginia. The younger Robertson had fathered a son out of wedlock, failed the bar exam, and adopted a bizarre brand of politically extreme evangelical Christianity that his father found unsettling, to say the least. The elder Robertson disapproved of his son's quixotic quest to build a national cable-television network, which only succeeded with the unexpected largess of seven hundred generous donors, from which evolved *The 700 Club*.

Though he has often waxed poetic about his humble origins, Robertson, as Ann Richards said of George Bush, was born with a silver spoon in his mouth. Shortly after graduating from Yale, Robertson moved to Brooklyn, where he worked to bring poor blacks to God. His religious conversion was so intense that he sold all his worldly possessions, much to the dismay of his pregnant wife. Moving to his native Tidewater area of Virginia in 1960, he purchased, with no cash down, an abandoned television station, which he gradually converted to twenty-four-hour Christian television programming.

Like Falwell's, Robertson's religious vision was inextricable from his financial one. Robertson, whom historian Garry Wills has called an "entrepreneurial evangelical," appealed directly to viewers for support and expansion. After buying the station, he began setting deadlines for viewers to send checks or risk losing *The 700 Club,* the talk show he hosted. By the early 1970s, *The 700 Club* was a fund-raising machine, with counselors talking with viewers on the air. After their problems were addressed, callers were enlisted as members. Before early-morning television chat shows were popular, *The 700 Club* provided viewers, who were predominantly housewives, with daily support for their relationship with God and a sympathetic ear for their grievances with the modern world. (One of the early attractions of the network were Jim and Tammy Bakker, who starred in a lively daily variety show.) As the show grew in popularity, Robertson expanded it by inviting prominent writers and politicians—not all of them conservative—to appear on the show. Eventually, Robertson created news programs with a decidedly conservative Christian slant presented as objective journalism. News bulletins, for example, would feature reports on cross-dressers and leather contingents at gay pride celebrations, while ignoring the rest of the parades. They also served as an uncritical forum for Robertson's allies in the increasingly crowded field of the religious right's leadership.

In his hagiography, John Donovan compares Robertson to Abraham Lincoln in his ability to combine religion and politics. A more apt comparison, however, might be Father Coughlin, with his elaborate conspiracy theories and lack of coherent analytic skills. Indeed, watching *The 700 Club* is to be transported to a parallel universe with its own system of logic and reason. A punishing God has his hand in everything that Robertson himself holds dear, down to natural disasters, like hurricanes and earthquakes, caused by homosexuals. Robertson often blurs the line between receiving or interpreting God's wisdom and simply promoting his own political and personal views via the Bible.

Donovan contends that Robertson is so conscientious about accuracy and fairness that he often stops himself in the middle of his *700 Club* monologues to correct even "a minuscule exaggeration." Yet Robertson's gift for hyperbole is legendary. He regularly compares American political skirmishes to military battles in which an assortment of enemies—liberals, environmentalists, gays—must be annihilated. Given his own checkered military background, the military metaphors are hypocritical. When the potential for actual combat arose, Robertson was nowhere to be found. Thanks to the high-level military connections of Senator Robertson, the younger Robertson was assigned to noncombat duty in Korea. Robertson's enormous financial success—his net worth is estimated at more than $200 million—has only strengthened his belief that God is on his side. In his writings, Robertson makes much of a philosophical principle he calls the "law of reciprocity." In simple language, the law means that if you give to God (especially via Robertson), you shall be rewarded, a lesson he apparently discovered in his own life. Indeed, Robertson landed in hot water with the Internal Revenue Service for privatizing his Christian Broadcasting Network, which he founded with tax-deductible contributions from supporters.

Despite his privileges, Robertson is fond of portraying the religious right as victims of precisely the groups he has had a strong hand in marginalizing. Upon their entrance into mainstream politics, conservative evangelicals have often adopted the left's language of oppression. Instead of gays, women, and racial minorities, it was evangelical Christians who were the real victims of intolerance. Even though there was no evidence they faced widespread discrimination, their moral beliefs, still dominant in many parts of society, supposedly face systematic exclusion from American society. God, who was on their side, was plotting his revenge on their behalf. Only their intervention in the world of politics could save the nation from his wrath. Robertson has often said that America has neglected its responsibility to the poor and the "oppressed." But his definition of the downtrodden is dubious: middle-class Christian families living in a secular world. Though Christian evangelical families undoubtedly struggle in an age of diminishing wages, underfunded schools, and crime epidemics, they don't differ from non-Christian families. Robertson opposes proposals to raise the minimum wage or make the tax system more progressive, thus alleviating the poor's share of the burden, and posits the elimination of homosexuality and abortion rights as the answer to the problems facing Christian families.

But the insistence on victim status for evangelical Christians generally did not lead to a heightened sensitivity toward other minority groups. Like Falwell, Robertson would have his own problem with anti-Semitism, only a more severe one. In 1995, Robertson came under fire for placing international Jewish bankers at the center of a conspiracy to overthrow the U.S. government in his 1991 book, *The New World Order.* In his defense, he cited a long bibliography that formed the basis of the book. Unfortunately for Robertson, one of his sources turned out to be Eustace Mullins, a David Duke mentor and Holocaust revisionist. It took Michael Lind, at the time an editor of the conservative digest *The Public Interest,* to raise the issue to national status. The mainstream press had failed to do its homework. Fixated on the irrelevant question of whether evangelicals should bring their biblical interpretations to politics, the press had overlooked the substance of Robertson's interpretations and his reliance on conspiracy formulas.

Such debates, which took place primarily in the pages of liberal Eastern publications, had little negative impact on the Christian Coalition. Robertson sent Reed out to sweet-talk the B'nai B'rith's Anti-Defamation League and the American Jewish Committee. In establishing the Coalition, Robertson and Reed knew that the key to success was local organizing. If you controlled a "disciplined charging army," dedicated to advancing your goals, as Falwell once described his followers, it mattered little what columnists at the *New York Times* thought. As the antigay initiatives of the early 1990s would come to demonstrate, the key to dominating national politics was grassroots organizing. Robertson had marshaled the foot soldiers; gay activists and their allies had not.

CHAPTER 2

Test Market

O N THE NIGHT OF JUNE 8, 1992, an unknown group of assailants broke into an office in Portland, Oregon. They stole a
fax machine and two computer systems, the kind of equipment in
which thieves regularly traffic. If they had done nothing else, the
break-in would have seemed to be just another urban burglary.
But the assailants had other goals in mind. They were not content
simply to steal. They wanted to close the office down. So they set
about systematically trashing it. They severed phone lines. They
poured photocopier toner onto desks and into other computers.
They stole the insurance papers for the group. When workers ar-
rived the next morning, their office was strewn with papers and
chemicals. It would be days before they could be fully operative
again.

The office targeted for such a methodical attack was the headquarters for the Campaign for a Hate Free Oregon. This group
was opposing an initiative proposed for the fall ballot that would
bar the state from "promoting" homosexuality and would void
existing local gay rights ordinances. Ironically enough given the
group's name, the Campaign for a Hate Free Oregon had been

the target of a hate crime. The incident in Portland that late-spring night was just one episode that year in a long, bitter fight over gay rights in Oregon. A similar battle was also under way in Colorado, where another antigay initiative was being promoted. To gay activists, both states were test markets for a new strategy by the religious right to build its infrastructure on the backs of gays and lesbians. As an issue that galvanized religious conservatives, gay rights presented a golden opportunity to build a strong political base in the churches that dotted every town in each state. The election would be a chance to see just how good an organizing tool an antigay initiative might be.

The ballot box had been the site of previous battles over gay rights ever since Anita Bryant led her crusade in Dade County in 1977. Over the years, the themes did not change much. In fact, Bryant's central message—protecting children from preying homosexuals—was still current in the campaigns fifteen years later, as the prevalence of "statistics" about gay pedophiles would prove. Electoral politics offered religious conservatives the chance to block the spread of nondiscrimination ordinances. But the luster of antigay campaigns had dimmed with some high-profile losses, particularly California voters' rejection of an initiative that would have prohibited gays from being teachers.

But as conservative evangelicals in the late 1980s were looking for ways to consolidate their local power bases, initiatives began to make sense again, this time as a tool for organizing at the grassroots level and thereby building a national political machine. In Oregon the religious right showed its peers around the nation that the ballot box was a useful weapon to have in its arsenal. There, a small, hitherto unknown group of religious activists took on the governor and, to the surprise of everyone, won. The ostensible cause for the battle was fairly innocuous. In 1987, then-governor Neil Goldschmidt, a Democrat, had issued an executive order forbidding employment discrimination on the basis of sexual orientation in the executive branch of state government. At the time, activists conceded that the move was largely symbolic, affecting only a handful of gays and lesbians.

Lon Mabon knew the order was largely symbolic, too, but

with far darker overtones. Mabon, an ex-hippie turned born-again Christian, was convinced that the success of gay activists signaled the moral decline of America. "If we take something that is wrong behavior and allow our government to transform it into what is good and acceptable—'what we should celebrate' is the term they use—that's going to have a dramatic effect on the moral foundation of our culture," he argued. As head of the Oregon Citizens Alliance, the politically ambitious Mabon had the weight of an organization behind him, even if outsiders saw it as an amateur operation. But Mabon had an uncanny talent for making fringe positions have an outsized impact on electoral politics. With its liberal reputation, Oregon did not seem the most hospitable place for a right-wing evangelical political group. But that reputation stems exclusively from Portland. The rest of Oregon is largely rural, blue-collar, and conservative. Moreover, the state has a long history of right-wing politics; it was a stronghold of the Ku Klux Klan in the 1920s. Neo-Nazi skinheads had made it their stronghold in the 1980s.

The Citizens Alliance had echoes of Pat Robertson's Christian Coalition, springing as it did out of another failed campaign. In the Alliance's case, it was a 1986 U.S. senatorial effort by Joe Lutz, a former Baptist minister. Running on an antiabortion conservative platform, Lutz challenged incumbent Bob Packwood in the Republican primary and walked away with 43 percent of the vote, a stunning showing for a candidate who had been expected to provide only token opposition. (Lutz launched another campaign against Packwood six years later, but was forced to abandon it in the wake of stories that he had left his wife for another woman and, after divorcing his wife, fallen behind on child support payments.) Lutz's supporters also backed a 1986 ballot measure that would have ended Medicaid funding for abortions. Again, they failed. But Mabon saw the campaigns as a springboard for a large-scale movement and formed the Oregon Citizens Alliance. While evangelical Christians had failed on the abortion issue, Mabon was determined to succeed on the gay issue. By developing a network in the churches of rural, blue-collar Oregon, he would be able to influence politics in Oregon for years to come.

Mabon was an unlikely leader for any political movement. Raised mostly in southern California, he was an indifferent student. Two years after his high school graduation in 1965, Mabon was drafted into the Army. He served sixteen months as a communications field wireman in Vietnam. The experience seemed to shake Mabon. When he returned to the States, he drifted around, experimenting with marijuana, LSD, and mescaline. He became the quintessential hippie—almost. Years later, he would joke that he was the only hippie ever to vote for Nixon. Eventually, his wanderings took him to Eureka in northern California, where he was born again. He kicked drugs, took over a local evangelical church, and met his wife-to-be, Bonnie. The Mabons settled in Oregon, where Lon was pretty much a failure as a businessman. He made two unsuccessful stabs at running retirement homes; he sold one and closed the other. It was only with the founding of the Citizens Alliance that Mabon finally found his niche. It was a calling. It was a living, too; he and Bonnie have earned a modest income from the Citizens Alliance ever since, and over the years other family members have drifted on and off the group's payroll.

⌒ In 1988, the Citizens Alliance announced that it would gather signatures for a measure to repeal Goldschmidt's executive order. Gay activists did not take the threat seriously, and with some reason. The Alliance and its founders had yet to have any sustained success. Although T. H. Bailey, an Alliance supporter, was chairman of the Republican Party when the group was formed, his tenure was brief and stormy. Party regulars were so enraged by Bailey's presence at the helm of the party that money quickly dried up and Bailey could no longer afford office space.

But the losses that the Alliance's backers were incurring in party politics were not fatal. The group had just not found the strategy that played to its strengths. A referendum on gay rights provided them that opportunity. The Alliance needed 63,578 signatures to place repeal of the executive order on the ballot. In just over two months, they pulled in 118,000 signatures. Volunteers circulating the petitions wore T-shirts that read I LOVE JESUS. Gay activists saw the Alliance as a fringe group that they could beat back with reason and hard cash. "As long as we can control the elements of the debate," Liz Kaufman, campaign manager for Oregonians for Fairness, the group opposing the referendum, said a few months before the election, "I'm confident of winning." However, the debate was shaped by the Citizens Alliance, which had a devastating motto. The name of their campaign group was the No Special Rights Committee. Every time the group was mentioned in the media, its message was mentioned as well. The message would become the battle cry of antigay campaigns nationwide.

Oregonians for Fairness did not kick into high gear until after Labor Day in 1988, as is traditional with campaigns. Officials in the campaign against the referendum, known as Measure 8, had no reason to think their effort was anything but traditional. They were successful at raising money and getting endorsements. The group's ads were slick, but did not mention gays or lesbians, referring instead to a "witch-hunt." Still, the effort seemed to be working; the polls put the antireferendum forces ahead. The campaign reassured gays and lesbians that defeat was a sure thing. Confident that they could rack up a solid margin at the polls, activists began to look to the next year, when they could push for a statewide nondiscrimination law. But on election day, Oregonians for Fairness discovered how unlike other campaigns this one was. Instead of losing, Measure 8 won with a respectable 53 percent of the vote. In the years to come, "no special rights" would be the club used against gays in dozens of elections in Oregon and elsewhere. The Oregon Citizens Alliance had found the formula it needed for success.

⌐ Mabon followed his triumph with a series of failures that nearly obliterated his power. In 1989, the same year the Citizens Alliance lost control of the state Republican Party, the Oregon secretary of state fined the group for violations of campaign laws. The next year, the Citizens Alliance came up with a measure that would have banned what the group called "convenience abortions." That initiative was defeated. In the same election, the Citizens Alliance fielded vice-chair Al Mobley as a pro-life independent gubernatorial candidate. Mobley pulled 13 percent of the vote, enough to allow Democrat Barbara Roberts, a gay rights supporter, to beat out moderate Republican Dave Frohnmayer.

The Citizens Alliance's efforts won it the enmity of mainstream Republicans, who were certain that Mobley was fielded solely to deny the pro-choice Frohnmayer the governor's mansion. The group also found criticism from within its natural constituency as well. The Oregon Association of Evangelicals complained that the Citizens Alliance was unwilling to forge compromises with moderates. The Citizens Alliance dismissed the complaint as the attitude of "gradualists," who had contributed to society's increased tolerance for abortion.

For its failures, and its arrogance, the Citizens Alliance suffered. Its leadership hit hard times, too. Mabon saw his income dry up. He fell behind on his taxes and his rent. For a while, it looked as if the Citizens Alliance had accomplished all it was going to accomplish. Then in a stroke of genius, the Citizens Alliance announced in May 1991 that it would start collecting signatures for an Abnormal Behaviors Initiative. The measure, as originally conceived, lumped homosexuality with bestiality and necrophilia as "abnormal, wrong, unnatural and perverse." Later, the initiative, and its title, were modified to ban state protections or funding for "promotion" of homosexuality, pedophilia, sadism, and masochism. The initiative would prove to be the Citizens Alliance's comeback vehicle. Within months, the group would regain its prominence in state politics, never again to lose it.

The timing of Mabon's announcement coincided with the death of a statewide bill banning discrimination on the basis of sexual orientation. The measure, supported by Governor Roberts, passed the Senate only to languish in the House, where speaker Larry Campbell, a Republican, refused to allow hearings on it. When Mabon filed the proposed ballot measure in May 1991, Roberts declared that it was written by people who were "flat-out paranoid." But to Mabon, the measure was a last stand to stop the state from hurtling toward sinfulness. "Unless somebody stands up and fights for what they believe are right and correct values, I think it's going to be a systematic downward trend," he said. Any quarter given to homosexuality was, to Mabon, promotion, and it had to be stopped. By his own sights, he was not bigoted. The measure would only be enforced against individuals who did not stay in the closet. "If a person keeps their sexual practices to themselves and does not try to force them into the public arena, then we're not after going after somebody," he declared.

⟶ In devising his initiative, Mabon was able to rely on outside counsel for assistance. In the Citizens Alliance's case, help came from Bruce Fein, who had been deputy attorney general in the Reagan administration and was now a fellow at the Heritage Foundation, the conservative think tank that had fueled the Reagan revolution. (Reagan was Mabon's hero, even though when he was governor Reagan had explicitly rejected the antigay Briggs initiative that would have barred gays from teaching.)

In a letter to Mabon, Fein declared the proposed—and revised—ballot measure to be "facially constitutional." Citing the Supreme Court decision in the Bowers case, which upheld Georgia's sodomy law, Fein argued that the state had a legitimate right to sustain "public morals." Gays and lesbians who "did not exploit their offices to encourage homosexuality by others" would not be penalized under the initiative, nor would the measure lead to any censorship or abridgement of rights. In short, Fein concluded, the proposed amendment "should survive any challenge to it made under provisions of the United States Constitution." The Citizens Alliance widely distributed the letter, adding its own interpretations in the margin, such as "sodomy is not a civil right." But the extremeness of its original proposal would shadow the revised initiative until the end of the campaign.

With the death of the statewide nondiscrimination bill in the spring of 1991, gay activists in Portland decided to try a more local approach. If it couldn't happen for the entire state, at least some protections should be in place in the state's biggest, and most liberal, city. The drive to get the Portland city council to pass a nondiscrimination ordinance was fairly easy, although opponents of the measure turned out in force at the city council hearings at the end of September. One senior at Portland State declared that gays could not be the targets of bigotry because they "live in nice neighborhoods, in well-furnished homes and apartments with expensive accouterments." The Citizens Alliance was on hand at the hearings to pass out flyers opposing the measure. Its literature depicted a male teacher in drag standing at the front of a classroom, with the caption "If gay rights becomes law, what prevents this type of thing from happening?" In fact, any teacher who attempted such a stunt would be dismissed for unprofessional conduct.

As expected, the Portland city council passed the nondiscrimination ordinance 3–0 in October. But passage allowed the Citizens Alliance to test the waters for its statewide measure. The group announced that it would gather enough signatures to force a voter referendum on the measure. It failed in this attempt, largely because of its own incompetence. Citizens Alliance supporters gathered plenty of signatures, but at malls in suburban Portland. Since the would-be voters weren't registered to vote in Portland, their signatures weren't valid.

The Citizens Alliance's setback on the Portland ordinance proved temporary. The group could still rally its troops among the evangelical faithful for future battles. It began distributing a forty-minute video with highly selected excerpts from the gay pride parade in San Francisco. The video, which featured a transvestite Christ and groups like Hookers from Hell, included the running subtitle "This is what gay rights means." Missing from the presentation were proud parents marching with their gay children or friendly religious groups. The video, which the Citizens Alliance sold for ten dollars, was widely used in churches.

⟳ Having been burned once, gay activists knew enough to take the Citizens Alliance seriously this time around. But the gay community was still pointing fingers over who was to blame for the 1988 defeat. In this atmosphere of distrust and bickering, rifts were inevitable. The nascent campaign lost the support of many well-connected gay men, who felt that campaign organizers—

many of them women—were intentionally ignoring the assistance that they could provide. (The women, for their part, felt that the men didn't like any campaign that they weren't running themselves.) Thus, many gay political movers and shakers largely sat on the sidelines. There were exceptions; John Baker, who was board chair of Right to Privacy, a statewide gay political group, poured countless hours into fighting Measure 9. But many others simply wrote checks and did nothing else.

The campaign against the Citizens Alliance took the name Coalition for a Hate Free Oregon and immediately began working under the assumption that the measure would qualify for the ballot. Among the activists on the Campaign's steering committee was Donna Red Wing, the head of the Lesbian Community Project in Portland. In a community known for its divisiveness, Red Wing had earned the respect of her peers. She brooked no nonsense, but she also had a warm personality and good sense of humor. Even Mabon respected her, and she in turn admired his political skills.

Red Wing had come to the gay and lesbian cause in a roundabout manner. Like Mabon, she was a former counterculture type, having lived as a teenager for a while in a commune in San Francisco's Haight-Ashbury district at the height of the flower power movement. Born Donna Olson, Red Wing grew up in the projects of Worcester, Massachusetts. She bounced around the antiwar effort, organizing a chapter of the left-wing Students for a Democratic Society at her high school. After becoming pregnant, Red Wing got married in 1969. With her husband, a painter, and son, Julian, she lived on a farm in western Massachusetts. But her husband became physically abusive, and after eight years, Red Wing escaped in the middle of the night with her son and just a bag of clothes. Working as a waitress, she enrolled at a local community college, finally graduating summa cum laude with a fine arts degree from Assumption College in Worcester. She went on to get her master's degree and became director of a social service agency dealing with abused children. During her tenure, Child Assault Prevention increased its client load tenfold.

It was in Worcester that Red Wing met Suzanne Pommerleau, an ex-nun who had become a lesbian feminist talk-show host. It was love at first sight. Eventually, the pair adopted the last name Red Wing together as a sign of their commitment to each other. After burning out at her job, Donna knew that she needed a change, so she and Suzanne, who changed her first name to Sumitra, moved to Portland after Donna was hired to head the Lesbian Community Project. As head of the Project, Red Wing was perhaps the most visible lesbian activist in the city. It was inevitable that she would be integral to the campaign against the Citizens Alliance. She was joined by other grassroots activists on the steering committee, such as Scott Seibert in Eugene and Kathleen Saadat, an African-American lesbian in Portland, all of whom were eager to fight the proposed amendment. They knew the battle would be hard; what they couldn't predict was just how hard it would be.

⤳ Before the Citizens Alliance qualified its statewide measure, it was able to put similar versions of it on the ballot in two rural towns, Springfield and Corvallis, in May 1992. For the Citizens Alliance, the vote would be a test of how well the measure would play in the rest of rural Oregon. Success would mobilize its followers with the prospect of victory in November. For gay activists used to concentrating their efforts on urban areas, the possibility of two losses would prove an embarrassment, showing how shallow their support was outside of a few liberal regions. As it turned out, the votes were split, with the measure passing in Springfield and failing decisively in Corvallis, which allowed each side to claim a win.

By the time the two local elections were held, the stakes in Oregon were rapidly escalating. Paul deParrie, an antiabortion activist who insisted he had no affiliation with the Citizens Alliance, filed a $12 million lawsuit against Red Wing, the Lesbian Community Project, Campaign for a Hate Free Oregon, Queer Nation, John Baker, and other gay activists, charging them with racketeering. DeParrie also cited Portland chief of police Tom Potter and his daughter Katie, an openly lesbian officer on the police force; Potter, who marched in the Portland gay pride parade and was active in the local chapter of Parents and Friends of Lesbians and Gays, was a particular irritant for conservative Christians, who felt he was abusing his office by promoting gay rights.

The lawsuit was eventually dismissed—deParrie was acting as his own lawyer, modeling his suit on ones that right-to-lifers had been slapped with—but not before deParrie put a scare into the people named in it. He also further divided the gay community, albeit indirectly. The American Civil Liberties Union agreed to represent some of the defendants, but not the ones involved with direct-action tactics. "They have engaged in very different behavior that others have been very careful not to engage in," said Stevie Remington, the executive director of the state's ACLU chapter. Thus Bigot Busters, a group that had tried to prevent the Citizens Alliance from collecting signatures for its petitions, and its founder, Bob Ralphs, were effectively ostracized by more mainstream groups for resorting to such strategies as filming Citizens Alliance volunteers in action. It was the start of a tactic that angry activists would dub the "good gay/bad gay" strategy.

The viciousness surrounding the campaign escalated with the passage of the Springfield measure. Suddenly the tensions that had been under the surface burst into the open. Just how brutal the campaign could be became appallingly clear with the attack on the Hate Free Oregon headquarters in June. More chilling than the damage was what the vandals stole: two complete computer systems that contained a list of thousands of volunteers and contributors, and, mysteriously, four telephones. (In the increasingly paranoid atmosphere of the campaign, workers began to wonder if the stolen phones had been bugged.) People who did not want to be identified as gay for fear of their jobs or exposure to unaccepting families woke up one morning to realize that their names were in the hands of people who clearly hated them for their support for the campaign. No one on the list was ever contacted by the vandals, but the anxiety the theft caused was very real.

At the same time, the public incidents of harassment against

Hate Free Oregon supporters grew. Ellen Lowe, a sixty-one-year-old heterosexual grandmother who was associate director of Ecumenical Ministries of Oregon, received a death threat. The volume of hate calls to the campaign's office soared. A wheelchair-bound woman in Springfield was spat upon by three youths who saw a bumper sticker on her car opposing the measure. The Citizens Alliance vehemently denied that it was responsible in any way for the explosion of incidents, particularly the vandalism at the campaign offices. "Citizens Alliance has also been the victim of numerous similar hate crimes in recent months," Scott Lively, the Citizens Alliance's communications director, said in a statement. "For everyone's sake, we hope that the perpetrators are caught and prosecuted to the fullest extent of the law." In fact, the Citizens Alliance was not to be outdone in the sweepstakes for victim status, even though it never endured anything of the magnitude of the attack on Hate Free Oregon's offices. There had long been harassment and insults of Citizens Alliance supporters as well. The Citizens Alliance headquarters had been vandalized, pelted with eggs, its locks glued shut. Mabon had regularly received death threats. "It's like the gates of hell have opened up," said Lively, leaving others to draw the conclusion as to who the forces of Satan were.

Yet if Mabon was willing to complain bitterly about the threats and vandalism the Citizens Alliance endured, he was unwilling to grant that gays and lesbians were more than equally at risk. As the campaign heated up, there was a frightening upswing in bias incidents against men and women perceived to be gay or lesbian. You didn't have to be involved in the campaign in any way to be worried. Incidents of verbal harassment and outright physical attacks by bashers who concluded people were gay on the basis of a bumper sticker or simply because of the way they looked rose dramatically. Many gays and lesbians in Oregon were suddenly fearful that they would be the target of an attack, even if they had nothing to do with the campaign. Their fears only added to the escalating tensions in the state. Yet Mabon dismissed reports of antigay violence as propaganda designed to generate sympathy. By the time the Citizens Alliance turned in 115,000 signatures to qualify the initiative at the beginning of July, 26,000 more than necessary, Oregon had fallen under a state of siege.

⟿ In arguing to voters that gays and lesbians did not deserve employment or housing protections, Mabon relied on the premise that gays were not a minority. "[H]omosexuals already have the same basic rights as everyone else," a 1992 Citizens Alliance flyer stated. "They want their choice of homosexuality to be given the same civil protections and preferences as being born black or Hispanic. This would be like granting affirmative action quotas to celibates or polygamists just because they claim to be born that way." The argument of a privileged class seeking further privileges played well among blue-collar workers, particularly in rural Oregon, which was reeling from job cutbacks in the timber industry. The Alliance repeatedly made the point that gays were supposedly privileged to disgruntled workers watching their livelihoods disappear. The timber towns, conservative and hostile to gays to begin with, were receptive to the argument.

Yet, the Alliance was not content with civil rights arguments alone. The group went much further, characterizing gay life and practices as repulsive and dangerous. In a voters' pamphlet distributed before the election, Phillip Ramsdell, the group's political director, outlined his version of gay sexual habits in graphic detail: "Studies by leading researchers show that the following practices are regularly engaged in by homosexuals: fellation 100%, fisting 41% (inserting fist and forearm into rectum), rimming 92% (licking rectum), water sports 29% (urinating on partners, drinking urine), mud wallowing 17% (defecating on partner), sado-masochism 37% (beating, piercing, another person for sexual pleasure), public sex 66% (public restrooms, bathhouses, parks), pedophilia 46% (sex with minors)."

The Citizens Alliance made particular use of the child molestation charges. Given that the Oregon ballot initiative would prevent schools from "promoting" homosexuality, pedophilia was the ideal argument for Measure 9, as the initiative was christened. Alliance literature contained numerous references to the North American Man/Boy Love Association (NAMBLA), a group that urges the repeal of age of consent laws. That NAMBLA is itself a pariah among most of the gay community did not stop the Alliance from implying that it was simply another gay organization by pointing to a NAMBLA ad in a gay newspaper. But the Alliance hurt itself through some ham-fisted efforts. Chief among those was a flyer, "Homosexuality, the Classroom and Your Children," that the group circulated in September. In the flyer, the Alliance dramatized its allegations in the fictional story of a twelve-year-old boy named Billy who lives in a mill town. Billy was being pressured by his fat friend Chuckie to have sex, who claimed that the entire political establishment of Oregon was on his side. "How can it be wrong?" Chuckie asked. "The police chief says it's OK. Our teachers say it's OK. The newspaper says it's OK. Even the governor says it's OK." Under the weight of so much authority, Billy relents. "Doing those things couldn't be wrong or those people would say so, I guess." The pamphlet not only conflated homosexuality and pedophilia. It went far beyond, saying that Governor Barbara Roberts and Portland police chief Tom Potter condoned children having sex. The pamphlet became an easy target for the No on 9 campaign, as Hate Free Oregon was renamed. "This is a sleazy, misleading tactic used by desperate people," said No on 9's campaign manager, Peggy Norman.

Still, no matter how firmly the allegations were knocked down, the visceral reaction that they created lingered. Gays—and the campaign focused far more of their attacks on gay men than on lesbians—seemed vaguely unsavory in their habits. To that already unsettling image, the Alliance introduced the worst "threat" of all: the specter of AIDS. In its statement of principles, the organization said that "there should not be laws granting civil rights protections based on behavior that is morally wrong or injurious to public health." It was not enough to object to nondiscrimination protections. The people who were covered by them were now being portrayed as a menace to society.

Given the threat many gays and lesbians felt from the initiative, it was not surprising that the No on 9 campaign saw a tremendous influx of money and volunteers. But not everyone was made to feel welcome. Some grassroots activists were left behind in the rush to develop a campaign strategy. When Peggy Norman, who had worked in campaigns for the National Organization for Women, was chosen to head the campaign, Red Wing phoned her twenty-seven times to welcome Norman and offer her assistance. Not one of the calls was returned. Others among the original steering-committee members also met with a chilly reception. The campaign refused to turn contribution and expenditure reports over to Scott Seibert, forcing him to file for them from the state secretary of state's office. After being ignored by the campaign, Kathleen Saadat struck out on her own, forming a coalition of black leaders to oppose the measure.

Gary Wilson, the pastor of the predominantly gay Metropolitan Community Church in Portland, was also shunned, although the campaign did try to use him at first. Officials asked Wilson to pass the word to direct action groups like Queer Nation to keep their activities low-key during the campaign so as not to cause any embarrassment. Wilson was suspicious that his goodwill with those groups was being exploited and remained cautious; soon he found himself cut off from the campaign as well.

Respected activists with years of grassroots experience, the ostracized group cared enough about winning the election to keep their mouths shut and do what they could to beat back the initiative. But they knew that the campaign in Oregon had been de-gayed. No on 9 insisted that gays were simply a smoke screen for the Citizen Alliance's real agenda, to open the floodgates of restrictive legislation. "This measure is really not about gay and lesbian rights," Peggy Norman insisted. "This is a measure about Oregon and which direction we will go." To an extent, the last part of that statement was true. The leaders of the Alliance knew from firsthand experience that opposition to homosexuality would resonate more widely with voters than opposition to abortion, another of its key issues. Success with Measure 9 would strengthen them and enable them to visit other matters dear to their hearts. But, as Red Wing argued, Measure 9 obviously was about homosexuality. Mabon's opposition to it was real, and he was not using it as a decoy for other concerns. Opposition to gays and lesbians was at the heart of what the Citizens Alliance was.

The image that No on 9 presented to voters was exemplified by its spokeswoman, Ellen Lowe, a straight grandmother with religious ties. No one questioned Lowe's ability. But Red Wing and her compatriots were increasingly frustrated that the campaign did not want to educate the public about gays and lesbians in society. They acknowledged the danger in framing the debate in those terms because of the very real possibility that the public would decide that if Measure 9 was indeed about opposition to homosexuality, then it was all in favor of it. Yet they were also worried that if No on 9 was run just like any other campaign, with a focus on how to win and nothing else, the long-term benefits to the gay community would be minimal.

In terms of its campaign message, No on 9 was amazingly successful. Its first television ad was a brilliant attack on the Citizens Alliance, featuring a teacher who complained that the Alliance would force her to raise issues she thought inappropriate. The use of a teacher gave enormous credibility to the argument, which flipped the "save our children" rhetoric of the Alliance on its head. But noticeably absent from the commercial were the words *gay, lesbian,* and *homosexual,* suggesting that maybe these words were too unsavory for children to hear.

While the campaign tried to be as heterosexual as possible, there was still a sizable gay presence. Many volunteers were drawn from the gay community, since gays and lesbians had the most at stake in the outcome. Even those who did not volunteer emptied their pockets at house parties, bar fund-raisers, and raffles to bankroll the campaigns. AIDS organizations saw donations plummet while people poured their money into No on 9. Nor was the campaign's leadership completely devoid of a high-profile gay presence, although it was largely national, not local. Gay and lesbian activists were advising the campaign, most notably Suzanne Pharr, head of the Arkansas Women's Project in Little Rock, who ended up as a consultant to the Oregon campaign.

The national gay groups described the battle in apocalyptic terms. "The entire national gay community sends its love, support, and heartfelt wishes for success," Urvashi Vaid, director of the National Gay and Lesbian Task Force, said in a speech during a visit to Oregon in October. "We who are gay, lesbian, or bi-sexual in this room tonight know that we live in a world bereft of justice and peace for lesbians and gay men. We are the last class of persons left without full citizenship rights in American society today." How bereft the audience was was open to ques-tion: Vaid was speaking at a $100-a-plate fund-raiser. The Citi-zens Alliance would have been hard-pressed to put together so pricey an event.

Both Vaid and Pharr, author of *Homophobia as a Weapon of Sexism,* saw gay issues as part of a broader left-wing agenda. In trying to explain the connection between race issues and gay is-sues, Pharr would write that former Ku Klux Klan leader David Duke, who had been shunned by the Republican Party when he ran for governor of Louisiana, was "following in a long line of racist politicians such as Wallace, Reagan, and Bush." Vaid and Pharr promoted an image of the gay community as part of a move-ment to create a new, more equitable political system, although most gays and lesbians probably wanted nothing more than to fit into the existing one. The rhetoric made it easier for the right wing to portray the gay movement as a fringe of the loony left. More to the point, it left little room for moderates and conser-vative libertarians who supported gay rights. For them, and for many gays and lesbians as well, gay rights was not a left-right issue; it was a simple matter of fairness.

~ By the time Vaid visited Oregon, the campaign was in full swing. The Citizens Alliance used whatever measures at its dis-posal to fight back, but it lacked the slickness of the No on 9 cam-paign. Mabon often jettisoned the question of civil rights altogether to tear into homosexuals. He told *USA Today* that gays and lesbians "are born with a weakness toward unnatural sex be-havior. They should fight it." If Measure 9 forced gays back into the closet, "that's probably better for society," he concluded. In-deed, Mabon was waging a cultural war, and he had no problems declaring as much. "Oregon is at the cutting edge," he declared. "We are the first troops of two opposing armies that are engaging each other. We are talking about fundamental questions, about what is right and what is wrong." When the Citizens Alliance was visited by former representative William Dannemeyer, who had made his reputation in the House as a vehement opponent of gay rights, the Orange County Republican sounded the same theme. "How we define the family unit is an important battleground in this cultural war," declared Dannemeyer, who once suggested that AIDS spread through "spores." "That's the essence of the fight over Measure 9."

After a while, the No on 9 campaign took on a life of its own. When Norman joked that the flood of supportive statements the campaign had procured from businesses and politicians amounted to an "endorsement du jour," sympathizers called the campaign headquarters to see how they could be the one to pro-vide the endorsement of the day. No on 9 became a chic cause among Hollywood celebrities, attracting donations from Debra Winger, Tom and Roseanne Arnold, and Kirstie Alley. The na-tional media made pilgrimages to No on 9's nondescript offices to chronicle the unique battle. The calls from reporters and talk shows were so numerous that the campaign's young, inexperi-enced press officer was swamped. Phil Donahue's show called three times without a response before turning to Seibert as a guest for its program on the initiative.

Avoiding the question of gay rights, the campaign turned into a referendum on the Citizens Alliance, whose many enemies were more than happy to damage the group as much as possible. Dave Frohnmayer, who would have been governor but for the Citizens Alliance, was a frequent critic of the initiative, as was Craig Berk-man, the moderate chair of the state Republican Party. Berkman in particular was a fierce enemy of the Alliance, fighting it for what he believed was the soul of the party. The religious right, he said, was "driven by a dominion theology, which says that Chris-tians should take over the government." The Alliance returned the enmity, successfully targeting Berkman for replacement after the election was over.

Although it seemed as if every major group inside Oregon op-posed the measure, the Alliance did get comfort from outside the state. The Christian Coalition donated $20,000 to the Alliance's campaign. In September, Ralph Reed, the Coalition's director, flew to Oregon to announce the formation of a state chapter of the group. The chapter's head: Lon Mabon, who had attended a Christian Coalition conference earlier in the year. "We would have come in here whether there had been a Measure 9 or not," Reed said. Given the foundation that the Alliance had already laid, the Christian Coalition could not resist building on it.

As the campaign entered its final weeks, the violence in Oregon escalated. By this point, the debate was no longer about homosexuality. It was a free-for-all that brought out the worst in people. The most fundamental rights—free speech, freedom of religion, personal safety—were jettisoned as dark, antidemocratic impulses surged to the surface. At its mildest, the harassment in Oregon took the form of the destruction of lawn signs supporting or opposing Measure 9. Someone, presumably gay activists, painted pink triangles outside the homes of Springfield city councilman Ralf Walters, who supported Measure 9, and Citizens Alliance spokeswoman Loretta Neet. Walters declared that "to a Christian, a pink triangle in front of one's home is as offensive as a cross burning on a black person's home or a swastika on a synagogue."

Worse still were the threats to personal safety. Mabon and other Alliance officials took to varying their routes to work in response to the death threats that they regularly received. But gay activists were the ones who saw the threats become real. Seibert twice had his home vandalized. Once, someone broke in and stole the contributor list to OUTPAC, the political group he had formed. Another time, in the middle of the night, someone threw a rock through his window. Attached to it was a note: "Remember that you are never safe and that we will always know what you are doing every day and at all times."

Red Wing in particular became a target for a flood of hate messages and threats. One caller would phone her daily to describe exactly how well he had done at target practice that day and how, come election night, he would "take her out." Red Wing called him the gun du jour caller. Another caller listed all of Red Wing's family members and threatened to break into her house.

"We could get you anytime," the caller told her. "You only have ten days left to live." Strangers showed up on her porch in a working-class Portland neighborhood, peering into her windows. The police took the threats seriously, equipping Red Wing with a cellular phone and the beeper numbers of officers who would respond twenty-four hours a day. They wired her house with a button that immediately alerted the police when triggered. Red Wing armed herself with a shotgun and several rounds of ammunition. The threats took such a toll that her partner Sumitra could only fall asleep if Donna was sitting in bed next to her with the shotgun across her lap.

Into this volatile environment, someone threw a bomb—literally. Early on the morning of September 26, a group of skinheads tossed a firebomb into the basement apartment of Hattie Cohens, a black lesbian, and Brian Mock, a gay white man, in Salem. Cohens died of smoke inhalation the same day. Mock lingered a few days before succumbing to his injuries. The skinheads who were arrested for the arson were not connected to the Citizens Alliance. But the gay community felt that the demonizing rhetoric used by the Alliance had set the stage that made murder inevitable. "Measure 9 really creates an atmosphere where people feel they can indeed go out and act out some of this behavior," said Sherry Oeser, a No on 9 spokeswoman.

But No on 9 had waited four days before issuing a statement about the bombing, infuriating grassroots activists like Red Wing. They felt the delay had to do with the victims themselves, who were not "good" gays. Although Mock had been viciously beaten by skinheads in an attack a few weeks earlier, he made for an unusual martyr: developmentally disabled, marginal, a little odd. Cohens was a strong-willed, outspoken woman—a prototypical butch dyke who had also spent time in jail, not exactly a victim with whom the public could easily identify.

The death threats and vandalism continued right up until the election. A few days before voters went to the polls, vandals broke into St. Matthew's Roman Catholic Church in Hillsboro and spray-painted "We hate gays" and "Yes on 9" on the walls, while also setting a fire in the rectory. Citizens Alliance supporters were also the target of attacks, although they received far less publicity, in part because they were so distrustful of the media that they dealt with it as little as possible. A Baptist church in Portland received a bomb threat, while someone in another church set fire to an Alliance flyer posted on a bulletin board, causing $30,000 in damage. The Portland Foursquare Church was repeatedly vandalized, with someone painting "Bigots" on its walls.

There were also derogatory flyers circulated by a handful of radical gay activists. One depicted a Christian fish symbol with the slogan "Vote No on 9 or We Shoot the Fish." Proponents of the initiatives were branded neo-Nazis with dreary regularity. One gay guest columnist in the *New York Times* spoke of a campaign of "purification," which took Alliance's censorship of gay books to the level of ethnic cleansing. Editors at *The Advocate*, the national gay newsmagazine, chose to illustrate a cover story about the Oregon campaign with a swastika and the headline "The Rise of Fascism in America."

It wasn't only the amendment's opponents who flung terms around with abandon. Leaders of the antigay campaigns were equally inclined to brand their opponents Hitlers at heart. The Citizens Alliance distributed a flyer proclaiming that gay tactics were drawn from *Mein Kampf*. Scott Lively would later go on to write a book, titled *The Pink Swastika*, suggesting that the entire Holocaust was masterminded by a handful of crafty gays in Hitler's inner circle, revisionism that twisted the presence of a small cadre of gays present in the early days of Nazism into justification for the Alliance's antigay stance. As the election approached, each side regularly described the other as a threat to American society.

~ By the final week of the campaign, No on 9 officials were hopeful of victory. The momentum of the campaign against the Citizens Alliance seemed to be too much for the group to overcome. The polls indicated a comfortable margin of victory, but still Norman and activists outside the campaign took nothing for granted. The campaign continued at full throttle up until election day. Fearful of violence, the Portland police were out in force in Oregon on election night. Gay-friendly sites were scattered throughout the city for people to watch election results together without fear. Norman obtained a bodyguard. Leaders of the Citizens Alliance had their own extraordinary precautions, including bulletproof vests and tight security at their headquarters. "In my twenty-six years with the Portland Police Bureau, I don't think we've ever taken the precautions we've taken on this election because we've never had the volatility, emotion, fear, and anger this election has," Chief Potter said. Police had identified thirty activists on both sides as potential targets.

As the results began to pour in in Oregon, activists heaved a sigh of relief. The initiative was failing and would ultimately go down to defeat 57 percent to 43 percent. The margin was contributed largely by liberal voters in Portland, who were also turning out in large numbers to vote for Bill Clinton. At Citizens Alliance headquarters in Wilsonville, Mabon refused to concede defeat. He had a point. He had been outspent four to one, but he had convinced 530,000 voters to side with his condemnation of homosexuality. By winning twenty-one of thirty-six counties, the Alliance had paved the way for more local-level initiatives.

In the end, the Citizens Alliance was fated to lose. Too many forces were arrayed against it. Virtually all of the mainstream Protestant denominations had condemned Measure 9, as had the Roman Catholic hierarchy. The state Democratic and Republican Party leaders were against it, even appearing together in a television commercial to say so. The major businesses in the state were opposed to it. US West, a telecommunications company, went so far as to buy space in the voters' pamphlet to condemn the initiative. The publisher of the *Oregonian,* Fred Stickel, a conservative Roman Catholic, made an unprecedented front-page appeal to the paper's readers to vote against Measure 9.

The celebration among gays and lesbians was unrestrained. At first, Red Wing was caught up in the exuberance. But at some point, she realized that the victory was largely Pyrrhic. At a rally just after midnight, she stood up and gave a speech. "It's not as if we won anything tonight," she reminded the crowd. "It's not like we lined up and won a nice prize. We did nothing more than run in place. That's not enough, given the price we paid." Measure 9 was a single battle in a long war, Red Wing warned the crowd. (As if to underscore just how long, nine days after the election, and four years after Measure 8 had passed, a three-judge panel finally threw out the results of the 1988 referendum.) Gays and lesbians were running the risk of confusing a campaign with the gay rights movement. A campaign was, as Red Wing put it, 50 percent plus one vote. A movement was a long-term education effort to win the hearts and minds of the population. It could not be done in the few months of a campaign. But a campaign could provide the groundwork for future education. The problem, Red Wing concluded, was that No on 9 did not look beyond election day, which meant that the Citizens Alliance would be able to return again and again with its antigay measures. The $2 million spent to beat back the Citizens Alliance did not bring people to a better understanding of gay and lesbian citizens. That was where the real work remained to be done.

Mabon seemed unfazed by the results. Even if the Citizens Alliance lost, the election results were still good for fund-raising. Three weeks after Measure 9's defeat, the Alliance sent out a plea for money to its supporters. The letter was an angry call to further battle. **"Come on, folks,"** Mabon wrote. "We can't let the homosexuals have this state! **In order to win,** they lied about the effects of Measure 9. They lied about homosexuality in the schools. They lied about who their opponents were by calling you and your family bigots and Nazis. *They* staged phony hate crimes. **They won by trickery and deceit and we cannot let them get away with it."**

The faithful stood by Mabon. "In our opinion, it was important to come out strong the first time and then modify the measure the next time," Lively said. Two months after the election, he would announce the formation of an Idaho chapter of the Citizens

Alliance and plans to file thirty-two local initiatives, more "moderate" versions of Measure 9, in Oregon. In 1994, Mabon would return with another statewide initiative. Though he would again fail, he would keep trying, promising to return in 1996. To him, election day was just one more battle in the long war that he was waging.

CHAPTER 3

Angels and Demons

EVEN AS THE STORM CLOUDS were gathering in Oregon and Colorado, the first national skirmish between the religious right and gay activists was already taking shape. The 1992 presidential campaign was a war by proxy through the national parties. Years of fund-raising and support were finally paying off for both groups. Now the time was arriving to demand a seat at the table, a say in each party's platform and power structure.

Although the campaign was fierce and polarizing, conservative Christians and gay activists could agree upon one thing. They disliked George Bush. In the four years leading up to his reelection effort, Bush had managed to antagonize both groups. Bush's outreach to the religious right did not satisfy their basic distrust of a man who once was pro-choice on abortion and who was a former member of the Trilateral Commission, an innocuous public-policy group that the right wing viewed as a vehicle for a world-government movement. Gay activists used Bush's ties to the religious right to bash him as well. If anything, they hated the president even more. Most of their anger centered on Bush's apparent lack of interest in AIDS. Although somewhat more moderate than the Reagan administration, the Bush White House repeatedly torpedoed AIDS education efforts because it considered prevention materials to be nothing more than gay erotica. The administration also refused to provide full funding for the Ryan White CARE Act, the bill named after the Indiana hemophiliac who had died from AIDS, which funneled money to cities in the epicenter of the epidemic.

In the one speech that Bush delivered on the disease while president, a fairly innocuous address in March 1990, Urvashi Vaid, then executive director of the National Gay and Lesbian Task Force, heckled him. The episode underscored the outsider strategy of many gay activists that peaked during the Bush years. Although the Task Force was a Washington-based organization, Vaid's action proved that the group was not part of the political establishment, nor did it aspire to be. Instead, it was drawing on the confrontational approach of direct-action groups such as ACT UP and Queer Nation, the latter launched just weeks after Bush's speech. With much of the political establishment impervious to the tragedy of AIDS, activists took to the streets for noisy, intentionally outrageous protests. By the time the 1992 presidential campaign was heating up, gay activism and protests had become, to many people, virtually synonymous. The activists had used their anger at being ignored and gotten the attention that they wanted. They had perfected the role of the angry outsider.

Leaders of the religious right thought of themselves as outsiders as well. They didn't take to the streets (although they certainly used the images of gay activists in the streets to proclaim the threat of an aggressive gay menace). But they were nonetheless angry at what they saw as George Bush's betrayal of their cause. As early as the summer of 1990, conservative Christians were fed up with Bush. Much of their ire stemmed from Bush's breaking of his 1988 campaign promise not to raise taxes. But that was not all. In a newsletter from Pat Robertson, the televangelist cited "the White House embrace of homosexual activists" as second in a list of reasons why the president's honeymoon was over. The administration's continued funding of the National Endowment for the

Arts, with its occasionally controversial (i.e., gay-themed) art, drove Robertson and his allies to a frenzy, making the agency a favorite target for their wrath. It was also an opportunity for organizing. "Had you and I 'learned the ropes' of the political world, no agency like the National Endowment for the Arts (NEA) could have spent public monies on homo-erotic photography, or pictures of Christ immersed in a vat of urine," Robertson wrote in a 1990 fund-raising letter.

The pressure the religious right brought to bear on Bush paid off. John Frohnmayer, the director of the National Endowment for the Arts who had defended the agency from political intrusions into its internal decisions, was forced to resign in May 1992. His successor, Anne-Imelda Radice, was more deft at steering through the political shoals around the agency, but she too came under intense criticism. Gay activists alleged that she was a lesbian and found a willing audience for their charges not just among the gay press but among right-wing publications like the *Washington Times*. The episode was an odd moment where the needs of gay activists and the needs of the religious right dovetailed. Both sides hammered away at Radice, gay activists because they wanted to brand her a traitor, and leaders of the religious right because they wanted to question her loyalty to their view. Bush came under attack for hypocrisy from all sides. For her part, Radice refused to comment on the charge on the grounds that her private life had nothing to do with her work at the agency.

Other incidents, which went virtually unnoticed by the mainstream press, took on enormous significance to the religious right. In 1991, the federal government granted $25,000 to the National Lesbian and Gay Health Conference to help fund workshops on AIDS education. The uproar was so great that Dr. William Roper, head of the federal Centers for Disease Control, had to apologize profusely. "I am not pleased that CDC is listed as a supporter on the front page of the conference brochure, giving the impression that we are supporting the sessions," Roper wrote in a letter to Richard Land, executive director of the Christian Life Commission of the Southern Baptist Convention. Bush used Vice President Dan Quayle as a kind of liaison to conservative Christians, but the move only made Quayle look like a true believer and Bush a reluctant convert.

The breaking point for religious conservatives came in February 1992. Twice before, gays and lesbians had been invited to the White House for bill signings. Then on February 13, National Gay and Lesbian Task Force officials, including Vaid, met with Robert Mossbacher, chair of Bush's reelection campaign. The meeting, done with White House approval, was largely a courtesy by Mossbacher to his daughter Dee, a lesbian activist. It was simply a chance for gay leaders to brief Mossbacher on a variety of concerns. With the Bush administration's track record, no one really believed that the session would produce any results. However, it did produce a backlash. The idea that Mossbacher would even *talk* to gay activists infuriated religious conservatives. They were not content to have the ear of the administration; they wanted to ensure that gay activists were completely cut out of the political discourse. Even the exchange of ideas was seen as tantamount to an embrace of gay rights, the ultimate betrayal. "Your meeting with homosexual activists is a slap in the face," Gary Bauer, head of the Family Research Council, the think-tank affiliate of the giant Focus on the Family, fumed in a letter to Mossbacher: "It leaves pro-family groups with the impression that the Bush staff's attitude toward our concerns is one of utter contempt." Eight conservative members of Congress, including Rep. Newt Gingrich and the rabidly antigay Rep. William Dannemeyer, sent Bush a letter urging the president "to re-establish yourself as a protector of traditional family values."

Bush scrambled to repair the damage he had done. Whereas gays were accorded a meeting with Mossbacher, fifteen evangelical leaders had the privilege in April of sitting down with the president himself. They used the occasion to extract a series of promises from Bush on gay rights. As the Reverend Lou Sheldon, head of the Traditional Values Coalition, recounted it, "Mr. Bush said to me, 'Reverend Lou, mark me down—I am opposed to the same-sex marriage thing, and their agenda.'" Bush, a moderate on social issues in the past, had to listen to people like Sheldon because they controlled key segments of the Republican Party appa-ratus. A Presbyterian minister and a former aide to Pat Robertson, Sheldon had formed the Coalition in 1981, after helping to pro-mote the unsuccessful California initiative in 1978 that would have led to the firing of gay teachers. The group, based in Ana-heim, California, grew to have twenty-five thousand churches on its mailing list and eventually opened an office in Washington, run by Sheldon's daughter Andrea. Sheldon's letters to his followers always struck the same note: the gay threat, or as Sheldon also called it, "the battle of the decade."

Sheldon's followers exerted considerable influence on the Re-publican Party in the key state of California. By 1991, the state party convention resembled a Coalition revival meeting. The min-ister credited them with forcing Gov. Pete Wilson to veto a gay rights bill in 1991 that he had promised to sign into law the year before. With the backing of Howard Ahmanson, heir to a banking fortune, Sheldon's goal for 1992 was to take over the California state assembly, and the Coalition had the skills to do it. Sheldon's clout wasn't limited to California, either. He provided key support to proponents of Colorado's antigay initiative. He had organized black ministers in support of Clarence Thomas's nomination to the Supreme Court. He had been a leader of the fight to oust Frohnmayer as head of the National Endowment for the Arts.

Bush's reassurances allayed the concerns of Sheldon and the other attendees at the meeting. Yet he did not entirely win them over. Religious conservatives had been pushing Bush to issue an executive order banning any protections for gays and lesbians and "affirming the traditional family," but Bush remained noncommit-tal, leading evangelical leaders to wonder just how far he was will-ing to go to promote their cause. That was of special concern, because they viewed the election in almost apocalyptic terms. Pat Robertson saw it as the last gasp of the liberal elite. "The strategy against the American radical left should be the same General Douglas MacArthur employed against the Japanese in the Pacific . . . bypass their strongholds, then surround them, isolate them, bombard them, then blast the individuals out of their power bunkers with hand-to-hand combat. The battle for Iwo Jima was not pleasant, but our troops won it," he wrote in an April 1992 report to Christian Coalition members.

The Mossbacher incident did prove one thing, however. Nothing could motivate the religious right and its followers like gay rights. Richard Land declared that among evangelicals "there is greater unanimity [on homosexuality] than even on the abortion issue." With Bush saddled with a recession, he would need something to whip up the troops, especially in the South, where Clinton had a natural advantage as a native. As it turned out, the issue of homosexuality was exactly the thing he needed.

⟿ For gay activists, the 1992 Democratic National Convention was a far cry from the 1988 convention that sent Michael Dukakis forth on his disastrous presidential quest. Although there were ninety-six gay delegates in 1988—about 2 percent of the total number of delegates—gays and lesbians felt effectively shut out by Dukakis's strategists. The welcome that they had found in the Reverend Jesse Jackson's presidential campaign, which became a haven for gay activists, was gone. The message that Dukakis campaign officials sent gay delegates was to keep a low profile and a closed mouth. Otherwise, they would risk jeopardizing Dukakis's ability to win. Dukakis went so far as to turn down the offer of three gay fund-raisers who promised to raise $1 million in contributions from the gay community.

As it turned out, of course, Dukakis was perfectly able to run his campaign into the ground without outside help from gay activists. But he was reflecting a view long held by many Democratic politicians. They were open to putting some pro-gay rhetoric into the party platform as an easy way to placate gay activists, but not much else. Attempts by activists to push for more visibility was met by warnings that anything that made the party look like the captive of special interest groups, especially gays, would lessen the chance of victory. Besides, where else did gays have to go? They weren't about to vote for George Bush, so they had little choice but to shut up and tow the party line.

By the beginning of the 1992 presidential campaign, the

Democrats' reticence was eroding. Partly it was a question of money; the gay community had the potential to contribute lots of money to the candidate of its choice. Partly it was a question of demands; after being satisfied for years with writing checks and being grateful that any candidate would take them, gay donors started to insist that they get something in return. Big-money gay contributors like James Hormel, a longtime party regular and heir to the meatpacking fortune, started threatening to keep their checkbooks closed until the Democrats made commitments to their cause. However, the biggest changes had nothing to do with the Democratic Party per se. AIDS had increased gay visibility to a level never before seen, and with it sympathy and understanding. At the same time, more and more gays and lesbians were open about their sexuality. In all sectors of society, from business to entertainment, Americans saw for the first time that many of their colleagues, friends, and family members were gay. Growing visibility at the personal level was matched by visibility in the new street activism of ACT UP.

The Democratic presidential hopefuls responded to the changing atmosphere. To one degree or another all five candidates who made it to the primaries at least paid lip service to gay issues. Every major candidate supported overturning the Pentagon ban on gays serving in the military. All promised increased AIDS spending. All said that the Democratic Party was the party of inclusion. Yet among the candidates there were clear differences. Sen. Tom Harkin of Iowa was probably the least relaxed with gay issues. Although he accepted $5,000 in 1991 from the Human Rights Campaign Fund (HRCF), a national gay political group, seven years earlier he had returned a $2,000 check from the same group. Harkin said many of the right things, but gay activists who met with him described him as appearing physically uncomfortable around them. When Harkin ventured into a heavily gay coffeehouse in West Hollywood in December 1991, he managed to talk for forty-five minutes without ever mentioning gays, lesbians, or AIDS. In private, Harkin was clearly more comfortable; he hired an openly gay man, Richard Socarides, to serve as his chief of staff. (Socarides's father, Charles, was a darling of the religious right. As a notorious antigay psychologist, he had led a lifelong crusade to "cure" gays and lesbians.)

Activists were also wary of Sen. Robert Kerrey of Nebraska because he had a mixed track record on AIDS issues. While he was a strong supporter of the Ryan White Act, which provided federal funds to cities hard struck by the epidemic, he had also voted for a bill sponsored by the ultraconservative senator Jesse Helms that would have fined or imprisoned health-care workers who had tested positive for HIV and failed to disclose their condition to their patients. (Harkin also voted for the bill.) What support Kerrey had in the gay community evaporated overnight in November 1991 over a joke that he was overheard telling at a political dinner in New Hampshire. In the joke, Jerry Brown, another Democratic contender, tells a man in a bar that he was interested in one of two women sitting nearby. The man tells Brown not to bother because both women are lesbians. When Brown asks how he knows, the man describes how he saw the pair perform oral sex. Brown tells the man he likes to perform oral sex on women, too, and asks if that makes him a lesbian.

The outcry was immediate. An HRCF spokesman declared that the joke "raised questions about whether he is smart enough to be president." Although the joke spoke more to Kerrey's sense of humor than his intelligence, the senator immediately begged for forgiveness. "It was an insensitive, stupid joke told by a hopefully temporarily insensitive, stupid politician," he apologized. (David Beckwith, Dan Quayle's press secretary, had to apologize a few days later for making a far more insensitive crack; he had joked that the good news about Kerrey's misfortune was that lesbians were angry with him and that the bad news was "they'll be coming our way to support us.")

Former California governor Jerry Brown was the most liberal of the candidates and certainly very supportive of gay rights, going so far as to endorse gay marriage. He saw gay rights as part of the need for "absolute change—change that weeds out the corruption and discrimination plaguing the system." It was a compelling message, and Brown understood the public's disenchantment with the status quo probably better than any of his opponents. But if it was the right message, it was the wrong messenger. Brown was saddled with his "Governor Moonbeam" image, which made his campaign quixotic. He never had a real chance to win the nomination.

That left Clinton, rapidly emerging as the party's anointed choice, and former Massachusetts senator Paul Tsongas. As a candidate, Tsongas presented some drawbacks. The conventional wisdom was that he was unelectable. He was a Greek from Massachusetts, and Democrats were already wary of repeating 1988 without choosing a candidate that similar to Dukakis. Like Dukakis, Tsongas was more earnest than charismatic, but at least Tsongas did have a dry wit. There were also questions about Tsongas's health; he had decided not to run for reelection to the Senate in 1984 because he was diagnosed with lymphoma. The cancer appeared cured, but concerns that it could recur lingered.

Of all the candidates, Tsongas was far and away the most pro-gay. Long before it had been popular, Tsongas had been a proponent of gay rights. In September 1979, the first year of his one term in the Senate, he had introduced the first federal non-discrimination bill to protect gays and lesbians. The bill met with a frosty reception; only New York Democrat Daniel Patrick Moynihan and Connecticut Republican Lowell Weicker agreed to cosponsor the measure. Even for a senator from liberal Massachusetts, the move was fraught with political risk. Gay political power was still nascent; the first national gay rights march came the month after Tsongas introduced his bill. The *Lowell Sun* hammered at Tsongas for his support of gay rights, once depicting him in an editorial cartoon clad in a tutu. By the time Tsongas decided to run for president, he was well aware of the political pitfalls surrounding gay rights.

Clinton could not match Tsongas's experience. In fact, Clinton could not point to any experience on gay issues. During a decade as governor of Arkansas, he had taken no public stands on gay rights. Not that he didn't have the opportunity. Arkansas politicians occasionally resorted to the most outrageous slanders against gays. At a 1989 conference about AIDS for state legislators, state representative Lacy Landers declared that the disease was divine just desserts. "The Bible says that any deviation will bring His wrath down, and that's what we've come to now." The following year a Republican running in a statehouse primary announced that he wanted to force gays to register with the state in order to tell their potential spouses that they had a "defective sexual preference." Clinton remained quiet during the attacks.

The most conspicuous silence came in 1977, when the state legislature passed a same-sex sodomy law. The original bill would have mandated prison terms of up to five years, but was watered down to make gay sex a misdemeanor. During hearings on the bill, members of the House Judiciary Committee "had a hard time repressing giggles," according to one contemporary news account. As the state's attorney general at the time, Clinton could have registered his disagreement with the bill, but did not. Other law officials did. John Hall, deputy prosecuting attorney of Little Rock, said that he saw "no compelling state interest" in turning people who had consensual sex into felons. When Clinton began his presidential campaign, he justified his silence by saying that he was working behind the scenes to kill the bill. "I did what I could to defeat it," Clinton said after he had the nomination sewn up. "I thought it was in error. There was no public statement. I just lobbied against it." Clinton's claim met with some skepticism within Arkansas. If Clinton did lobby against the measure, he "made sure he didn't get caught doing it," John Starr, managing editor of the *Arkansas Gazette-Telegraph,* told ACT UP activists. As governor, Clinton was not exactly in the forefront of AIDS issues either. The state provided no confidential testing for HIV, and what testing there was was done for a fee. Until 1991, the state had spent none of its money on AIDS. By the time Clinton was running for the Democratic presidential nomination, expenditures on AIDS totaled less than $165,000.

Clinton's sins of omission worked to his advantage in his presidential campaign. He could present himself as unloosed from the narrow-mindedness of Arkansas, able to speak openly about his beliefs for the first time. And if he failed to distinguish himself during his tenure in Little Rock, at least he had not done anything horrendous. He was a cipher on gay issues and could invent himself any way that he wished. To prove that he was a believer in gay rights, Clinton relied heavily on campaign promises and soothing statements. His first remark about gay issues came in October 1991, not long after Gov. Pete Wilson, a Republican, had vetoed a bill prohibiting antigay discrimination in housing or employment after promising activists during his 1990 campaign that he would support the measure. (A year later, Wilson signed a watered-down version of the bill, much to the displeasure of the conservative Christians who controlled the state party.) "I didn't see anything wrong with that bill," Clinton commented during a visit to Los Angeles. "This is a very diverse country and we have to try to . . . reach some accommodation about what choices should be left to individuals, as opposed to the choices that should be made by government." Clinton's remarks astonished gay activists in Arkansas. It was the first indication they had had that Clinton cared about their issues.

As much as Clinton courted gay voters in southern California, he still remained coy about the issue within Arkansas, as if he were courting gay voters everyplace except his home state. He refused to answer questions that local journalists, such as Anne Clancy, editor of *Spectrum Weekly* in Little Rock, and local gay activists had about his sudden conversion. "While our governor becomes the favored presidential candidate of gay and lesbian organizations around the nation, homosexuality remains a crime in Arkansas," Clancy wrote in one column. "Lesbian, gay, and bisexual rights sit on the back burner of a stove that's not even hooked up, much less lit." When the Arkansas Gay and Lesbian Task Force profiled the presidential candidates in its newsletter, it concluded that Tsongas "has the strongest gay-rights record of any Democratic presidential contender." It was a frank assessment from the people who knew Clinton best.

⟿ Clinton's sudden emergence as the candidate of choice for gays and lesbians was engineered by David Mixner, a corporate consultant in Los Angeles. Through his charm and reassurances, Mixner allayed the concerns that gay activists had about the candidate. Mixner had a genuine and deep commitment to the cause of gay rights, and he sincerely believed that Clinton would prove a boon to that cause. With his guidance, Clinton wended his way through the gay money circuit. As far as the gay community went, Mixner created Bill Clinton. The pair met on Martha's Vineyard in 1969, at a reunion of twenty-five staffers from Sen. Eugene Mc-Carthy's presidential campaign. Just three days apart in age, they hit it off, and Mixner would join the long list of Friends of Bill that Clinton acquired over the years. Clinton would leave the retreat to return to Oxford and become involved in antiwar demonstrations. Mixner was already neck deep in the antiwar movement. In the fall of the same year, he organized the Vietnam Moratorium and even convinced labor leader Walter Reuther that he should endorse it.

At the time of the Martha's Vineyard reunion, and for the following eight years, Mixner was deeply closeted. He told friends that he had been engaged to a young woman who had died in a car crash. Later, Mixner would say he simply made her up. "We all did that sort of thing in those days," he told the *New York Times,* although the *Boston Globe* later reported that the "fiancée" was actually a football player that Mixner had a relationship with when he was a freshman in college. When Mixner came out, among the three hundred people he informed by letter were Bill and Hillary Clinton. As a political operator, Mixner had his share of successes. He persuaded Ronald Reagan to oppose the Briggs initiative in 1978, which would have banned gay teachers from the classroom. He advanced the cause of gays and lesbians in national politics by bringing them into Sen. Gary Hart's 1984 presidential quest. As the 1992 campaign got under way, he formed Access Now for Gay and Lesbian Equality (ANGLE), a collection of wealthy gay southern Californians.

Mixner had his share of failures as well, but his failures were more spectacular than most people's. He resigned as manager from Los Angeles mayor Tom Bradley's 1977 reelection campaign, telling reporters that he had terminal cancer. He didn't. Instead, he was suffering a crisis as he came to terms with being gay. Actress Shirley MacLaine, a friend from the antiwar movement, helped Mixner find a therapist and even let him stay at her house as he recovered. The other failure in Mixner's political past involved the Great Peace March for Nuclear Disarmament in 1985. Five thousand people were to march from Los Angeles to Washington, D.C., to protest the arms race. Mixner's belief in the idea led him to ignore fundamental planning problems that had developed. He raised only $3 million of the $15 million estimated necessary for the cross-country trek. The timing of the march was unusual as well. The antinuclear sentiment that had led 1 million people to turn out in New York's Central Park for a rally in 1981 had already peaked.

The march got off to a shaky start, with only twelve hundred of the projected five thousand marchers showing up. Mixner had to bow out after three days when he sprained an ankle. The lack of money for the march soon became all too apparent. Within two weeks, Mixner had to fly to the Mojave Desert to tell the marchers that the trek was off. Several hundred managed to struggle on to Washington on their own anyway. One of them, Joseph Broido, a Democratic Party activist, was later to tell Clinton that Mixner's performance during the march was a precursor of just how much Mixner would underestimate the difficulty of repealing the military ban on gays. The following year, Mixner redeemed himself by working tirelessly to defeat a California state initiative that would have allowed people with AIDS to be quarantined. Some of Mixner's critics—not always distinguishable from his friends—felt that he had a bit of a messiah complex. Sprinkling his speeches with quotes from Gandhi and Martin Luther King Jr., Mixner did at times appear to be angling for the role of *the* leader of the gay movement. That position was to elude his grasp, but with Clinton's ascension Mixner did become the preeminent political power broker of the gay movement.

Just how good a job Mixner had done in selling Clinton to the gay community quickly became clear to Tsongas's supporters. When they went to look for money in southern California in the fall of 1991, they found it was already in Clinton's pockets. "David ate our lunch," Vincent McCarthy, Tsongas's liaison to the gay community, told the *Boston Globe*. With Mixner's help, the gay community there, and eventually throughout the country, had come to see Clinton as their candidate. The fact that Clinton looked as if he had the nomination sewn up added a pragmatic urgency to the endorsements. In that headlong rush to embrace him, Tsongas, with his support of gay rights dating back to the 1970s, was lost in the dust. Also lost was the Arkansas sodomy law. While most of the gay activists lining up behind Clinton relied upon his promise to lift the military ban as proof that he was a friend of the gay community, they did not demand the candidate do something about the one thing under his immediate control.

It took Michael Petrelis, Steve Michael, and Wayne Turner, a trio of gadfly activists who constituted the ACT UP Presidential Project, to force Clinton's hand on the matter. Threatening a massive demonstration in Little Rock—the potential size of which was probably exaggerated—they and local Arkansas AIDS activists managed to secure a meeting in May with Clinton's chief of staff, Betsy Wright, and through her, Clinton's first public statement on the sodomy law, condemning it. It was the first contact local activists had had with Clinton's gubernatorial office since he'd refused to issue a proclamation for National Coming Out Day in 1989. Yet because Petrelis in particular had managed to offend most of the gay leadership with his blunt criticism and often irritating style, the accomplishment went largely unnoticed. Dubbed "America's nastiest activist" by *The Advocate,* Petrelis lived up to the title, his critics felt. At the notorious demonstration at St. Patrick's Cathedral in December 1989, which offended all but the most hard-core activists, Petrelis stood in a pew, screaming, "Stop killing us, Cardinal O'Connor!" At a gay bar in Washington, he once threw a drink in the face of Rep. Steve Gunderson, taunting him to come out as a gay man, which the Republican did three years later.

Petrelis's animosity wasn't directed solely at people. He also regularly trashed the national gay organizations for what he saw as their ineptness. They were, in his view, unresponsive to their members, slow to respond to attacks, and lacking in vision. But his tactics tended to overshadow his observations and allowed people to downplay his political savvy. Despite the concession that he had wrung from Clinton, Petrelis was so ostracized because of his past actions that no one heeded his advice to demand more of the candidate.

⌒ By the time that the activists met with Betsy Wright, Mixner had consolidated Clinton's position in the rest of the country. He arranged a meeting with gay and AIDS activists in New York at which Clinton charmed potential antagonists who were not impressed with his record on gay issues and stopped them from jumping ship to Jerry Brown. But it was a fund-raising event in California arranged by Mixner that would forever seal Clinton's connection to the gay community. In his letter inviting people to attend, Mixner declared, "Bill Clinton is our friend." "This is a chance for our community to show that we are a force to be reckoned with," said David Wexler, a gay attorney in Hollywood, in another invitation. "We will not get our rights until we put forth the money and effort necessary to elect people who will protect our rights. A good showing in terms of people and cash raised will make a powerful statement that we are committed to doing what is necessary to attain our goals." The letters underscored the belief that money was the most powerful lever the gay community could have.

By the time of his May fund-raiser, Clinton was rapidly achieving a kind of honorary membership in the gay community. (The apotheosis of this would be a doctored photograph of Clinton and Gore that would appear later in the campaign; the Democrats' heads were superimposed on the torsos of two bodybuilders wearing only skimpy shorts, their arms around each other.) His appearance in West Hollywood, which raised over $100,000 for his campaign, was nothing short of a love fest. Six hundred fifty gays and lesbians plunked down at least $100 to hear Clinton talk about one of his favorite themes—"we don't have a person to waste." Gays and lesbians were part of that theme. Clinton spoke about how he would like to have people like David Mixner and San Francisco supervisor Roberta Achtenberg in his administration "because America needs you." He outlined his objection to the military ban and his commitment to "a Manhattan

Project on AIDS" run by one person "who can cut across all the departments and agencies, who has the president's ear and the president's arm."

Yet, it wasn't the promises that made the speech a success. It was the emotion behind them. "What I came here today to tell you is, I have a vision and you are a part of it," Clinton declared. He was clearly moved when he spoke about the toll from the AIDS epidemic. "If I could wave my arm for those of you that are HIV-positive and make it go away tomorrow, I would do it, so help me God I would," he said at the end of his speech. "If I gave up my race for the White House and everything else, I would do that." By the time Clinton was done, people were in tears. At long last, here was a candidate who not only tolerated them, but wanted them as partners in the political process. After years of feeling like pariahs, gays and lesbians were finally being welcomed with open arms. It was a profound, moving experience for a people used to being shunned.

In the process, Clinton was transformed from a moderate Southern politician with no record on gay issues into the gay community's Moses, ready to lead his people out of bondage under Pharaoh Bush. Hundreds of videotapes of the speech flooded the gay community in the months that followed. They were handy for raising funds. They also raised hopes, higher than they had ever been raised. By the time Clinton headed for the Democratic National Convention, many gays and lesbians expected Clinton's victory would also mean that they would finally win their rights.

~ Even as Clinton was playing to the gay community's hunger for a hero, the religious right was pouring its energies into making sure that it could depend upon whomever it supported. Candidates like California governor Pete Wilson and George Bush had burned them once they'd assumed office, proving that campaign promises were idle. The only way to prevent that from happening again was to decide who the candidate was in the first place. On a state-by-state basis, conservative Christians were taking over state Republican parties and transforming them into vehicles for their own concerns, especially homosexuality. The same month as Clinton's West Hollywood address, the Washington state Republican Party adopted a platform that demanded that gays and lesbians be barred from employment as teachers or health care workers. (The platform also condemned yoga classes and witchcraft in public school.) In Iowa, the state Republican platform called for rigid enforcement of sodomy laws and mandatory reporting of the names of individuals who tested positive for HIV. In Harris County, Texas, which includes Houston, the party went so far as to declare that homosexuality "leads to the breakdown of the family and the spread of deadly disease."

By controlling the local machinery, Christian activists were able to achieve national influence. Nowhere was that more evident than in the 1992 national Republican platform committee. The national platform, neatly bound with a flyleaf that showed people sitting in the pews of a church, was a litany of conservative causes, including social issues. It called for contact tracing for people who test positive for HIV. It stated its opposition to nondiscrimination legislation, gay adoption, and gay marriage. It harshly rejected the "irresponsible position" of businesses that had stopped contributing to the Boy Scouts of America because it was denying gays the right to serve as scouts and scoutmasters. The Boy Scouts, the platform declared, "are defending decency in fulfillment of their own moral responsibilities."

In 1988, gay groups had been allowed to testify before the platform committee. The opportunity was mostly a courtesy, letting activists from the National Gay and Lesbian Task Force air views that the platform did not reflect. In 1992, the committee was not interested in etiquette. Gay activists were denied any speaking time. In the past, that would not have been so surprising, but in 1992 the committee was not just rejecting gay activists. It was also rejecting Republicans. Since 1990, a contingent of gay Republicans, sailing under the name Log Cabin Club, had been trying to convey the idea that gay rights and the party's philosophy were not inimical. They had their first success the year they were formed, with the gubernatorial elections of Pete Wilson in California and William Weld in Massachusetts. By reneging on his promise to Log Cabin leaders about supporting a gay rights bill, Wilson was a terrific disappointment, leading some gay Republicans to resign from the party. But Weld came through, emerging as the most pro-gay governor in the country. He appointed gays and lesbians to visible positions in his administration and tackled such thorny issues as gay teen suicide rates.

Among Weld's appointees was Rich Tafel, who would go on to become the executive director of Log Cabin. The buttoned-down Tafel was hardly anyone's image of the average gay activist, including that of more liberal gay leaders. An ordained Baptist minister with a degree from the Harvard Divinity School, Tafel felt at home with the Republican Party's conservative bent on fiscal and defense policy. He had the distinction of being just about the only gay leader to support the Persian Gulf War. There were probably more gays and lesbians like Tafel than the media, or even many gay activists, realized. Forty percent of the Human Rights Campaign Fund's contributors identified themselves as Republican. But until Tafel and Log Cabin came along, the party did not have to deal with a public gay face. Republican gays, such as Marvin Liebman, had traditionally stayed in the closet. Liebman did not feel comfortable enough to come out until the year Log Cabin was founded, when he was in his late sixties. By the time of the 1992 presidential election, Liebman was concluding that for Republicans, gays and lesbians "have replaced the communists as the Number One Menace to all that they pronounce is good and traditional in American life." Coming from Liebman, who founded the anticommunist group Young Americans for Freedom, it was a sad conclusion to reach.

Confronting an increasingly antigay party with the issue of gay rights took courage. Tafel got all kinds of flak from conservatives like L. Brent Bozell, a fund-raiser, who told Tafel in one broadcast confrontation, *"We're* standing for family values, and you're just going to have to make up your mind whether you can live with that." But Tafel got just as much criticism from gay activists, who saw Log Cabin as nothing more than a collaboration with the enemy. Barney Frank, the openly gay congressman from Massachusetts and a highly partisan Democrat, derided the group as "Uncle

Tom's Cabin Club," adding, with some justification, that the group was better at preaching Republican values to gays than gay rights to the Republican Party. Still, Tafel's willingness to challenge his Republican peers on gay rights, as fanciful as the task might seem, was an important reminder to the party of its libertarian roots and an even more important attempt to educate the public at large about the political diversity of the gay population. Gay activists also needed to be reminded of the ideological diversity of their community.

Yet, as the platform showed, the religious right was not inclined to take libertarian stands on gay rights or abortion. No one was happier about that than Phyllis Schlafly, head of the Eagle Forum. Schlafly was one of the most intelligent and dynamic figures on either side of the political spectrum, something her enemies did not always credit her for. They preferred to look at some of her more provocative statements such as calling a group of pro-ERA demonstrators a "lesbian chain gang." At various times, Schlafly declared that women who were modestly "virtuous" were not subject to harassment and that the atomic bomb was "a marvelous gift that was given to our country by a wise God." It was easy to dismiss such remarks as the product of a simple ideologue. But with a law degree, graduate work in political science, and numerous books to her name, Schlafly was a formidable figure. She was an early supporter of the Reagan revolution, but her expectations for a Pentagon appointment after Reagan's election were dashed. Not long after, the Eagle Forum began to lose ground to Beverly LaHaye's Concerned Women for America. Yet with eighty thousand members in the Forum and over two hundred and fifty radio stations carrying her message, Schlafly was still an important leader in conservative circles.

Schlafly was exultant about the platform. "Total victory, none of this litmus-test, big-tent garbage," she declared. The committee had stopped "wimpy politicians" from turning the strong language into pablum, a feat that she described as "one of the cleanest, clearest victories we have had." But just as she was savoring the triumph, she was hit with a devastating report that undermined her credibility. According to *QW,* a gay magazine in

New York City, and later confirmed by the *San Francisco Examiner,* Schlafly's son John was gay. Schlafly complained that the report was timed to damage her, just as she was about to enjoy her triumph within the party, but she stood by her son, who lived at home. "He is my son and I do love him," she told the *Examiner.* "What else is there to say? I'm not going to comment on his life." But the author of such pamphlets as "The ERA-GAY-AIDS Connection" also said that she stood by her beliefs. For his part, John, a staunch Republican himself, said, "I don't think she is in any way bigoted."

The revelation put Schlafly in the same quandary as Charles Socarides and pointed to one of the persistent problems facing antigay activists. Within their families and circles of friends, there were bound to be gays and lesbians whom they loved. Schlafly and Socarides were unique only insofar as their secret came out; other conservative Christians, including one of the most prominent couples in the religious right leadership, also had children who were gay. That simple fact left them open to charges of hypocrisy, like those leveled against Schlafly, and gave gay activists the opportunity to gloat. After being frozen out by the platform committee, Tafel had his revenge. In a statement he issued after John Schlafly's homosexuality was revealed, Tafel declared with a straight face, "My sympathy goes out to her son and her family."

⁓ Long before the issue of gay offspring became a national issue, Barbara Bush let it be known that she supported tolerance for gays and their families, much to the chagrin of conservatives. In 1990, Paulette Goodman, president of the Federation of Parents and Friends of Lesbians and Gays (PFLAG), asked Barbara Bush for some "kind words to some 24 million gay Americans and their families, to help heal the wounds, and to keep these families in loving relationships." Bush responded in a May 10, 1990, letter. "You sound like a caring parent and a compassionate citizen," the first lady wrote. "I firmly believe that we cannot tolerate discrimination against any individuals or groups in our country. Such treatment always brings with it pain and perpetuates hate and intolerance. I appreciate so much your sharing the information about your organization and your encouraging me to help change attitudes. Your words speak eloquently of your love for your child and your compassion for all gay Americans and their families."

The tone of the letter—its genuine warmth, its compassion, its graciousness—was what people had come to associate with Barbara Bush and what would make her the most popular figure at the Republican convention in Houston. Had the president written the letter, conservative Christians would have howled. However, the respect that Barbara Bush commanded made her a difficult figure for the religious right to attack. Publicly, they praised her, but letters like the one to Goodman made them wonder if she wasn't soft on their issues. Her influence on her husband added another layer to their distrust of the president. Even during the campaign, the first lady was not silent. Asked during one interview whether issues of "personal preference," such as abortion and homosexuality, belonged in the party platform, she answered that "the personal thing should be left out of, in my opinion, out of platforms at conventions." Such statements could hardly be comforting to Schlafly, Sheldon, and other conservatives.

Caught in the cross fire was George Bush. With Clinton wooing the gay vote and conservative Christians fuming about homosexuality, the media was bound to start asking the president about his views. His answers reflected his apparent ambivalence about the issue. On one hand, he echoed his wife's sentiment that families should care for one another. When he was asked in an NBC interview how he would respond if one of his grandchildren were gay, Bush's first response was, "I'd love that child." On the other hand, Bush was relying on the family-values issue to win him votes, so he couldn't suggest that homosexuality was acceptable. Tripping over his syntax, Bush added, "I would put my arm around him, and I hope he wouldn't go out and try to convince people that this was the normal lifestyle, that this was the appropriate lifestyle, that this was the way it ought to be. But I, I—you know, for me, I think the Bible teaches compassion and love. But I would say I hope you wouldn't become an advocate for a lifestyle that in my view is not normal and propose marriages, same-sex marriages is a, is a normal way of life."

Bush was wrestling with his personal values and political instincts in the exchange. He did not want to appear mean-spirited, yet he did not want to appear pro-gay. The conflict was no different from the attitudes of many voters. While they might not like homosexuality, they did love their family members and did not want to see them come to any harm. The family values rhetoric of the religious right did not allow for that kind of shading, however. Sheldon, for instance, declared homosexuality to be "deviant" and, contrary to accepted medical standards, "a developmental disorder." In adopting the family-values campaign, Bush was signing on to something with which he was clearly not altogether comfortable.

At times, in fact, Bush sounded just like the average American grappling with the issue. Barbara Walters asked the president in an interview if he would "knowingly" appoint a gay cabinet member. Bush's response was honest, although a reflection of the days when gays and lesbians weren't open about their lives. "We have no litmus test on that question here, and there aren't going to be any," Bush said. "And I would say, how do I know?" Because refusing to discriminate against gays in employment resonated with a majority of voters, the religious right looked upon it as the camel's nose under the tent. In their view, to give on that point would lead to all kinds of gay rights legislation. Richard Land of the Southern Baptist Convention expressed "outrage and a sense of betrayal." Sheldon condemned Bush's comment as "a terrible blooper." The Traditional Values Coalition leader also condemned Bush campaign officials for merely talking to the *Washington Blade,* a gay newspaper. He made it clear what the stakes were for Bush. Homosexuality, Sheldon said, "galvanizes our public more than right-to-life. It is absolutely a vital issue to Bible-believing Christians."

Bush's instincts differed from H. Ross Perot's. The independent candidate, queried by the ubiquitous Walters in May, had declared that, for pragmatic reasons, he would not appoint a gay man to his cabinet. "I don't want anybody there [who] will be a point of controversy with the American people," Perot said. "It will distract from the work to be done." Perot also said that he doubted that gays in the military was "realistic." Perot's stance caught his gay supporters, who had formed a committee to back his candidacy, by surprise. In April, Perot had said that sexual orientation was a private matter and pledged to "go night and day" to increase AIDS research funding. His gay supporters saw in Perot the opportunity to marry conservative fiscal policy with libertarian social values. Under pressure from his gay followers, Perot issued a statement in which he promised to prohibit antigay discrimination and strictly enforce hate-crime laws if he was elected. A few days after the statement, Perot withdrew from the race. With his departure, gays and lesbians felt that they had no choice. Their candidate had to be Clinton.

∼ The Democratic National Convention in New York City in July was, for many gays and lesbians, a triumph, a celebration of their arrival at the heart of political power. Out of the 4,000 delegates and alternates present, 133 were gay or lesbian—35 more than in 1988. Just two months before the convention, the National Gay and Lesbian Task Force had hosted a meeting with Ron Brown, chairman of the Democratic National Committee, and demanded that a gay man or lesbian and a person with AIDS address the convention in prime time. They got their wish, in San Francisco supervisor Roberta Achtenberg and environmental lobbyist Bob Hattoy.

Achtenberg's convention appearance was the culmination of a remarkable journey. Just four years earlier, she was a political outsider, the head of the National Center for Lesbian Rights, a legal group in San Francisco that was a pioneer in handling lesbian custody cases. Achtenberg decided to challenge the San Francisco Democratic machine candidate for an assembly seat on the grounds that the gay community would do better to have one of its own in office than just a friend. Achtenberg was easily defeated in that race, but two years later she had been elected to the San Francisco Board of Supervisors. Even by San Francisco standards she was progressive, but she endorsed the more moderate Clinton early in his campaign, bringing with her key support in northern California and the gay community. By the time of the convention, she had vaulted into Clinton's circle. For her work, after Clinton's election she was rewarded with a job in the Department of Housing and Urban Development, winning confirmation only after a grueling Senate debate during which Sen. Jesse Helms called her "a damn lesbian." She would move to Washington with her partner, Mary Morgan, who had been a judge in San Francisco, and their son, Benjamin.

In her speech, Achtenberg called on the country to "rededicat[e] ourselves to social justice." She mentioned that she was raising a child. "It is a matter of justice that all people should be allowed to work free from discrimination and that lesbians who choose to serve their country in the military are entitled to do so," she proclaimed earnestly. "As a nation, we must stand for the proposition that all people are of equal value." She also took a swipe at Republicans, whose leaders "are scapegoating people like me—and families like mine—by charging that we are destroying America."

The other gay speaker, Hattoy, was new to AIDS activism. A lobbyist for the environmental group the Sierra Club, he had been diagnosed with AIDS just weeks before the convention. He had been planning to move to Little Rock to work on Clinton's campaign; instead, he informed Clinton of his diagnosis and resigned from the campaign. When Clinton tapped him to give an address on AIDS to the delegates, Hattoy admitted to having "a moment of true homosexual panic." With characteristic humor, he admitted that he did not worry so much about death, "but when they said my hair would fall out if I had the [chemotherapy] treatment, I was torn."

Hattoy's speech was an emotional high point for many delegates. "If George Bush wins again, we're all at risk," he said. "We must vote this year as if our lives depended on it. Mine does. Yours could." As he spoke, gays and lesbians with tears in their eyes hugged each other on the convention floor and cheered. The phrase *vote as if your life depended on it* became the motto of gay activists everywhere; the nominally nonpartisan National Gay and

Lesbian Task Force used it in its preelection flyers. The idea had been around since 1984, the first presidential campaign during the AIDS epidemic. But this year was different. Mondale had little chance of winning, while Dukakis, who looked like a strong contender during his convention, avoided gay and AIDS issues altogether. Clinton was the first candidate who looked as if he cared *and* who looked as if he could win. Exasperated by the previous defeats and the unending loss from AIDS, gays and lesbians were desperate for a change in AIDS policy. The sad truth was that the virus would continue to claim lives without regard to who held political office. The most that people could hope for was a stronger commitment to AIDS prevention, research and care that would result in the faster development and release of drugs and treatment—no small thing, but not huge, lifesaving advances.

Unlike the 1988 convention, this convention seemed much more willing to embrace, even celebrate, the gays in its ranks. The media was fascinated by the novelty of gay delegates and rushed as a group to profile them. In the onslaught, however, some warning signs about Clinton's commitment to the delegates were obscured. His promise to give an interview to *The Advocate,* the national gay newsmagazine, as Tsongas had done, never materialized. And when the draft of Clinton's acceptance speech was originally circulated, gays and lesbians weren't included. Only through the intercession of Mixner did the nominee include them in a laundry list of people who were deemed outcasts in the politics of division. By contrast, Tsongas in his address did not have to be reminded of his principles. "When will lesbian and gay teenagers who discover their identity feel that an American president will respect what they are?" Tsongas asked the crowd. "When will they be free to pursue their lives without the ravages of rejection and discrimination?" By then Tsongas was just an also-ran, and his speech seemed like simply one more pleasant affirmation of gay rights.

⌇ "Well, we took the long way home, but we finally got here." With those words, Pat Buchanan, the conservative commentator who had given Bush a run for his money during the primaries, opened his prime-time speech on the first night of the Republican convention in Houston. What followed was the kind of red-meat oratory that made Buchanan the white knight of the religious right. "My friends, this election is about much more than who gets what," Buchanan said, his voice ringing with righteous thunder. "There is a culture war going on in our country for the soul of America. It is a cultural war, as critical to the kind of nation we will one day be as was the Cold War itself." The audience, particularly the brigade of well-scrubbed young men and women who populated the Astrodome, loved it. Waving signs reading FAMILY RIGHTS FOREVER, GAY RIGHTS NEVER, they cheered Buchanan with a fervor that they never showered on Bush.

Buchanan used his speech to attack the Democrats and their allies, including gays and lesbians: "A militant leader of the homosexual rights movement could rise at the convention and exult, 'Bill Clinton and Al Gore represent the most pro-lesbian and pro-gay ticket in history.' And so they do." The delegates laughed wildly. Buchanan also condemned the "amoral idea that gay and lesbian couples should have the same standing in law as married men and women." Letting Buchanan set the tone of the convention may have been a political mistake, but his address was also an honest reflection of the beliefs of many of the delegates. He was simply standing on the shoulders of Pat Robertson, who estimated that 750 out of the 2,210 delegates were members of his Christian Coalition. But whereas Robertson presented an elfin, cheery appearance, Buchanan came off as belligerent and proud of it.

Yet, by Buchanan's standards, he was relatively tame in Houston. In the past he had called gay groups fascist and said that "anybody who doesn't think that the homosexual lifestyle and AIDS are related is a blockhead." In a June speech, Buchanan regaled his audience with the story about how his announcement speech had been disrupted by AIDS activists, a problem anticipated by his security chief. "Just as my speech got to the point where I talked about compassion for the forgotten American, they were body-slamming an AIDS activist," Buchanan told the cheering crowd.

The media had not been paying close enough attention to Buchanan, Robertson, or any other religious right heroes to understand the subtle changes that they adopted for the Houston convention. Robertson's convention speech was uncharacteristically subdued, failing to mention such standard themes as the connection between natural disasters and gay activism that were a regular part of his *700 Club* appearances. Exposed to the religious right for the first time, many correspondents were clearly surprised at what they saw. Yet Houston was mild compared to the battles in local Republican parties, and the rhetoric there was low-key compared to the defamatory statements of the evangelicals in their fund-raising letters.

Even as Buchanan was speaking inside the Astrodome, gay and AIDS activists were outside protesting. The demonstration quickly devolved into a melee, with police on horseback charging the protesters. Suzanne Pharr, taking a break from organizing in Oregon, was in Houston as co-organizer of VOICE '92, a coalition of gay and AIDS groups. In an overheated response, she compared the police action to sexual assault: "The purpose of police brutality against oppressed people, like the rape of women, is to threaten and terrorize all who belong to that group. The objective of the police brutality in Houston was to threaten all of us in the gay and lesbian community."

The incident was just about the last hurrah of direct-action groups like ACT UP and Queer Nation. After the election, their membership would dwindle and chapters would fold. A combination of burnout, death, and changing political fashions made protests fewer and farther between. Interest in the groups, both in the media and the gay community, faded. For the religious right, however, the groups would remain an ominous, outsized, and handy threat for years to come.

The entire convention week in Houston soon became a battle outside the Astrodome between gay activists and conservative Christians. Gay activists interrupted a convention-related speech by President Bush and another by Jerry Falwell. Activists at such events would brag about how they disguised themselves in "conservative drag," dressing in tacky clothes and wearing bad hairstyles. A few activists privately cringed at the protesters' amused boasts, believing that they revealed a superior attitude bordering on classism toward the middle-American core of the religious right. For his part, Falwell enjoyed the interruption. "Those are some of our enemies," he declared to his audience. Afterward, infected by the pugnacious tone of the convention, he said about the protesters, "I could whip four of them at one time."

Actually, Falwell had reason to be grateful to the demonstrators. They had been instrumental to his comeback. After folding the Moral Majority in 1989, he had been mired in financial problems at his Liberty University. But beginning in 1991, he started on a new antigay campaign, a "national battle plan" to put an end to "the radical homosexual movement." In a July fund-raising letter for the Liberty Foundation, Falwell expressed sympathy and disdain for gays. "We surely love their souls," he wrote. "And we must reach out to them with the Gospel. But we must awaken to their wicked agenda for America!"

From that start, Falwell soon escalated his claims, alleging that AIDS activists were out to kill him. "It is truly a miracle that I am alive today," he began a fall 1991 fund-raising letter. "I sincerely believe that certain persons fully intended to take my life." The specific incident to which Falwell was referring was an October 1991 protest in Los Angeles over California governor Pete Wilson's vetoing of the statewide nondiscrimination bill. Falwell had the misfortune of staying in Los Angeles at the time, and demonstrators massed outside the hotel calling his name. In his letter, Falwell had himself and his son cowering in the hotel kitchen while a waiter prayed for them, but in fact police escorted Falwell from the hotel before any protesters broke in. The scene contrasted sharply with Falwell's boast of pugilistic prowess at the Republican convention.

Then Falwell claimed the week before the convention that Queer Nation sent him urine infected with the AIDS virus. The package, delivered to his university office, contained "human urine, vulgar, terribly hard-core pornography and a letter that said whoever opens it, he is infected," and a death threat. Without any independent confirmation, it was hard to tell how much of Falwell's re-creation of events was factual. In truth, conservative Christian leaders regularly receive hate mail and death threats. Yet any AIDS activist knows that a urine sample is a scientifically improbable source of infection. However, gay activists did nothing to help the matter. "Unfortunately, I don't know anything about it," John Woods, a Queer Nation member in San Francisco, said. "But it sounds like a great idea to me." The incident showed just how thoroughly yoked together Falwell and the protesters were. Just as Falwell was using the report to raise funds, Woods happily admitted that the incident was "more publicity for us."

⁓ For members of the religious right, the Republican convention served the same purpose as the Democratic convention did for gay activists. By providing Buchanan with an unexpectedly strong showing against an incumbent president, they had proven their political clout. By promising to support Bush, they were able to extract promises that would consolidate their gains should he be reelected. At the convention they showed that they already had a seat at the table; now they would have a say in who sat at the head. Their clout allowed the Republicans to be dubbed the party of God, just as the Democrats were dubbed the party of gays.

The battle cry of the convention in Houston was "family values," and the Astrodome was flooded by it. Potential successors to Bush repeatedly paid homage to the theme. William Bennett, former drug czar and secretary of education, used his speech nominating Quayle for vice president as an opportunity to address the question, often invoking religious terms. He spoke of the GOP's holding to "our sacred *old* covenants." He quoted Lincoln about appealing to the "better angels of our nature." He described children as "gifts of God." Bennett also spoke about gays and lesbians, although without using those terms. He chose instead to use the outdated phrase "alternative lifestyles." "Heaven knows, there are a lot of them," he told the convention, getting a laugh. And he haughtily expressed tolerance of a sort: "Within very broad limits people may live as they wish." But Bennett still dismissed gays and lesbians as somehow leading less worthy lives. "And yet we believe that some ways of living are better than others—better because they bring more meaning to our lives; to the lives of others; and to our fragile, fallible human condition. Marriage must be upheld because in marriage between husband and wife—and in fatherhood and motherhood—come blessings that cannot be won in any other way."

In the crush of coverage about the extreme rhetoric of the convention, this kind of damaging attack was bound to seem mild by comparison. It was a more subtle dismissal of gays and lesbians than Buchanan's belligerence. But Bennett was saying that not only did gays and lesbians lead less meaningful lives, they contributed less to society in general. The sense that individuals prove their worth on a case-by-case basis, and not as a class—one of the fundamental tenets of Republican philosophy—fell by the wayside. Heterosexuals were simply better people than gays and lesbians, not because gays did demeaning things in bed but because their lives were emptier. It was a class structure based on a certain type of morality.

Bush campaign officials saw the "family values" issue as a wedge to use against the Democrats. Charles Black, a senior campaign adviser, charged that Clinton had "adopted the gay agenda." An unidentified campaign official told the *Washington Post* that "our purpose is to define George Bush and the Republican Party as the proponent of fundamental social norms in terms of the family, in terms of sexual behavior, and in terms of reward for work. Conversely, we intend to define Clinton and the Democrats as advocates of individual fulfillment, without regard to generally held values and beliefs."

The problem for Bush was, once the issue was unleashed, he had no control over it. Conservative Christians were not constrained by following a more abstract idea of what "family values" meant. They knew exactly how to define them, and they said so during the convention. Sometimes the definition was mostly theological. At a "God and Country Rally" during the convention, singer Pat Boone said, "We're here to reelect the living God as our source of life. And unless we do that as a people, it doesn't matter a whole lot who we elect as president." After William Weld gave his convention address—effectively censored by party officials who did not want him to refer to his support for gay rights or abortion rights—James Smith, director of government relations for the Christian Life Commission of the Southern Baptist Convention, dismissed it as "not a view that Christians hold of the role of government. We believe government was created by God to reward those who do good and punish those who do evil, according to the Scriptures." At other times, the language was even more explicit. In his address to the convention, Pat Robertson contended that the Democrats would "destroy the traditional family." The proof: Clinton's pledge to lift the ban on gays in the military. It was an early signal of the battle to follow after Clinton's election.

⁓ There were legitimate issues to discuss about the fraying moral fabric of society. Undoubtedly, people were concerned about their families and the pressures on them. The availability of drugs, a mediocre school system, the demands of work—all of these things made modern family life difficult. The idea that families must somehow compartmentalize their faith, the one thing that helped to sustain them through difficult times, and keep it separate from their public lives only frustrated and angered people already carrying enough burdens. But in Houston, the debate was framed as gays versus morality. Gays and lesbians became, depending on the party you listened to, angels or demons, when they simply were much like everyone else. The debate didn't serve evangelicals well either. Gay activists all too easily were able to characterize conservative Christians as antigay bigots and nothing else. The questions of government involvement in personal morality and the concerns that motivated them to become politically involved in the first place were obscured by that image. In the constant divisions of "us" and "them," conservative Christians and gays alike ended up in both categories, depending upon who was doing the dividing.

By the time the convention was over, conservative Christians were giddy. "I think it's the best convention the Republicans have had in my recollection," said Falwell. Lon Mabon, head of the Oregon Citizens Alliance, was equally pleased by the event. Visiting Houston from Oregon, he declared the gathering was "like an

OCA convention." Moderate Republicans like Sen. Richard Lugar and Sen. John Chafee were appalled. Former housing secretary Jack Kemp, himself a possible presidential contender with impeccable conservative credentials, shrewdly noted, "You can win an election, but you cannot govern the country by dividing the American people."

Yet the religious right soon found out there were limits to their political muscle. Voters were unimpressed by the "family values" theme. Bush failed to get quite the postconvention "bounce" that he had expected. When all the shouting was over, what most concerned voters was still the economy. Only 23 percent of those polled by the *New York Times* considered homosexuality an important issue to them during the campaign. Unlike conservative Christians and gay activists, most voters did not care primarily about a social issue; they cared about getting out of the recession.

Republicans did not entirely abandon "family values" during the rest of the campaign, but they certainly backed away from the issue. Vice President Dan Quayle, a favorite of the religious right, went so far as to deny that he agreed with his supporters and urged gays to vote for him and Bush. "I don't think you heard any of that rhetoric coming from me," Quayle said on a Los Angeles call-in radio show. "You didn't hear it coming from the president." (During his acceptance speech at the convention, Quayle *had* said that "Americans try to raise their children to understand right and wrong, only to be told that every so-called 'lifestyle' is morally equivalent. That is wrong.") The vice president went so far as to say that the White House had an official nondiscrimination policy when it came to gays. It did not. In fact, Tyler Franz, a Bush campaign worker, had alleged earlier in the year that he had been fired solely because he was gay.

Quayle had a private nondiscrimination policy, however. As *The Advocate* reported, in anticipation of a run for the presidency in 1996, which he later scuttled, Quayle hired a ghostwriter, whom Quayle knew to be gay. Of course, that is what all the arguments about nondiscrimination ordinances come down to, the ability of qualified people to do their job without threat of dismissal. At that moment, Quayle and his allies on the right could not have been further apart.

⟶ As far as gays and lesbians were concerned, the Houston convention was the last straw. It was just a matter of waiting until election day to cast their votes for Clinton. The Democrats did their best to make sure that they got as many of those votes as possible. In West Hollywood, for example, the party set up a store-front where passersby could register to vote, buy campaign merchandise, or volunteer to help in the campaign. It was a model of efficiency and service that paid off on election day. Pollsters put Clinton's share of the gay vote, always a nebulous thing to pin down, at about 75 percent. In the end, Mixner estimated that the gay community poured as much as $3 million into Clinton's campaign fund, or roughly one dollar out of every eight. Gays and lesbians were euphoric. "This is a great day for lesbian and gay Americans, and a great victory for all Americans," said Tim McFeeley of the Human Rights Campaign Fund. "The election of our lives is over. . . . Now the hard part begins."

Yet, a few activists were concerned that the community had failed to learn some critical lessons from the campaign. For one, too many people continued to confuse the election with the movement. Tom Swift, a staffer at the Human Rights Campaign Fund, was assigned to the West Hollywood campaign office. He was horrified to see the office vanish two days after the election. "It all just got rolled up," he would later recall. "The community failed to recognize what a valuable and unique entity it was." To them, it was just a campaign office; to Swift, it was a phone bank and database of volunteers that could be mobilized when the movement required. It was from exactly such an operation that the Christian Coalition sprang. And activists on both sides seemed unaware that a victory at the ballot box would not resolve the issue once and for all, because the loser would simply make inroads somewhere else. What both sides wanted to accomplish simply could not be done by a vote.

That kind of thinking, however, was lost in the joy of the election. Gay activists formed a transition team to get résumés of gays and lesbians to the White House for job openings. Plans were made for the inauguration, right down to the appearance of a gay band. In gratitude, Clinton sent a letter to gay activists attending an annual National Gay and Lesbian Task Force conference held just after the election. "Hillary and I would like to thank you all for the advancement of human rights for gay and lesbian people everywhere," Clinton wrote. "I would also like to take this opportunity to thank every one of you for your tremendous support during our campaign for change." The warmth of the letter would quickly cool with Clinton's inauguration.

CHAPTER 4

No Special Rights

G AY ACTIVISTS' VICTORY CELEBRATIONS FOR CLINTON and for the defeat of the antigay initiative in Oregon were tempered by the success of another antigay ballot measure in Colorado. After attracting little attention throughout the summer and fall, Colorado suddenly emerged as the emblem of the culture war, of supreme importance to both sides. For the religious right, Colorado was proof that its antigay message carried weight at the ballot box; for gay activists, it was proof of just how far they had yet to go.

Like any other overnight success, the antigay initiative in Colorado was years in the making. Opponents of gay rights were a substantial, well-formed group in the state well before election day, 1992, far more so than they were in Oregon. U.S. senator Bill Armstrong had been a vociferous opponent of gay rights in Congress. Colorado boasted numerous chapters of conservative national organizations, such as the Traditional Values Coalition, and was headquarters for some of the national groups themselves. Chief among these was Focus on the Family, which moved to Colorado Springs in October 1991. Founded in 1977 by Dr. James

Dobson, the group has since grown to a massive operation with a $100 million annual budget, employing 2,200 people in a forty-seven-acre, custom-built complex. By 1995, its magazine was reaching 2 million homes, while its thirty-minute daily radio show was being carried by more than two thousand stations.

Dobson earned a Ph.D. in child development from the University of Southern California in 1967. Three years later, he published *Dare to Discipline,* in which he heartily—too heartily for some critics—endorsed corporal punishment for children. The book struck a nerve among readers, selling 2 million copies and making Dobson a wealthy man. With the founding of Focus on the Family, Dobson's empire quickly grew. In 1988, he was able to take over the Family Research Council, a Washington-based think tank, where he ensconced Gary Bauer, a former Reagan administration official, as its head. The following year, Dobson scored a coup with a videotaped death-row interview with serial killer Ted Bundy, in which Bundy blamed his murderous ways on his exposure to pornography. ("Ted, how did it happen? Take me back," Dobson began the interview, in his best Barbara Walters manner.) Dobson's stature among conservative believers was confirmed that same year when Jerry Falwell pointed to Dobson as an heir to the legacy of the Moral Majority.

Dobson had long been critical of homosexuality. It was, he felt, "a perversion." In *Parenting Isn't for Cowards,* published in 1987, Dobson described his "tranquil" and "moral" high school days when "homosexuals were very weird and unusual people." Focus on the Family literature took "strong exception to the activist movement that seeks to gain special privileges and protected minority status for the homosexual community," claiming that there was "no evidence" gays were discriminated against. "Radical homosexual 'social reformers'" were out "to redefine the family, permit homosexual 'marriages,' be able to adopt children and recruit the young." The only answer for gays and lesbians, according to Dobson, was to rely on God's grace to try to become heterosexual.

By the time Dobson moved to Colorado Springs, the area had become especially congenial for religious conservatives. In 1990,

Alice Worrell, a local city official, had become something of a one-woman evangelical chamber of commerce, recruiting conservative groups to the area to take advantage of depressed real estate prices and the state's liberal tax code. Within a matter of years, the Springs emerged as a mecca for the religious right, much as San Francisco did for gays and lesbians. Citizens Project, a local group that monitored the right wing, estimated that fifty right-wing organizations were in the area.

David Noebel, head of Summit Ministries, an unaccredited Christian "college" in nearby Manitou Springs, was an early pioneer. Noebel was part of the religious right long before it had achieved its current power, with strong ties to the old-line conservative groups. (Noebel was a member of the John Birch Society until 1986.) He had joined Summit, which offered programs and seminars for Christians, at the age of twenty-six as a student in its first class after failing in a Republican congressional primary in Wisconsin. Two years later, in 1964, Noebel was the dean. The institution had its share of troubles. Founder Billy James Hargis, an anticommunist crusader, held an anti-integration rally in conjunction with Summit in 1963. Summit had its property-tax exemption turned down three times by Colorado, which rejected the argument that it was a religious organization. The biggest scandal came in 1974, after five students—four of them male—accused Hargis of having sex with them in his office. Hargis resigned and Noebel took over.

The Summit rebounded from its problems, growing with endorsements from Dobson, whose son Ryan attended programs there, and the Reverend D. James Kennedy, the head of Coral Ridge Ministries in Coral Gables, Florida. Some of Noebel's philosophy was old-fashioned for the students. He was a fiery crusader against rock music, including the growing field of Christian rock. To him, rock was nothing more than coitus accompanied by electric guitars. One of his early books was titled *Communism, Hypnotism and the Beatles*. In another, *The Marxist Minstrels: A Handbook on Communist Subversion of Music,* Noebel declared that the communists were "rendering a generation of American youth neurotic, through nerve-jamming, mental deterioration and retardation." But Noebel was also one of the first members of the old religious right to see homosexuality as the issue that would rival, and eventually surpass, communism among religious conservatives. As early as 1977, Noebel was warning that the nation was "rotting within" and that "homosexuality is only an issue when a nation is rotting morally." He went on to author an antigay tract titled *The Homosexual Revolution* and to pepper his lectures on gay rights with such slurs as "fairies" and "fruits." By 1989, the Summit was so popular that fourteen thousand people requested applications to attend its programs.

The antigay backlash in Colorado began in October 1990, when the Denver city council approved an ordinance banning discrimination on the basis of sexual orientation in housing, employment, and public accommodations. (Religious groups were explicitly excused from adhering to the ordinance, as is typical of such laws.) Infuriated conservatives formed Citizens for Sensible Rights and began collecting signatures for a referendum on the law for the May 1991 ballot. But it was in February 1991 that a series of events converged to lead evangelical conservatives to launch a statewide campaign against gay rights. In Denver, the state legislature held public hearings on a hate crimes bill that included enhanced penalties for physical attacks based on sexual orientation. At about the same time, the Colorado Springs city council was considering adding sexual orientation to the local nondiscrimination ordinance.

This was too much for conservative Christians, who mobilized against the legislation. The opponents included Tony Marco, a freelance copywriter and marketing consultant in the Springs, who went to Denver to testify against the hate crimes bill, prepped by reading material that Noebel had given him. In Marco's view, the legislation not only was unnecessary, since gays were already protected under existing laws against crime, the bill was an assault on morality, because for the first time the state would identify gays and lesbians as a class.

In his testimony, Marco raised a series of questions intended to turn the debate away from the growing violence gays and lesbians faced. Would necrophiliacs have the right to work in funeral parlors? Would pedophiles have the right to work in day-care centers? Would bestialists have the right to work on a farm? The questions were meant to shock, and they did. Marco was convinced that the law meant he could be sent to jail just for speaking out against homosexuality. The bill took misdemeanors and felonies committed against an individual on the basis of sexual orientation, race, religion, or gender and reclassified the charge to the next highest level, thus stiffening the penalties. It would not have infringed on free speech or criminalized actions not already against the law. Still, the bill died in committee with seven Republicans voting against it and five Democrats voting for it.

Marco and his supporters immediately turned their attention to the Colorado Springs measure. They turned out hundreds of supporters at a council hearing on the measure and flooded council members with thousands of letters and postcards. "They made a choice, that's their lifestyle," said Kevin Tebedo, one of Marco's allies. "That's fine. But where do we draw the line? I reject opening this code to choice. Then we would need to open it to alcoholics or drug addicts." A handful of local gay and lesbian activists tried to salvage the proposed legislation. Chief among them was Robin Miller, an attorney working in McGraw-Hill's legal-publishing division. Low-key and articulate, Miller had moved to the Springs from San Francisco, going from being just one more lesbian in the gay hub to being one of the few openly gay people in the city. She would become the lesbian that the religious conservatives would demonize in their literature, usually as a "homosexual lawyer."

"Antigay bigots want us to remain illegitimate and invisible," Miller argued at the time. "Employment, housing, and public accommodations are inherently public by their nature and must be open to members of the public. Individuals are not to bring their biases into those areas. They are entitled to their private biases, but they cannot act on that." The argument did not sway the city council. Spooked by the turnout at the public hearing, the council stripped the sexual orientation provisions from the proposed law. By April, conservative Christians had claimed their second victory.

~~~ In the months that followed, Colorado saw a series of angry skirmishes around the issue of gay rights. In March, state representative Charles Duke refused to vote for a measure commemorating the Holocaust because the bill was "defaced" by the mention of gay victims. (In the wake of the 1995 Oklahoma City bombing, Duke was identified in the media as one of the most ardent supporters of the militia movement, suggesting that the federal government was behind the explosion.) But the greatest battle was being waged over the effort to repeal Denver's nondiscrimination ordinance. The group sponsoring the referendum, Citizens for Sensible Rights, turned in eleven thousand signatures to qualify the measure for the May 1991 ballot.

Most of the city's political leaders opposed the measure, but not all. Mayoral candidate Steve Schweitzberger, who had little chance of winning, suggested that the ordinance was forcing families to leave Denver. "You talk about trying to attract people [who] want to raise their families here and have Christian values," Schweitzberger said at a candidates' forum. By passing the ordinance "you've just told them that this city is not the place." Citizens for Sensible Rights played to the disgruntled voter who was feeling put upon by big government for whatever reason. "What's happening in our cities when these kinds of ordinances have been allowed to stand is that they've been destructive to the liberties of the little guy," said Richard Heckman, a spokesman for the group. But lack of money and an amateurish operation hobbled the referendum effort.

Gay activists relied on endorsements from everyone from Mayor Federico Peña to Rep. Pat Schroeder, the House Democratic liberal whose intelligence and wit had earned her a national profile. Activists were able to portray the referendum's supporters as extremists who wanted to undo legitimate laws. Ultimately, the referendum failed 55–45 percent, in large part because liberal Denver was not receptive to the arguments of Citizens for Sensible Rights. There were other reasons as well. The referendum campaign lacked a compelling message. "The little guy" approach appealed to simmering voter anger among white men in particular, but it wasn't strong enough in conveying just why they should be angry. And in a liberal city like Denver, "the little guy" was not reflexively antigovernment in any case.

The success left activists heady. "We had it from the start," bragged Sue Anderson, who was the head of the Gay and Lesbian Community Center in Denver. "This was a hate campaign." But there was ample cause for concern as well, although few paused to consider. If 45 percent of the voters in liberal Denver sided with the antigay arguments, what did that say about the depth of antipathy to gay rights? And what did it say about the feeling in more conservative parts of the state? Activists would soon find out to their dismay.

Throughout the spring of 1991, Marco, Tebedo, and Noebel brainstormed about how to defeat the state's gay rights movement once and for all. A group of conservative Christians began to meet regularly in Colorado Springs under the banner Colorado Coalition for Family Values, using the phrase so popular at the Republican convention in Houston well before its appearance in the national spotlight. At the first meeting, Noebel provided the benediction. The *Coalition* was dropped from the group's name when a local radio talk-show host suggested that it smacked too much of Marxism—an odd objection that had certainly never been raised against Pat Robertson's Christian Coalition. But it did reflect upon Marco's past. In the 1960s, Marco was a self-described Marxist involved in campus protests. He numbered feminist Kate Millett among his erstwhile friends. He also had gay friends when he lived in New York City, including one man whose lover was one of the original Stonewall rioters. As for himself, "I was far from being a paragon of sexual abstinence," Marco told a radio talk-show host in February 1991.

As Colorado for Family Values grew, it attracted important support. Will Perkins, a prosperous Colorado Springs Chrysler dealer, helped bankroll the group during its formation. Bill Armstrong, a Republican who had just retired after two terms as U.S. senator in order to, in his words, "praise the Lord, have some fun, and make some money," signed on to Colorado for Family Values, giving it the high-profile, experienced figure it needed for fund-raising. Armstrong, who had sponsored antigay legislation in the Senate, was a valuable asset. His presence would block any attempt to put together a united bipartisan front among the state's politicians against an antigay campaign, a tactic that worked particularly well in Oregon. Colorado for Family Values was afforded the respect that came from its affiliation with a former U.S. senator.

Colorado for Family Values found important help from outside sources as well. Marco was also able to turn to the National Legal Foundation, a conservative think tank that focused on legal issues, for advice. Marco had already received assistance from the Foundation during the fight over the Colorado Springs nondiscrimination ordinance. And Marco himself had a critical connection to Pat Robertson; for three years, Marco had served as a senior writer for the sophisticated direct-mail efforts of the televangelist's Christian Broadcasting Network in Virginia Beach, Virginia.

The final version of Colorado for Family Values' ballot measure was far more subtle—and palatable—than the draft initiative being floated in Oregon. Coloradans would see no mention of necrophilia or bestiality in their measure. No mention would be made about schools or state funding. Instead, the measure would amend the state constitution to prevent "protected status based on homosexual, lesbian or bisexual orientation." The law would not only prohibit the passage of a statewide nondiscrimination or hate-crimes law, but would void existing ordinances in Denver, Aspen, and Boulder.

Colorado for Family Values formally announced the measure—and the group's existence—in July 1991. "If having sex becomes all it takes to consider [someone] 'ethnic,' with full minority rights and privileges, the concept of ethnicity will have lost nearly all its meaning and value," Marco said. Gay activists knew that Colorado for Family Values was working on a statewide measure following its success in Colorado Springs. The activists' attempts to knock the initiative off the ballot through court challenges proved futile. They would have to rely on the voters. "We think the electorate will see through the bigotry and hatred of the Colorado Family Values Coalition and its initiative," said Arthur Powers, a spokesman for the Colorado Gay and Lesbian Task Force.

⟿ While conservative Christians were able to turn to such national powerhouses as Focus on the Family right in their own backyard, gays and lesbians in Colorado had no such advantages. They did not have the experience of organizing on a statewide basis. In fact, there was no truly statewide gay group in Colorado. Rather, there were activists in cities and towns around the state, some of them with organizational affiliations, some not. Each region was fairly autonomous of the others. As might be expected, Denver dominated.

The formation of a gay campaign began after Colorado for Family Values announced its intentions. The original idea was to form an entirely new group for the campaign, with representation from around the state. Along the way, however, Equal Protection Colorado, which ran the campaign against the Denver referendum, took control. For the group's supporters, the decision made sense. After all, Equal Protection had already run a campaign, and Denver was bound to be critical. There wasn't enough time to start entirely from scratch, and with hundreds of volunteers left over from the Denver campaign, why should the community be at square one? Judy Harrington, the Equal Protection proponent who would end up running the campaign, had important connections to the Democratic Party in the state, having worked in Sen. Gary Hart's campaigns, including his presidential bids, experience few could match.

Those reasons made sense at the time, but they masked two critical flaws. For one, having beaten back the referendum by only a 10 percent age point margin, Equal Protection was in no position to rely on Denver to provide the margin of victory in a statewide battle. Without building respectable margins elsewhere, or at least keeping losses to a minimum, the campaign was bound to lose. A full statewide effort was required. Moreover, the choice of Equal Protection was, in the eyes of activists like Miller and Powers, railroaded through, over the concerns of activists in the rest of the state. Whatever the merits of Equal Protection, they were obscured by the way that its supporters rode rough over the feelings of activists elsewhere. The ill will that this created split gays and lesbians into two camps at a time when unity was essential. In the eyes of many activists, the campaign became Denver versus everyone else, when it should have been everyone versus Colorado for Family Values. Powers was later to say that the seeds of loss were sown when Equal Protection took over.

〜 Colorado for Family Values had its problems as well, primarily between Marco and Tebedo. Given his experience with the Christian Broadcasting Network's efficient fund-raising operations, Marco had little patience with the foul-ups the group experienced at the start and blamed Tebedo for them. At one point Marco described Tebedo's duties as those of "a mechanic." The group ran into financial problems, and its signature-collection drive foundered. Marco resigned as executive director in October 1991, citing financial problems, although he was still involved in the campaign. By the beginning of the new year, the group had only four thousand signatures, less than a tenth of what it needed by March.

Still, the group had been able to put together a coalition of local representatives from a variety of national religious-right groups: the Traditional Values Coalition, the Eagle Forum, Concerned Women for America, and the Christian Coalition. Those conservative activists could marry grassroots organizing with support from the national level. When Focus on the Family featured Colorado for Family Values on its radio program, the group was flooded with requests from listeners who wanted to help. The national groups saw the issue as an important test of their political skills and of their ability to stop gay activists in their tracks. A success in either Colorado or Oregon would be an important start to turn what evangelicals saw as a rising gay tide.

What finally mobilized conservative Christians in Colorado was a remark at a February 1992 press conference by Bill McCartney, the immensely popular University of Colorado coach. McCartney had come under criticism by CU president Judith Albino for identifying himself as the CU football coach in Colorado for Family Values materials. Albino ordered an investigation (before talking to McCartney) to see if any university policies had been violated. In responding to the attack, McCartney said that his faith motivated his political activity.

"I have very clear guidelines—it's all spelled out in Scriptures," the coach said. "I embrace what Almighty God has said about these things to me when I read the Scriptures. Homosexuality is an abomination of Almighty God." Gays and lesbians, he added, were "a group of people who don't reproduce, yet want to be compared with people who do reproduce." The statement, similar to others by conservative opponents of homosexuality, ignored the growing number of gay and lesbian parents.

McCartney's views were hardly new. In 1990, he had founded Promise Keepers, a Christian men's movement, which revived— and revised—the idea of muscular Christianity for the 1990s. *Seven Promises of a Promise Keeper* told men to "take back" their role as leaders of their family from their wives. The group also stressed the need for sexual purity, which included turning away from homosexual desires. Jerry Falwell praised Promise Keepers for its potential as "the foundation for a desperately needed national spiritual awakening." By 1995, Promise Keepers was attracting hundreds of thousands of men to its conferences, held in stadiums throughout the country. The group had grown to have an annual budget of $65 million and a staff of 300. In 1989, the coach had also endorsed Operation Rescue, the controversial antiabortion group. Indeed, McCartney seemed to court controversy; on one occasion he questioned date-rape charges that had been brought against two of his players, and he had required all team members to join in pregame prayers until the ACLU challenged the practice in court.

Predictably, McCartney's remarks, delivered while he was wearing his CU sweater, created an uproar. Rep. Pat Schroeder declared in a letter that McCartney was "preaching hatred" and "hate mongering." At a protest outside the university's athletic center two days after the coach's press conference, one hundred students listened to CU student-union president Samantha Levine demand that "this university must keep this man in line." (During the rally, some football players mocked gay male students by affecting effeminate mannerisms.) Illana Zhenya Gallon, a spokeswoman for CU's gay student group, said that McCartney's statements proved that "it is not safe to be lesbian, gay, or bisexual at the University of Colorado."

Tensions rose on the campus. Gallon reported receiving a hate message after her remarks. Tebedo canceled a scheduled appearance. Pink triangles were spray-painted on the women's studies building. One news report noted darkly that the triangles, more usually the calling card of gay activists than of gay rights protesters, were depicted "the way Hitler used them, with the point down." The negative publicity would have crushed anyone else. But McCartney refused to back down. A few days after his press conference, he told a gathering of conservative Christians at an abortion-alternative clinic that "I've been called a hate monger and self-appointed ayatollah, but my heart is not against any man or person." He then went on to say that gays and lesbians are marked by "internal upheavals that literally drive a person stark raving mad. That torment makes [them] the most miserable of all people." As a final note, he said that homosexuals "burn with lust."

McCartney's own family was hardly a pillar of moral rectitude, at least as he would define it. McCartney had a ferocious temper and a history of alcohol abuse. His daughter Kristyn had engaged in highly publicized affairs with several of his players, bearing a child by the star defensive tackle out of wedlock. McCartney's own marriage had, by his admission, suffered while he pursued his high-powered career. At Promise Keepers meetings, a tearful

McCartney, who left his coaching job in 1994 to run the group, told his audience how much he regretted his neglectful ways.

But in 1992 none of that seemed to matter, largely because to many Coloradans McCartney was a hero. He was buoyed by the idolatry fans afforded him for coaching his team to the national title the year before, upsetting Notre Dame. Proving that there was no such thing as bad publicity, Colorado for Family Values began to reap the benefits of the editorial condemnation of McCartney's remarks about homosexuality. The initiative's supporters credited the uproar with galvanizing previously apathetic Christians. At a press conference a week after McCartney's initial statement, Will Perkins characterized the criticism of McCartney as political correctness at its worst.

Indeed, Perkins turned the issue on its head: it was McCartney who was the victim. "Simply for voicing his difference of opinion with the politically correct party line, he became the latest target of gay activists' campaign of intolerance," Perkins said. McCartney did have the right to his opinion, and some gay activists wanted him not to speak at all, Perkins charged, characterizing all gays and lesbians as "extremists" who relied upon totalitarian techniques of silencing opposition that had been perfected by Hitler.

Ironically, what drew support for the Colorado for Family Values initiative was the very thing that Marco had said he wanted to avoid: a biblical condemnation of homosexuality. Despite the incendiary rhetoric he had used in the fight over the statewide hate crimes bill, Marco now preferred to frame the statewide measure as a civil rights issue. Anything else, he believed, risked a backlash. But it wasn't as a civil rights issue that the ballot initiative finally garnered support. It was as a scriptural matter. That was the banner under which the troops rallied. When the deadline for presenting the signatures to qualify the measure rolled around a month later, Colorado for Family Values was able to turn in 85,500 signatures, far more than the 49,000 needed. Gay activists were expecting the measure to qualify; what they were unprepared for was the extent of support for the measure. Colorado for Family Values had collected signatures in every county in the state, in virtually every rural hamlet. It proved that their network and supporters went far beyond Colorado Springs. Gov. Roy Romer acknowledged that the issue would prove to be a touchy one. "I want to say to all the people of Colorado who find this an uncomfortable issue, we need to continue our learning curve," he said at a press conference.

Taking the advice offered to candidates by Pat Robertson's Christian Coalition, Colorado for Family Values had kept itself out of sight. "We operated a stealth campaign," Tony Marco boasted to the Christian Coalition newsletter. "We went under their radar. They never knew what strength we had." Marco envisioned that the campaign for Amendment 2, as the measure became known, would focus on the issue of who was entitled to civil rights. In a letter to Tony Ogden, then head of Equal Protection, after the amendment was proposed, Marco stated explicitly that he wanted the campaign to be civil.

"We are concerned over the expressed fears of 'gays' that such a campaign as will be conducted over this issue will result in heckling, protest or violent abuse of those practicing their behaviors," Marco wrote. "Let me say at the outset that as responsible, law-abiding citizens, we intend to do all within our power to ensure that *no unpleasantness* takes place. We would be greatly distressed to see Colorado's 'gay' citizens victimized by any sort of abuse. (Note: We do not regard the citing of authentic, documented medical information about homosexual behavior as 'abuse.') Our goal is not to arouse hatred, but in fact to extend a hand of hope to 'gays.' Our opposition is not to the humanity of 'gays,' but to the granting of legal sanction and special rights to homosexual/bisexual/lesbian behavior."

For many activists, the letter was easy to dismiss as posturing. For one thing, the "authentic" information that Marco wanted to cite was anything but legitimate, consisting of a hodgepodge of false data and out-of-context facts. But Marco was one of the few conservative Christians to countenance any connection between antigay rhetoric and physical attacks on gays and lesbians. (In Oregon, Lon Mabon, for example, consistently denied the *existence* of antigay violence.) What Marco wanted was to save gays and lesbians from what he saw as the sin of homosexuality. He had a personal stake in this crusade; his wife, Joyce, had a lesbian daughter by a previous marriage who was raising a child with her partner. "It breaks my heart every day because I know the pain she's in," said Joyce, who was born again after her 1972 conviction for selling cocaine. "I can love my daughter and not agree with her lifestyle."

Marco wanted restraint, but restraint was not what motivated opponents of gay rights. They were mobilized by the threat gays were perceived to present to children and the public health. That is why religious right groups employed such incendiary antigay rhetoric in their fund-raising letters. It paid off. Colorado for Family Values was no exception. In his fund-raising letter for the group, former senator Armstrong argued that gays were not "concerned about the health crisis which may result if militant homosexuals succeed in forcing acceptance of their promiscuous behavior." The costs will be astronomical, Armstrong said. "AIDS and its consequences will cost America $60 *billion* in 1991 alone—of which Colorado will pay its share." Ultimately, Marco's stance would lead to a rift between him and the rest of Colorado for Family Values' leaders, who chose to ignore his advice. The campaign would trot out all of the accusations about gay sexual behavior that Marco wanted to keep under wraps.

If the Colorado campaign could be summed up in a phrase, it would be "no special rights." It was the sound bite that Colorado for Family Values used to frame the debate. As much as the "special rights" phrasing was to haunt gay activists throughout the 1990s, its history was far longer than most activists knew. The Oregon Citizens Alliance used it to brilliant effect in the 1988 referendum on Governor Goldschmidt's executive order prohibiting antigay discrimination in state agencies. In fact, the idea had already been floating around for some time before that. In 1982, a campaign in Lincoln, Nebraska, to prevent the inclusion of gays in a nondiscrimination ordinance was led by the Committee to Oppose Special Rights for Homosexuals.

Other antigay activists refined the theme. In his 1985 book,

Are Gay Rights Right?—which the religious right in Colorado relied upon for its campaign—Roger J. Magnuson described nondiscrimination ordinances as "special legal privileges that give a unique protection" based on sexual behavior. "Homosexuality ought not to be elevated to an extraordinary, legally protected behavior," Magnuson, a Harvard-trained lawyer, wrote. "While promoted as an act of compassion, such privileged treatment is compassionate neither to the homosexual, who is not helped by social encouragement of his life-style, nor to society at large, which in increasing measure is experiencing the costs—social, medical, and psychological—of disordered sexual behavior of all kinds."

Colorado for Family Values was even sharper in its use of the phrase. Tony Marco and other Amendment 2 supporters hammered away at attempts to equate sexual orientation with any other category of minority. "If having sex becomes all it takes to be considered 'ethnic,'" a Colorado for Family Values flyer declared, "then the concept of ethnicity, as well as legitimate minorities' hard-won gains, will have lost nearly all their meaning and value." Instead, Colorado for Family Values outlined its own criteria to qualify as a true minority. The group must "show that they're discriminated against to the point that they can't earn average income, get an adequate education, or enjoy a fulfilling cultural life." In addition the group must show "unchangeable physical characteristics like skin color, gender, handicap," and "clearly show that it is not politically powerless." The standards were so loose and legally untenable that they could deny virtually anyone rights; the first argument had been used in the past against Jews, and by focusing on physical traits, Colorado for Family Values would deny nondiscrimination measures protecting its own members' freedom of religion.

Colorado for Family Values buttressed its arguments that gays were not the same as racial minorities by turning to respectable sources. Colorado for Family Values literature featured quotes from Ignacio Rodriguez and John Franklin, past chairs of the Colorado Civil Rights Division, a state agency, arguing that gay rights would, in Rodriguez's words, "erode and seriously damage the legitimate civil rights protections" of blacks, Hispanics, and women. From this point of view, civil rights was a zero-sum game. If gays got protections, someone else had to lose theirs.

"No special rights" defined the issue for voters with a crushing finality, especially at a time when civil rights protections in general were under increasing scrutiny. Voters almost did not need to listen to the arguments about how nondiscrimination measures were "special rights." They just knew, from the ads, that they were. In Colorado especially, where the slogan was fresh, the damage it did was inestimable. The specter of affirmative action quotas and other "preferences" was a powerful scare tactic. No reputable supporter of nondiscrimination measures has ever suggested that companies be made to go out of their way to hire gays and lesbians. But the quota argument struck a chord with voters ignorant of the real, and limited, impact of the kind of protections gays and lesbians were seeking. (It was also yet another precursor of the battle over affirmative action that erupted in 1995.) Moreover, by emphasizing that gays were not a "legitimate" minority recognized by the federal government but instead were seeking minority status based on behavior that most people found offensive, Colorado for Family Values could salve the conscience of voters concerned that they were taking a stand against civil rights.

Gay activists could rebut the arguments behind the "no special rights" slogan. Too many people had lost their jobs simply because they were gay and had no legal recourse unless they enjoyed legal protections. Preventing job discrimination was not a special right. But gay activists could not counter Colorado for Family Values' slogan on its own short, catchy terms. In fact, many activists thought that the rebuttal was self-evident. *Special rights? No one in their right mind would buy that.* Opponents of Amendment 2 never understood how deeply that message resonated with voters until after election day. Robin Miller later said that it was the biggest mistake the campaign made. But even if Equal Protection had known how successful Colorado for Family Values' slogan was, activists would have been hard put to come up with an effective counter.

The "no special rights" tune that Colorado for Family Values sang in public was far different from the one it sang in the church choir. In a public forum, Kevin Tebedo would say that gays were "asking for special advantages, and they don't deserve it, that's all." But at church meetings, he used entirely different rhetoric. "You see, we say we should have separation of church and state, but you see, Jesus Christ is king of kings and the lord of lords," the pugnacious Tebedo told one congregation during the campaign. "That is politics; this is rule; that is authority. So whose authority is going to rule?" The idea that the campaign was an effort to establish Christ, as interpreted by Colorado for Family Values, as the final civil authority was a powerful catalyst for conservative Christians.

The campaign coincided with a time of unparalleled political organizing on the part of conservative Christians around the country. In Colorado alone, the Christian Coalition, Focus on the Family, and Citizens for Responsible Government were holding seminars about electoral politics for their followers. There was even a book, *A Christian Guide to Colorado's Political System,* to explain to evangelicals how to break into the process. The national gay groups, such as the National Gay and Lesbian Task Force, took advantage of the initiatives to raise funds and organize as well. But with nowhere near the resources of the religious right groups, the gay organizations' efforts were limited by comparison. Without the experience of a vast national network to draw upon, national gay groups could not compete. Such inadequacy left local activists to reinvent the same wheel time and again and proved to be one of the most enduring failures of the national gay movement.

~ The special rights slogan was not the only argument used in the antigay campaigns. Both the Oregon and the Colorado campaigns saw the use of well-worn claims about homosexuality, bolstered by pseudoscientific evidence. Fund-raising letters focused on the threat gays and lesbians, invariably described as "militant," posed to society. Bill Armstrong described gays as "pleasure-addicted" in one Colorado for Family Values letter, people who have "no use for the traditional family, for traditional moral standards, or for traditional religion." The characterization of gays as destructive and harmful to society had three components. First, gays were licentious and promiscuous, and their practices abhorrent and perverse. Second, homosexuality and pedophilia were so closely related as to be for all intents and purposes synonymous. Finally, because of AIDS, gays posed a health threat to and financial drain on the rest of the population.

Colorado for Family Values backed up these statements with a variety of statistics that sounded impressive, even if they were invariably phony or mischaracterized. Using sex surveys and passages from gay writers, the group put together a lurid depiction of homosexuality. Some of the material was visual. For example, the campaign made use of a video using footage from the 1990 gay and lesbian pride parade in San Francisco filmed by a Traditional Values Coalition supporter in Concord, California. San Francisco's parade, notable for its carnival atmosphere, attracts a wide range of marchers, from corporate-employee groups to motorcycle-riding lesbians. Not surprisingly, the video selected the frankest depictions of sexuality among the participants and concluded that this was what the gay community was all about.

Colorado for Family Values blandly stated that it was just reporting the truth. "We didn't stage the parade," said Perkins. "These are actual, factual things that happened." Equal Protection's Harrington mounted a game defense. "That's like depicting straights based on a video of Mardi Gras," she said. But for voters unfamiliar with gay behavior, the video seemed to confirm that it was alien and unrestrained. Flyers saying falsely that gays ingested "the fecal material of 23 different men per year" only served to confirm fears that gay sexual habits were disgusting. In fact, no comprehensive, scientifically balanced study of gay sexual practices has ever been completed. Even the National Opinion Research Center survey of 3,400 respondents that was released in 1994 did not include a large enough sampling of gays and lesbians to reach any conclusions about what they did in bed. But the lack of information only played to the strengths of Colorado for Family Values. Without any data to refute the charges, conservative Christians could portray gay sex as inhuman and nauseating, which they did with a kind of prurient vigor.

That the religious right produced at least the veneer of science to justify its antigay activity was an admission of secular society's reliance upon objective evidence in dealing with important issues. The right could just as readily have turned solely to biblical interpretation to make its point, since that was the irreducible basis of its position. But science, even the brand practiced by antigay activists, had a genuine value in political arguments. Far better to convince voters using ostensibly factual material than to preach at them. Yet, the religious activists were using the trappings of science only, without adhering to a rigorous methodology. They knew what results they wanted, and they got them. It was science in the service of the Bible.

Paul Cameron of the Family Research Institute, the one-man band of antigay science, was a frequent Colorado for Family Values representative during debates in Colorado, inevitably stirring up controversy with his views (although David Noebel was Colorado for Family Values' official education adviser). When Colorado for Family Values used Cameron's figures to argue that gays were responsible for up to half of all child molestations—the figure grew over the years—the group found itself in the uncomfortable position of arguing with a former Miss America, Marilyn VanDerbur Atler, an incest survivor who said the figure was a fabrication.

As it turned out, the figure, although equally untenable, was meant to apply to incest cases only, Perkins argued. But whatever the figure, it underscored the homosexual threat. "We feel that clearing this up is doubly important, because the authenticity of this rather shocking data sheds some greatly needed light on the kind of lifestyle militant gays are demanding that Colorado give protected-class status," Perkins said. A study released two weeks later by two pediatricians of 387 cases of suspected child molestation in the files of Denver's Children's Hospital found that in only one of the cases was the molester gay.

⟶ Correcting years of stereotypes and misinformation was a formidable task under the best of circumstances. Early on, Judy Harrington, campaign manager for Equal Protection, had stressed that " 'message' is so central to the campaign as to nearly overlap with 'strategy.' It's a statement of why you should win and/or why your opponent should lose." The message in this campaign, she concluded, was that "voters don't respond so much to issues as to values." The argument that Equal Protection used against Amendment 2 was that it was discrimination. A television commercial that played well with focus groups, depicting a couple talking about their gay son, concluded with the tag line "Let's leave family values up to families."

The group steered clear of the thorny issue of Colorado for Family Values' theocratic leanings. But far worse, Equal Protection decided to stay away from the issue of homosexuality as well. In doing so, the campaign employed the kind of good-gay/bad-gay standard that had proven so divisive in Oregon. Groups that seemed a little unusual to the public were kept at arm's length from Equal Protection, although their money was certainly welcome. This was particularly true of the leather community, the segment of the gay population who see leather regalia as a powerful and erotic image. Campaign officials were wary that pictures of bare-chested men in leather chaps and caps would be used against the campaign. Yet the videos that Colorado for Family Values were distributing used just that image anyway. More important, other than their after-hours attraction to leather, there was little to distinguish members of the leather community from the rest of the gay population or, for that matter, the general population; they paid taxes, held jobs, and voted. Furthermore, the leather community had been instrumental in mounting the earliest charitable response to the AIDS epidemic. The leather community was so incensed by the campaign's actions that it formed its own anti-amendment campaign.

Equal Protection made another mistake, even more critical, in avoiding the gay issue in the campaign. Officials decided for the most part to leave the Cameron statistics unrebutted for fear of pulling the campaign off its message. Instead, it took Colorado for Family Values' hits—a strategy all too reminiscent of Michael Dukakis's losing presidential bid four years earlier. It was more than a bad campaign tactic. Coloradans were left with a flood of antigay images that would shape their opinions of gay life for years to come.

Despite the viciousness of Colorado for Family Values' depictions of gays and lesbians, the campaign against Amendment 2 was relatively low-key compared to the one in Oregon. For one, the media attention was so focused on Oregon that at one point Equal Protection was reduced to sending a reminder to the press that Colorado was facing its own battle. But the atmosphere was entirely different in Colorado as well. Amendment 2 was one of ten ballot initiatives, and it never emerged as the most compelling of the bunch. The business community, which provided critical assistance to the No on 9 campaign in Oregon, was distracted by Colorado ballot measures that would have alternatively limited tax rates and raised the sales tax. Because the sales tax increase would have been earmarked for education, teachers' groups, another key component of the No on 9 coalition, were devoting most of their energies to it and not Equal Protection's effort.

Colorado for Family Values had another advantage over the Oregon Citizens Alliance. The religious leadership in Oregon was nearly unanimous in its condemnation of Measure 9. Not so in Colorado. True, the initiative was lambasted by mainline Protestant clergy. Bishop Roy Sano, regional head of the United Methodist Church, said that a vote against the measure was "a clear issue of simple justice." In a fit of ecumenical hubris, Tebedo dismissed Sano as a "liberal" who "doesn't speak for his congregations." But the opposition had one key holdout: the Roman Catholic bishops of Colorado decided to remain neutral about the measure. The silence of the Colorado bishops hurt the campaign against Amendment 2; voters were able to interpret neutrality as a sign of passive endorsement of the initiative.

Harrington and other Equal Protection officials felt confident going into the last days of the campaign. Colorado had seen some harassment and threats, but nothing of the scale of what happened in Oregon. The relative quiet seemed to mean that Colorado for Family Values had failed to electrify the electorate. The polls also predicted the defeat of Amendment 2. The day before the election, Equal Protection could point to a poll showing the measure failing 54 percent to 40 percent. But the poll was a kind of early warning. The Denver referendum in 1991 lost by 10 percentage points, but the polls had shown it losing by about 30 points. The dirty secret of polls was that people lied on some issues so as not to appear bigoted. Gay rights was one such issue.

⟶ On election night, gays and lesbians watched in disbelief and horror as the votes were tallied. The state was going for Clinton. But it was also approving Amendment 2. Predictably, Colorado Springs was voting for the measure by a huge margin. But areas that Equal Protection had thought it could count on were falling away—the Denver suburbs, Pueblo, and other traditional Democratic strongholds. By the end of the evening it was clear how successfully Colorado for Family Values had controlled the debate. Amendment 2 had passed 53 percent to 47 percent. Even Colorado for Family Values' members were astonished.

The only people more astonished were gays and lesbians. They stormed the Democratic victory celebration in Denver to remind the revelers that the night was not a total triumph. Several hundred opponents of Amendment 2 gathered outside the celebration until Governor Romer and Mayor Wellington Webb addressed the crowd. "The Democrats win and are in their glory," said Sue Larson, a lesbian activist from Boulder who had been a field organizer for Equal Protection. "Meanwhile, we're sitting on a cannon."

In the weeks and months that followed, Colorado was consumed by Amendment 2, far more than it ever was before the election. A movement for a boycott quickly materialized, as gays and lesbians in other parts of the country—many of whom never had plans to go to Colorado in the first place—vowed now to punish the state for its vote. Boycott Colorado, a group in Denver that kept track of and added pressure for the boycott, gained a national following. Within weeks, several city governments, including Atlanta and New York, as well as a variety of unions, announced that they supported the boycott. Colorado was dubbed the Hate State, but for many gays and lesbians in Denver, Boulder, and Aspen, it was still far friendlier than many other parts of the country.

The boycott effort became positively glamorous when Barbra Streisand announced that "we must now say clearly that the moral climate there is no longer acceptable, and if we're asked to, we must refuse to play where they discriminate." (Streisand later moved away from her remarks, saying that she wasn't actually calling for a boycott.) Mayor Webb, who was an honorary member of Equal Protection's board, traveled to New York and appeared on the *Arsenio Hall Show* to try to contain the damage. He and Governor Romer became the target of angry gay activists, despite their strenuous opposition to the antigay measure.

Boycotts often work better when they are threatened; the execution can be sticky and divisive. Ultimately, the boycott of Colorado proved to be just that. The boycott actually hardened attitudes; a poll in the *Denver Post* showed that 43 percent of those surveyed indicated that the boycott made them *less* likely to support a repeal of Amendment 2. In short, people didn't like the vote, but they liked outsiders looking down on them even less. Some activists in Colorado expressed the feeling that they were being picked on by outsiders who knew little about their state. To them, some of the boycott rhetoric smacked of holier-than-thou posing that actually helped enemies of gay rights elsewhere. After all, what was the sense in sending ski business from liberal Aspen, where city officials had condemned the vote, to conservative Utah, where a sodomy law was still on the books? The effort also took its toll on relations between gays and racial minorities, who were on the front lines of the tourism and convention industry and thus likeliest to suffer any falloff in trade. The boycott became the burning issue, not Amendment 2.

But the boycott, which petered out by the summer, was the least of the gay community's problems. What followed the election was an unprecedented display of finger-pointing, backbiting, and infighting. Instead of training their sights on Amendment 2, gay activists formed a circle and began shooting at each other. Some second-guessing was inevitable, given the confidence that Equal Protection had displayed before election night. But many campaign officials refused to talk after the election, fueling the resentment activists had harbored against the group since it took the reins of the campaign the year before. Those Equal Protection staffers who were around found themselves the targets of outrage by betrayed gays and lesbians. Larson, who had poured countless hours into the campaign, had people come up to her and blame her for the loss, even though she had done invaluable work in organizing gays and lesbians in rural areas.

Even those activists not associated with the campaign were sniping at one another. A variety of new groups sprang up, often at cross-purposes with one another. Most would die, with a few notable exceptions, such as Ground Zero in Colorado Springs, which was effective in keeping the real issue—the strength of the religious right—before gays and lesbians. But overall, the atmosphere was thick with distrust. A number of activists, including Miller, would eventually leave the state altogether to escape surroundings that now seemed threatening and poisonous. With the passage of Amendment 2, the atmosphere in Colorado was "like slogging through pea soup," Miller said.

By good luck and planning, a group of gays and lesbians in Denver had a contingency plan. Attorneys Mary Celeste and Patrick Steadman and other activists had developed a strategy for challenging the measure in court should it pass, something they thought would never happen. What they thought was an academic exercise became the basis of the lawsuit against Amendment 2. Among the plaintiffs were tennis star Martina Navratilova, who lived in Aspen, and Richard Evans, Webb's liaison to the Denver gay and lesbian community. The group was able to secure former state Supreme Court justice Jean Dubofsky as their lead attorney, while also receiving help from Lambda Legal Defense and Education Fund attorneys in New York.

One beneficiary of the vote was Paul Cameron. Not only had he worked for the winning side, suddenly he was one of the few "experts" that the state could turn to to defend its case in court. In a shocking development, state attorney general Gayle Norton's office paid Cameron thousands of dollars to appear as a witness in defense of Amendment 2. Only when word leaked out about

Cameron's hiring did Norton seem to realize how serious a blunder it would be to call a witness who had been rebuked by judges in his past court appearances for his unprofessional standards. While Cameron had already been paid, he was not called at the trial. Still, he was able to claim a newfound legitimacy as a government-approved expert. He found Colorado Springs so hospitable that he moved his enterprise there in the fall of 1995.

Colorado for Family Values quickly took advantage of the turmoil in Colorado following the election. The group immediately sent out a fund-raising letter warning supporters that the gay threat was even greater than before. "The entire national homosexual establishment—their multimillion-dollar Washington lobbying groups, their wealthy Hollywood allies, their friends in the national press—have converged on Colorado, telling the same tired lies—lies Colorado voters rejected—to a national audience," Colorado for Family Values warned. "And worse yet, they've vowed revenge on anyone who supported Amendment 2."

A handful of actions by a small group of gay activists confirmed Amendment 2 supporters in the correctness of the election result. The worst of the actions was the desecration of a Catholic cemetery outside of Denver in January, ostensibly in protest of the Church's policy against condom use. Signs at the cemetery read "BVM [Blessed Virgin Mary] Sez: No Latex No Sex" and "Jesus Died of AIDS." The offensiveness of the protest was a public relations nightmare for gay and lesbian activists trying to win support in their fight against Amendment 2. Four members of ACT UP who had previously been defiant about the propriety of the incident eventually plea-bargained to the crime and apologized "with our deepest, heartfelt sincerity."

There were future skirmishes, including one where protesters threw packages of Kool-Aid with condoms attached at worshipers in a Colorado Springs church. On the packages was the phrase "Remember Jonestown," a reference to the cult that committed mass suicide by drinking poison-laced Kool-Aid. Even without those actions, Colorado for Family Values members were not happy about what followed the passage of Amendment 2. They were also unprepared for it. Denver District Court judge Jeffrey

Bayless quickly enjoined Amendment 2 from taking effect, leaving its supporters to claim that the court was ignoring the will of the people. Politicians like Romer and Webb were also telling everyone that the vote was wrong. A group of Amendment 2 supporters formed BACK OFF and held a rally in front of Perkins's car dealership during which they destroyed Streisand tapes.

Emboldened by its success, Colorado for Family Values began to flex its muscles, eventually offering seminars, cash, and advice to other campaigns, especially in Cincinnati in 1993. The victory that the group boasted about was short-lived; after the election, Colorado for Family Values lost all the court challenges to Amendment 2, leading to an appeal to the U.S. Supreme Court in the fall of 1995. The group also lost one of its founders. Marco had gone from advising the campaign to testifying at the trial that temporarily overturned the measure that he thought the "no special rights" argument was "irrelevant."

"You risk giving gay activists ammunition to make their charge that Amendment 2 is what they've said it is: a hateful, fear-mongering and mean-spirited piece of work," Marco wrote in a memo to Perkins. "You risk rousing violent animosity toward gays, to which gay militants will react in kind, as extremists on both sides come out of the woodwork." Colorado for Family Values would lose its credibility if it continued "rubbing the faces of the state's people in repulsive, extremist homosexual behavior."

Marco's main point—"it is easier to nauseate than educate"—fell on deaf ears. Perkins said that Marco had "the right to his own opinion," but added that Colorado for Family Values had no plans to change its strategy. In the short term, at least, Perkins's decision was correct. After all, it was hard to argue with success. The campaign included vehement attacks on homosexuality and it produced a victory that few had anticipated. The religious right had proven itself a force to be reckoned with in the state, and the money that was filling Colorado for Family Values' coffers only underscored the value of the antigay literature and statistics. Perkins soon became a kind of elder statesman for the religious right, providing advice to antigay groups around the country. Tebedo, on the other hand, went on to become an embarrassment to Colorado for Family Values. Increasingly interested in the far-right movement for state sovereignty, Tebedo left Colorado for Family Values in November 1995 in the wake of his vigorous defense of an "ex-gay" counselor who the *Denver Post* alleged had masturbated with clients and engaged in sexually explicit phone conversations with them. Tebedo and Perkins said the parting was amicable, but Tebedo had apparently become too much of a loose cannon for the group to tolerate.

Unlike Perkins and Tebedo, Marco was focused on a long-term plan to win the hearts and minds of voters. The inflammatory tactics of Paul Cameron and antigay videos played well to conservative Christians, but after the initial shock wore off, other voters would wonder just why Colorado for Family Values was so obsessed with gay sex habits and why the image of gays and lesbians the group presented did not square with their own experiences. Marco certainly believed the rhetoric that Colorado for Family Values used; as a practical matter, he just felt that it was inappropriate for public discussion. His ultimate goal was theological. "Our deeper purpose is to bring a message of hope to individuals who, because of alienation or rejection, have chosen to go down the wrong road," he wrote in one Colorado for Family Values tract. He was simply laying all his cards on the table—that this was primarily a religious effort and that its aim was to bring people the message of salvation. (Marco went on to found Dove-Tail Ministries in Colorado Springs to help homosexuals "change" their sexual orientation, part of a burgeoning industry in creating "ex-gays.")

If Colorado for Family Values failed to win hearts and minds, gay activists did not do any better. In their justifiable concern to avoid a referendum on homosexuality, Equal Protection's leaders missed a chance to let the public know just what it meant to be gay or lesbian. The courts might save gays and lesbians from the excesses of the initiative, but that was no substitute for educating the public at large that in Colorado, as throughout the country, gays and lesbians were not pedophiles and serial killers, but fellow productive citizens. As the success of Amendment 2 showed, that was a lesson that too many people had yet to learn.

CHAPTER 5

The Stroke of a Pen

THE ELECTION OF BILL CLINTON unleashed unparalleled expectations among gays and lesbians. After twelve long years
living under the burden of the AIDS epidemic and chilly relations
with the Reagan and Bush administrations, gay activists were convinced that this was their time in the sun. They had played an
instrumental role in the election of the most pro-gay president
in American history, who as a candidate had made sweeping
promises to end all formal discrimination on the basis of sexual
orientation. Finally, their days as political pariahs were coming to
a felicitous end. They could now sit back with pride and watch
Clinton make history on their behalf. The jubilant celebration cul-
minated in a glittery January 1993 inaugural ball in downtown
Washington, D.C. Tuxedo-clad gay leaders toasted one another's
contribution to the new president's hard-fought victory with expensive champagne. Hobnobbing with such gay celebrities as k. d.
lang and Melissa Etheridge, the pop singer who had come out
with great fanfare earlier in inauguration week, same-sex couples
danced late into the night.

For David Mixner, a friend and key gay adviser to Clinton, the most cherished promise was lifting the ban on gay and lesbian service personnel in the military, one of the last bastions of officially sanctioned antigay discrimination in American life. Since the imposition of the ban in 1943, hundreds of thousands of gays had been expelled from the ranks, causing incalculable pain and suffering. Mixner saw ending the ban as the gay movement's top priority. Almost from the beginning of his campaign, Clinton, at Mixner's urging, had made his pledge to overturn the ban central to his strategy of appealing to gay and lesbian voters. Later, during his regular strategy sessions with gay activists as well as the president, Mixner maintained the complacent optimism of the campaign, assuring other equally sanguine gay activists that Clinton's lifting of the ban was as easy as "a stroke of a pen." The phrase, a seemingly apt reference to Clinton idol John F. Kennedy's famous pledge to eliminate racial segregation upon occupying the Oval Office, would become a painful reminder of just how unrealistic gay leaders had been about the fight that loomed before them and their president.

But as Barney Frank knew, eliminating the military ban would prove to be every bit as time-consuming, tumultuous, and tricky as ending segregation. The openly gay Massachusetts congressman, who was elected to the House in 1972, had seen his share of "done deals" come terribly undone. Even before the inauguration, Frank circulated a strongly worded memo to gay leaders warning them that storm clouds were gathering on the horizon. Frank knew that while the gay groups were passively waiting for the president to implement in January his campaign pledge to lift the ban, the religious right and its more secular conservative allies had surreptitiously gained a foothold among the Pentagon brass, who would be the final arbiters of any change in policy, had lined up heavy hitters in Congress, and had stirred up fervent opposition to lifting the ban among their legions of grassroots supporters. Without massive countermobilization, Frank realized, the stroke of a pen would more likely be that of the gay community on the terms of its political surrender.

Indeed, the religious right already had its sights trained on

Clinton and the reeling gay rights groups. The gays-in-the-military fight furnished the religious right, building on intensive antigay organizing from Maine to Oregon, an almost perfect opening to take its campaign national. By contrast, gay groups had no such organized plans. In only three months, the gay groups and the religious right had effectively switched roles they had assumed during the Reagan and Bush administrations. Gay activists were now insiders trying to persuade a sympathetic White House to adhere to a principled campaign pledge, while the right was on the outside screaming bloody murder.

For gay activists, expecting an immediate overturning of the ban was perhaps a bridge too far. The battle over the ban had taken place on many fronts for at least two decades—in the media, in the courts, on college campuses, and within the military itself—with little expectation even among the most fervent anti-ban activists that it would actually be lifted before the millennium. But by 1991, while little-known Arkansas governor Bill Clinton was gearing up for a presidential bid, a small group of gay activists, many of them military veterans, began to catch the attention of the larger gay community. For the first time, the national media began to take seriously the growing antiban movement. An August 27, 1991, article in the gay magazine *The Advocate* charged that Pete Williams, an assistant secretary of defense, was a closeted gay man. Williams, who neither denied nor confirmed the allegations, maintained a high-level security clearance and had been the Pentagon's star spokesman during the just completed Operation Desert Storm. His lofty, high-profile position forced Defense Secretary Dick Cheney to choose between scrapping his trusted aide or undermining the security rationale for the ban on gays in the military, epitomized by the argument that gays and lesbians are susceptible to blackmail by virtue of their sexuality. Never a die-hard proponent of the ban, Cheney admitted on national television that the rationale was "a bit of an old chestnut" that he had "inherited" from his less enlightened predecessors.

But other factors played into Cheney's partial retreat from the ban as well. An internal Pentagon report questioning the security rationale had just generated national publicity. Prepared by the Defense Personnel Security Research and Education Center, a Monterey, California, think tank funded by the Department of Defense, *Homosexuality and Military Personnel* noted that "both patriots and traitors are drawn from the class 'American citizen,' not specifically from the class 'heterosexual' or the class 'homosexual.'" Of 117 cases of espionage unearthed within the Department of Defense since 1945, only 7 were committed by gays or lesbians. Pentagon officials tried to keep the report's findings secret, but its conclusions were made public by Rep. Gerry Studds, who with Barney Frank, also from Massachusetts, was at the time the only other openly gay House member.

Pentagon officials and Capitol Hill pols weren't the only ones placing the issue on the table. Active-duty gay and lesbian service personnel were publicly acknowledging their sexual orientation in growing numbers. The best known among them was Margarethe Cammermeyer, a decorated Vietnam veteran who was being considered for the head nursing position in the Washington State National Guard when she was discharged under the ban after telling her commanding officer that she is a lesbian. Others included Tracy Thorne and Keith Meinhold, both of whom had nearly flawless military records, making their stories difficult for the media or military officials to ignore. With gay service members refusing to go quietly, the judicial system entered the fray. Cammermeyer, Thorne, and Meinhold, for instance, would each go on to challenge the policy in court. In a six-month period during the presidential campaign, federal courts issued four separate rulings challenging the Pentagon ban. In September of 1992, Los Angeles federal district judge Terry Hatter Jr. barred Meinhold's discharge in a stinging condemnation of the ban. Meinhold's attorney, John McGuire, who was himself a gay veteran, ably steered the case through repeated challenges, each round of which drew media attention to the antiban movement.

Pressure to lift the ban was simmering on many fronts, but it was Clinton's campaign pledge to lift the ban that brought it to a boil. During his tenure as Arkansas governor, when he had only a tiny organized gay constituency whose demands he could brush aside, Clinton assiduously avoided gay rights questions. He showed no such reservations on the campaign trail, though, first pledging to overturn the ban in October 1991 in response to a question during an appearance at Harvard University's Kennedy School of Government. Clinton felt that a high-profile position on the issue was the best bet to wrest away the gay voting bloc and its dollars from Paul Tsongas, the former Massachusetts senator and proven gay ally. Especially during the early Democratic primaries in the Northeast, where Tsongas posed a stiff challenge, Clinton needed votes from hard-core Democrats, a category many gay activists fit. Forces greater than the Democratic front-runner, however, kept breathing life into his promise even as the primary season wound down.

It was a pledge that Clinton would raise many times on the campaign trail, each time heightening expectations of gay activists and reinforcing the issue's role as the key litmus test for candidates seeking gay support. But Clinton and Mixner had badly misjudged the political climate surrounding the ban. The Bush-Quayle campaign was reportedly ready to capitalize on the issue in the fall, backing away only after polls showed voters had been turned off by the extreme tone of the Republican convention. By September, Quayle, who was the administration's unofficial liaison to the religious right, was telling everyone who would listen that he did not support the exclusion of gays and lesbians from his party. Having shot itself in the foot, the GOP had to watch its potentially crippling barrage languish in the arsenal.

The Republican campaign's silence on the ban caused Clinton to severely underestimate the resonance of the military issue with voters of all stripes. Adding to Clinton's lack of realpolitik was David Mixner's unfounded optimism. As a military foe dating back to the Vietnam War, Mixner was surprising in his naïveté. Antiwar social reformers like him should have been the first to assess accurately the Pentagon's long tradition of resistance to egalitarian reforms and its prerogative in doing so.

As much as the Arkansas governor coveted comparisons with Harry Truman, he seemed unschooled in the lessons of the Missouri Democrat's battle to integrate the armed forces a half century earlier. Truman won that battle despite intense hostility from the military establishment, but only with a grim determination that Clinton did not seem to share to vindicate a principle. Coupled with Clinton's unpopular history as an antiwar protester and alleged draft dodger, this made hopes of his prevailing in a public relations showdown with the military politically unrealistic.

For his part, the ordinarily savvy Clinton was little better than Mixner at accurately gauging the political winds. At a November 12 press conference in Little Rock just days after his election, Clinton cited Cheney's "old chestnut" remark and promised once again to "move forward" in a "prompt fashion" by issuing an executive order lifting the ban within days of his inauguration. Because it was a slow news day, dozens of reporters pounced on the comments, pushing them into headlines nationwide. Heartened by Clinton's words, gay activists found their already unrealistic expectations of the president's power and resolve to lift the ban confirmed. "We figured the president of the United States was powerful enough to get it done with an executive order if he really wanted to," Tim McFeeley, then executive director of the Human Rights Campaign Fund, would later say, reflecting on the military-ban battle. "With Democratic majorities in both houses of Congress, we didn't think it would be a problem."

By the time he was ready to take office, in fact, Clinton had raised expectations so high that nothing short of the swift and complete elimination of the ban would satisfy gay activists or the media, which weighed his every breath on the subject against his many ambitious promises. Yet within months Clinton went from promising an executive order lifting the ban, to delaying it pending further study, to floating a compromise that gay activists deemed a betrayal. By the end of the debate, he was borrowing the religious right's rhetoric, declaring that his opposition to the ban did not mean he condoned "the homosexual lifestyle." When he ultimately suggested a compromise that was deemed unacceptable by gay activists and a sign of weakness by his opponents, the president was tagged with the image of an unprincipled waffler that would come to haunt his entire administration.

⌒ In the days leading up to his inauguration, Clinton was still promising to place the order at the top of his agenda, hoping to slip it through an unsuspecting Congress with several less controversial abortion-related orders while still flush in his honeymoon period. But issuing an executive order would turn out to be far more complicated than the "stroke of a pen."

Largely because of his promise to lift the gay ban, the days following Clinton's inauguration amounted to more hell than honeymoon. By the end of January, the rumblings of opposition had risen to an outcry. Colin Powell, the powerful and popular chairman of the Joint Chiefs of Staff, advised midshipmen at the Naval Academy in Annapolis, Maryland, to resign in protest if the president carried out his campaign promise. While publicly taking a wait-and-see approach, Sam Nunn, chairman of the Senate Armed Services Committee, was already strategizing with other congressional supporters of the ban to beat back the president's proposal. Prodded by the religious right, callers jammed the switchboards at the White House, congressional offices, and radio call-in programs. In the infancy of the debate, calls favoring the retention of the ban outnumbered those opposing it by ratios of hundreds to one. The White House immediately went into the crisis mode that would come to exemplify the media's perception of its political operation. With no one in the White House designated to handle the issue, in the hope of heading off the mounting opposition Clinton himself held a series of late-night meetings with Nunn, who was still smarting from being snubbed for the top defense appointment. The president hosted solemn meetings with the Joint Chiefs at which he attempted to mollify their intense anger at not being consulted earlier about the proposed policy change. When the emergency gatherings came to nothing, the outpouring of opposition forced Clinton to announce in late January that he would suspend issuing the order for six months, until

July 15, pending further consultations with the increasingly confident and insistent pro-ban forces.

⌢ The religious right, meanwhile, quickly came to view the gays-in-the-military issue as the Alamo of the "culture war." When Clinton raised the issue, conservative activists pounced on the political opportunities it created to weaken a presidency it saw as the ultimate expression of morally lax liberalism. It also provided them with the evidence they had been seeking that antigay campaigns would succeed not only on the local level, but in national politics, as well.

Immediately upon Clinton's election, the gays-in-the-military issue became a staple for the religious right's direct-mail marketing, raising millions in contributions and providing a coherent, compelling enemy against which to organize. Pat Robertson railed against the proposal on *The 700 Club,* charging that allowing gays in the military would be providing "preferred status to evil. Let's give preferred status to the good." Jerry Falwell rallied the troops on *Old-Time Gospel Hour,* and Beverly LaHaye, president of Concerned Women for America, blasted homosexuals on her live radio broadcasts, which were carried by more than one thousand radio stations nationwide. Paul Weyrich's satellite network, National Empowerment Television, linked conservative political groups for strategy sessions in more than ninety congressional districts. Secular conservatives such as Rush Limbaugh stirred up grassroots antigay passions during his daily talk radio broadcasts. Together, the pro-ban forces reached into the homes of the vast majority of Americans with their antigay bile.

Caught off guard by the strength and vehemence of the opposition, gay activists were forced to hastily throw together a campaign to rally support for lifting the ban. The Campaign for Military Service, an umbrella organization composed of the National Gay and Lesbian Task Force, the Human Rights Campaign Fund, and more than a dozen other political, religious, and civil rights groups, did not get off the ground until early February, when the pro-ban firestorm was well under way. Mixner, the campaign's founder, would serve as its chief fund-raiser and titular head. Yet the combination of the pro-ban forces' strength and head start and Campaign for Military Service's tardiness and debility allowed the religious right to control the terms of the debate. While couching its argument in the rhetoric of God and country, the right's lobbying campaign had at its core the belief that prejudiced service members had the right not to associate with open homosexuals. By allowing gays to serve openly, they argued, heterosexual service members would somehow be victimized.

Because military enlistees serve in particularly close confines with one another, the right's demand had more currency than when invoked in other areas of American life. Gary Bauer, president of the right-wing Family Research Council, insisted that gay activists were seeking to impose themselves on heterosexuals, not fighting for equal treatment. "[Homosexuals'] notion of 'civil rights' would mean a jackboot on the back of the 99 percent of society that still follows the norms of nature," he said in a column written for his group's newsletter during the gays-in-the-military debate. Underlying such sentiments was the notion that gays and lesbians should simply shut up and go away. Bauer was the religious right's connection to Washington's conservative establishment. With the wealth and clout of James Dobson's Focus on the Family behind him, he was also one of Washington's most influential lobbyists. With the advent of the military debate, Bauer would establish crucial links with right-leaning, evangelical military officials.

Unlike gay groups, whose influence in Washington extended only marginally into other liberal interest groups, the right had a more entrenched position from which to wage a national battle. By the onset of the military debate, Bauer had already parlayed an expressed concern for traditional nuclear families, which he claimed were being beaten down by a range of determined foes, especially gays and lesbians, into a well-fortified political niche in Washington's interest-group politics. Though Bauer admitted that Family Research Council did little if any original research, as its name implied, the group published regular position papers attempting to refute mainstream social science on topics ranging from gay teenage suicide to the biological roots of homosexuality. Data from the "studies" was then funneled into the group's vitriolic fund-raising letters. In Family Research Council literature, the picture Bauer painted of his own family was as angelic as his descriptions of his political opponents were demonic. Fund-raising letters highlighted Bauer's idyllic picnics and backyard cookouts with his wife, Carol, and his three children, Zachary, Elyse, and Sarah. A 1994 Christmas letter mailed to the group's supporters came replete with a color photo of the happy Bauer clan. But underneath Bauer's romanticization of the American family lay contempt for those who do not conform to the structure of his family. The steady platefuls of antigay literature that Bauer dished out during the military debate were liberally sprinkled with ad hominem references to gays as "perverts," "weirdness on parade," "unnatural," and not "normal." That Bauer could get away with schoolyard name-calling and promulgating the image of gays as nothing more than "jackboot" thugs, drawn directly from fascist movements of the 1930s, telegraphed just how debased the public discourse would become as it progressed toward Clinton's deadline.

⟶ Meanwhile, under the radar of gay rights groups, potential allies fell away, only to hamstring the antiban forces further. Colin Powell made his objection to Clinton's plan clear as early as August of 1992. Powell publicly denied rumors that he felt strongly enough about the issue that he would resign were the ban lifted. For a draft-dodging president whose credentials with the military establishment were next to nonexistent, that threat alone, coming from America's most respected military leader since Eisenhower, was more than enough to give Clinton a serious case of cold feet. As the debate wore on, Powell, a black man whom the press was already treating in glowing terms as chief-executive material, would help inoculate the pro-ban forces from charges of prejudice, to which the largely white religious right was particularly vulnerable. He was also crucial to rebutting comparisons between racist and antigay discrimination. In an October 1992 letter to Rep. Patricia Schroeder, a ranking member of the House Armed

Services Committee, Powell laid out his view that the race/sexual-orientation analogy does not hold. "Skin color is a benign, nonbehavioral characteristic," he wrote. "Sexual orientation is perhaps the most profound of human behavioral characteristics."

For years, gay rights groups had employed the analogy between sexual orientation and race. But while the comparison had a superficial ring of truth, it was more complex than they admitted, especially in the military context. Coming as it did from the white boys' and girls' club of the gay rights leadership, the analogy would prove particularly difficult to defend. Perry Watkins, a black Army sergeant who served as an openly gay man for sixteen years before being discharged and winning from the Supreme Court the only reinstatement of a gay service member in U.S. history, complained bitterly that he was ignored by the gay activists leading the debate. "Here I am, the most qualified person to speak to the issue of gays in the military, and I was excluded from the discussions," he later said. But Watkins, who had a reputation for flamboyance and a flair for drag, was deemed a loose cannon by the gay groups, which were especially conscious during the military debate of countering the image of irresponsible gay pleasure seekers promoted by the religious right.

The gay groups' hopes to rebut Powell in the political arena relied largely upon the black civil rights community and Ronald Dellums, an African-American who had inherited the chair of the House Armed Services Committee when Les Aspin was appointed secretary of defense. In his eighteen years in the House, Dellums, a decorated World War II veteran, had earned a reputation as a fierce champion of gay rights and an outspoken opponent of the ban. Like Powell, he had faced rejection from the military for his skin color. But unlike Powell, Dellums viewed the gay ban as an equally rank form of injustice. Nevertheless, the new chairman remained uncharacteristically quiet during the debate. The dovish Dellums held only two days of hearings in June, allowing Nunn's high-profile Senate hearings to dominate the news. As perhaps the most liberal member of Congress, Dellums commanded little weight with the Pentagon or the political establishment.

Prominent black political support did give antiban forces some short-lived hope, but not until April, as the battle neared its conclusion. The Campaign for Military Service secured the endorsement of civil rights groups such as the National Association for the Advancement of Colored People and the Leadership Conference on Civil Rights, an umbrella civil rights group. Fearing alienating their more conservative constituents, both groups had traditionally been reluctant to support gay causes publicly, so their signing on was a crucial boost for gay activists. Such backing allowed the Campaign to arrange for an array of civil rights leaders, including Coretta Scott King, the president of the Martin Luther King Jr. Center for Nonviolent Social Change, and Joseph Lowery, president of the Southern Christian Leadership Conference, to speak on its behalf. The impact of the support, however, was weakened by its proximity to the July 15 deadline and diluted by the civil rights groups' unfamiliarity with gay rights causes and internal dissension over the endorsements.

Powell, by contrast, would prove a stopper. A career military officer who had gained a reputation as a team-playing political pragmatist, he was much better positioned to speak authoritatively on the issue than any of the gay organizations' black allies. Having benefited both from the desegregation of the armed forces by President Truman in 1948 and decades of military affirmative-action programs, he was also vulnerable to charges of hypocrisy. But with the gay activists unable to get their message across and the media's kid-gloves treatment of Powell as the hero of Operation Desert Storm, the allegation never took root. Indeed, in defending the ban, Powell was reflecting not only the views of the military brass; many African-Americans had also begun to see gays and lesbians as pretenders to the throne of disadvantage, a characterization fanned by religious-right propaganda. Homosexuals have "no right to stand on the shoulders of the African-Americans," wrote Willie and Gwenevere Richardson, publisher and editor, respectively, of the monthly newsletter *National Minority Politics,* a right-wing publication.

Gay opponents of the ban did little to dispel the notion. In press interviews, Joe Zuñiga, a twenty-year-old openly gay former

Army sergeant, compared himself to Rosa Parks, the civil rights pioneer who had refused to sit in the back of a segregated bus. Antigay blacks saw gay men like Zuñiga, who is Latino, as "Liberace in Rosa Parks drag," as Harvard professor Henry Louis Gates Jr., an African-American opponent of the ban, quipped. More accurate parallels between race and sexual orientation never got a hearing. As black critics of Powell were quick to point out, race has not always been considered a "benign characteristic." In a report to the secretary of the navy during the 1942 debate over desegregation of the military, for instance, the General Board of the Navy asked, "How many white men would choose, of their own accord, that their closest associates in sleeping quarters, at mess, and in the gun's crew should be another race? . . . The General Board believes that the answer is 'few, if any' and further believes that if the issues were forced, there would be a lowering of contentment, teamwork, and discipline in the service."

Unwittingly or not, Powell's role in the military debate boosted the fortunes of the religious right, which had long sought ways of driving a wedge between gays and lesbians and traditional minorities. "The backlash is on the streets among blacks and black pastors, who do not want to be aligned with homosexuals," crowed the Reverend Lou Sheldon, the white chairman of the Traditional Values Coalition, at the growing opposition of conservative black churches to the efforts to lift the ban.

Besides a racial credential, Powell also lent decorum to the pro-ban arguments, which would otherwise have been dominated by the shrill antigay canards of the religious right. He laid out his views in the cautious manner befitting his rank, carefully praising the "proud, brave, loyal, good Americans" who wished to serve their country as openly homosexual. But the intense heat of the religious right's rhetoric boiled just beneath the sheen of Powell's propriety, often leaving the impression that he supported their extreme views. Only once, when Concerned Women for America ran a full-page ad in *USA Today* touting his opposition to lifting the ban, did Powell object to the religious right's antigay campaign. "I have never made the statement that 'allowing homosexuals in the armed forces would destroy the military,'" Powell said in an April 16, 1993, letter to *USA Today*. "To the contrary, in answering a question during remarks at American University, I stated that I have never been of the view that allowing homosexuals in the military would break the armed forces of the United States."

Powell, however, seemed more interested in disassociating himself from the taint of the religious right than in shielding gays from its extreme and defamatory rhetoric. As a supporter of government affirmative-action programs, Powell might have been more skeptical of his bedfellows. Sheldon's Traditional Values Coalition and LaHaye's Concerned Women for America, to name just two examples, have a well-established history of opposing civil rights protections for blacks. In 1991, for instance, Sheldon took to the airwaves to oppose civil rights legislation, then pending before Congress, with the fallacious charge that it instituted "quotas." Powell's contribution to the pro-ban forces would quickly be forgotten by the religious right. As he geared up for a possible presidential bid in the fall of 1995, Bauer openly derided him as soft on homosexuals and other social issues, calling him "Bill Clinton with ribbons." Coming from Bauer, the appellation was hardly a compliment.

～ If Powell was the Pentagon's public face, Lt. Col. Robert Lee Maginnis was its private one. In the summer of 1992, Maginnis, inspector general of the Army, began compiling background information for a series of articles that would circulate among Pentagon brass warning of the dangers of permitting open gays and lesbians in the hypermasculine military setting. He was a conservative with deeply held religious beliefs, and his research would take him to the popular Washington, D.C., gay bookstore Lambda Rising to gather what he considered damaging information about gays and lesbians to bolster the military's defense of the ban.

In January of 1993, Maginnis was tapped by the Army to serve on a five-member panel known as the Homosexual Working Group to assess the impact on the military of lifting the ban. Like the Family Research Council's, Maginnis's work relied heavily upon discredited antigay research. His carefully footnoted articles were filled with references to Paul Cameron, president of the Family Research Institute, and Joseph Nicolosi, a therapist who was dedicated to "converting" gay patients to heterosexuality, a practice the American Psychological Association considers a form of patient abuse.

In his eagerness to support the ban, Maginnis anointed himself a psychiatrist and went on wild antigay tangents. "Homosexual men have trouble establishing male relationships characterized by mutability and equality," he theorized in a May 1993 article, "Homosexuals and Unit Cohesion," published by the Association of the United States Army, a professional group. "This is attributed to an underlying feeling of masculine inferiority which becomes the basis of envy and resentment toward heterosexual men. Consequently, the homosexual has difficulty relating to other men as equals, due to this resentment and because of the heterosexual's sexual and romantic significance to the homosexual. Additionally, heterosexual men who possess power and authority over the homosexual become particular symbols of masculinity, which only intensifies the homosexual's same-sex desire."

The Pentagon rewarded Maginnis for his speculative work by anointing him the unofficial adviser and researcher for the Military Working Group, a task force that Aspin appointed to study the ban and that would play a key role in its retention. While Maginnis was rummaging through gay bookstores for evidence of depravity, a far better qualified and less blatantly prejudicial voice was all but ignored by the Military Working Group and other Pentagon decision makers: Lawrence Korb. A high-level Pentagon official and ban defender during the Reagan administration, Korb had become an outspoken critic of the ban as its fallout in squandered skills and costly enforcement mounted; he eventually left the Pentagon to assume a post as a senior fellow at the Brookings Institution, a Washington, D.C., policy-analysis group, where he critiqued the ban in the measured tone of an expert. In pro-ban military circles, Korb was considered a turncoat, a traitor to the cause whom activists like Bauer and Maginnis went to elaborate lengths to discredit.

Like Korb, gay activists were left largely outside the debate as the compromise was hammered out between the White House, the Pentagon, and Congress. The Campaign for Military Service did not even gain a meeting with the Military Working Group until late in the spring. In one of the few bright spots of the campaign, Michelle Benecke, a Campaign for Military Service legal counsel, helped persuade the group that the public was less willing to tolerate the antigay witch-hunts that had come to epitomize the terror the ban inflicted on gay and lesbian service members. With the exception of Benecke, who served as a battery commander in the Army air defense artillery, and a few others it apparently never dawned on the activists to take the activities of Military Working Group seriously until late in their lobbying efforts.

Though Maginnis began his antigay crusade in the summer of 1992 and had a long paper trail of opposition to the integration of women in the armed services, gay activists never identified him or the Pentagon as a key source of opposition. The gay leadership's reliance on liberal rhetoric as a substitute for accurate background information and a clear assessment of the opposition hampered its understanding of the magnitude of the battle they were facing. Uncovering the crucial links between the Pentagon and the religious right could have allowed gay groups to question the fairness of the Working Group, protest the ban negotiations as biased, and secure concessions. Neither did antiban groups apply pressure on Powell to elicit an explanation for the antigay propaganda machine operating under his auspices.

Only later would the gay groups elucidate the unholy alliance between the religious right and the military brass. Indeed, it took sharp questioning of Maginnis one year later during a court hearing to bring to light the inner workings of the Pentagon in the midst of the debate. In the deposition, conducted by Beatrice Dohrn, a staff attorney for Lambda Legal Defense and Education Fund, a gay group, Dohrn adroitly coaxed Maginnis into acknowledging his ties to Bauer and admitting that his views could be traced in part to a 1981 incident in which he discovered that one of his soldiers, who may or may not have been bisexual, had a taste for women's clothing while off duty. But like the gay activists' campaign in general, the exchange between Dohrn and Maginnis, one of the few in which an antigay activist was ever forced to come clean about the tenuous basis for his views, constituted too little too late.

As the Military Working Group was preparing its analysis, a plethora of veterans and active-duty personnel groups, which opposed lifting the ban in overwhelming numbers, were backing Maginnis's efforts. An umbrella organization dubbed the Coalition to Maintain Military Readiness included such behemoth groups as the Veterans of Foreign Wars, the American Legion, the Retired Officers Association, the Navy and Marine Corps Leagues, the National Guard Enlisted Association, and the Naval Reserve Association. Gay groups and their liberal allies had no similar military muscle to flex. The largest gay military group—Gay, Lesbian and Bisexual Veterans of America—was a fraction of the size of even the smallest antigay veterans groups.

The activists' lack of familiarity with the military translated into a dearth of prominent allies with military connections. On June 10 the gay groups received a rare boost when former Arizona senator Barry Goldwater, a strident pro-military conservative and former chair of the Senate Armed Services Committee, sided with them in a *Washington Post* opinion piece. But coming at the tail end of the battle, Goldwater's support did little to lift the sagging fortunes of the antiban forces. The gay group's overtures to others were even less successful. Former president Jimmy Carter, a former naval officer who had advocated lifting the ban during an appearance on Cable News Network's *Larry King Live,* declined the groups' pleas to lobby Congress on their behalf. Even retired military officials who supported lifting the ban, including several with openly gay family members, privately admitted to Campaign officials that they feared a backlash from their peers were they to speak out publicly.

The activists' reluctance to confront the reality of Pentagon politics reflected their ambivalence about tackling the military ban in the first place and the rifts the issue created among crucial liberal allies. Many gay leaders got their start in activist politics during the antiwar movement of the 1960s and 1970s. The National Gay and Lesbian Task Force, for instance, did not institute its Military Freedom Project until 1988. Both Mixner and Torie Osborn, who took over the Task Force as Clinton was inaugurated, were active in antiwar protests two decades earlier. Neither could escape the suspicion that by fighting to lift the ban they were lending credibility to an institution they had spent much of their lives assailing. Similar conflicts erupted among gay groups' natural allies, especially among Quakers and other liberal-leaning religious denominations whose credibility was crucial to neutralizing the religious right's invocation of Christian moral teachings to justify their staunch pro-ban dictates.

Spared such fretful soul-searching, pro-ban forces solidified the nascent alliance between the religious right and military policymakers. In fact, Maginnis's work on gay issues at the Pentagon amounted to a long audition for a leading role with the religious right. In May, Maginnis coauthored a policy paper on the ban with Robert Knight, the director of cultural studies for Bauer's Family Research Council; the pair's piece was published in *Insight,* the group's newsletter. Maginnis retired from the military, effective July 9, as the president prepared to announce his compromise. On August 1, he assumed a position as one of the Family Research Council's full-time policy analysts.

⟶ While the effort to lift the ban was marked by misinformed players and strategic missteps, the campaign to retain it appeared flawless. It had on its side one of the most powerful advocates for the military in the country and an influential Democrat to boot, Sam Nunn. Despite his promises that congressional hearings would be fair to all sides, Nunn, as chairman of the Senate Armed Services Committee, deftly shifted the debate from discrimination to concerns about morale, discipline, and privacy. If gay groups had any hopes left of winning the battle, the May hearings put them to rest.

Like Powell, Nunn was careful to couch his argument in narrow terms. Conceding many points to opponents of the ban, the senator went out of his way to avoid the antigay slurs that were the bread and butter of the religious right. During a November 15, 1992, appearance on CBS's *Face the Nation,* for instance, Nunn sought to portray the issue as a careful balancing act. "We've got to consider not only the rights of homosexuals but also the rights of those who are not homosexual and who give up a great deal of their privacy when they go into the military," he said. But as the debate tilted in favor of the ban, Nunn's careful balancing act between competing rights tipped heavily in favor of "those who are not homosexual."

A quintessential Washington establishment figure, Nunn tried to keep the religious right's wild rhetoric at arm's length. Before the 1994 Republican takeover of Congress, the Christian right and its inflammatory propaganda were still considered beyond the pale of political respectability. As a Democrat, Nunn was uncomfortable with the affinity religious conservatives had traditionally shown for the Republican Party. However, focused on achieving a clear-cut victory, Nunn, like Colin Powell, did little to discourage the right's verbal gay-bashing. As opposition to lifting the ban grew, Nunn's antigay rhetoric increasingly reflected the religious right's. And while Nunn did not regularly resort to denigrating homosexuals as a class to justify the ban, his history suggested that he shared the religious right's underlying antipathy to gays and lesbians. In 1982, under the guise that they were security risks, the senator dismissed two male aides after discovering that they were gay. Asked during a May 1993 appearance on NBC's *Meet the Press* if he considered heterosexuality "morally superior" to homosexuality, he responded, "I'm not only saying that, I'm saying the family structure in America has deteriorated, and that's one of our big problems." Nunn was never asked to explain the connection between homosexuality and the supposed deterioration of the family structure in America.

Nunn's committee chairmanship furnished his antigay impulses a national platform. His fact-finding mission on a Navy submarine just days before the start of the Senate hearings illustrated the way in which his interests dovetailed with the religious right's.

Dozens of reporters tagged along, and in photos published across the country that became the defining image of the debate, committee members surveyed cramped living quarters, bunk beds, and communal showers. The photos, and accompanying quotes from sailors, conveyed the idea that gays would not be welcome in such close—and ostensibly heterosexual—confines. Nunn and Virginia senator John Warner, who accompanied him on the trip, cleverly invoked what has long been one of the religious right's favorite themes: portraying gay men as sexual predators. (Lesbians were absent from the fact-finding mission altogether.)

Religious conservatives expressed exactly the same concern, but more brazenly and with even less compunction over its inaccuracy. In advertisements that ran in newspapers serving large military communities, for instance, Bauer's Family Research Council warned: "Without the ban, America's young service men and women will be forced by law to share barracks and showers with homosexuals. . . . Military families with children could face living next to openly homosexual couples in base 'family' housing, and would have to compete with homosexuals for already overburdened medical services." Bauer's unstated message was clear: gay men were pedophiles who would defile heterosexual families and spread AIDS in military hospitals. (The ad, of course, encouraged readers to make large contributions to the Family Research Council.) Freedom Alliance leader Oliver North emphasized his own experience in a January 8 "priority alert" fund-raising letter. "In military barracks, totally private living accommodations are nonexistent," North wrote. "I know, I've spent years in the Fleet Marine Force."

By focusing the hearings on privacy, Nunn effectively shifted the debate away from discrimination that gays and lesbians regularly faced to the supposed indignities and anxieties heterosexual service members would allegedly suffer at the hands of open homosexuals among their ranks. Military officials had long acknowledged that there had been only isolated cases of same-sex sexual harassment or rape (in which the perpetrators were as likely as not heterosexual) reported, and that homosexuals spent their time blending in, not ogling other men in the showers. According to the military's own statistics, the much more serious and wide-spread problem was men's harassment of women.

While posing as advocates of law and order in the ranks, Nunn and religious conservatives conveniently ignored the far more serious and systematic conduct-related problems facing the military. In the widely publicized Tailhook scandal, which was revealed in the months preceding the gays-in-the-military debate, male officers were charged with sexually harassing dozens of female personnel at a Navy convention in Las Vegas. By placing culpability on sexual identity rather than conduct, the pro-ban forces distorted the behavior and the service records of both the vast majority of homosexuals who behave in an upright manner and of heterosexual women, who remain the targets of sexual harassment in the workplace. In the two-day House hearings, which followed the Senate hearings and received comparatively little press coverage, the gay groups were unable to convey the complicated analogy between the gay ban and the sexual harassment of women to a large audience. As an argument, it was far more subtle than sensational images of sex-crazed homosexuals attacking cowering heterosexuals in communal showers, which tapped into still-pervasive stereotypes.

As a legal enshrinement of antigay prejudice, the ban inevitably fostered mistreatment of service personnel who were gay or just suspected of being so. And as gay servicemembers could testify, epithets like *queer, fag,* and *sissy*—in their baseness and dehumanization, recalling the religious right's broadsides—were routine parts of military discipline. Yet the gay ban's contribution to harassment and even violence never became part of the debate, despite evidence that was hard to ignore. In October of 1992, Allen Schindler was beaten to death by a fellow sailor just days after it became common knowledge among the crew of the USS *Belleau Wood* that he was gay. Schindler, twenty-two, was so badly beaten that his mother, Dorothy Hadjys, had to search for tattoos on his body to identify him. The killer, Terry Helvey, confessed and received a life sentence from a military tribunal, but only after rumors circulated within the military that Helvey had merely been responding in legitimate outrage to Schindler's alleged sexual overtures. Two days before his death, realizing that his revelation made it unsafe for him to stay in the military, Schindler contacted an attorney.

Gay groups, however, made little use of Schindler's case and thus never made gay-bashing—a potential black eye to ban defenders—a crucial part of their campaign. Hadjys, a deeply religious woman who delivered a stirring speech at the April 1993 Gay and Lesbian March on Washington, D.C., implicating the ban in her son's death, never became a centerpiece of antiban efforts. It took Michael Petrelis, the maverick gay activist who had pressed Clinton for concessions during the presidential campaign, to bring Schindler's case to the fore. Financed by a grant from gay billionaire David Geffen, Petrelis shuttled back and forth between Washington, D.C., and Sasebo, Japan, where the *Belleau Wood* was stationed when Schindler was murdered. Petrelis convinced reporters to take a second look at the antigay aspect of the case and the military's clumsy attempt to conceal it.

Despite Hadjys's absence, the Senate hearings on the ban did pack at least one highly emotional punch. Riveting testimony came from an unexpected source: Marine colonel Fred Peck. On May 11, Peck told the Senate panel that his son Scott, a college student, was gay. The nation watched as a prominent military official struggled to balance his devotion to a family member with his loyalty to military policy, a situation that is far more common than supporters of the ban were willing to concede. "I love him as much as any of my sons," Peck told the panel. "But I don't think there's any place for him in the military." But Peck's reasons for supporting the ban despite his awareness of his son's sexual orientation was not what Nunn and the religious right had in mind. Peck, well aware of Allen Schindler's fate, explained that he was afraid that his son would be a victim of harassment and even violence were he allowed to serve as an openly gay man. What few of the reporters who pounced on the story actually grasped—or bothered to articulate—was that Peck had inadvertently delivered a stinging indictment of the ban.

In the procession of prominent speakers he called to testify,

Nunn made sure that there were few surprises of the sort Colonel Peck presented. Thus, the hearings reflected his views almost exclusively. When Goldwater, a retired Air Force major general and World War II veteran who has a gay grandson, was scheduled to appear before the Senate Armed Services Committee, Nunn scuttled the appearance at the last minute, replacing him with retired general Norman Schwarzkopf, commander of the allied forces during Operation Desert Storm and a ban defender. Nunn was apparently concerned that as the godfather of American conservatism Goldwater was the one person in America who could destroy Nunn's precarious logic defending the policy and snatch victory from the hands of the pro-ban forces.

Having lost control of the debate, Clinton did what he did best during the early days of his administration—backtrack. As early as May, trying desperately to focus his administration on the economic issues he had campaigned on, Clinton was floating the idea of a "compromise" that would segregate gay and lesbian troops from their heterosexual counterparts. Gay activists rejected the proposal as outrageously discriminatory, with Mixner appearing on ABC's *Nightline* to denounce it, and pro-ban forces termed it an insult to the integrity of the armed forces.

~ For the Campaign for Military Service, the Senate hearings were a political Waterloo. For an entire week, national television audiences digested antigay sound bites delivered by the nation's greatest military heroes. But the Campaign still had one last card up its sleeve. The group had prepared a slick television advertising campaign featuring Zuniga, who was named Army Soldier of the Year shortly before coming out publicly, which it planned to unveil on Memorial Day weekend. What the group overlooked was that by that late date, most members of Congress had already solidified their position on the issue. The Campaign, operating as if it were an electoral campaign, built for a big finish rather than a painstakingly constructed, solid support base in Congress and the public.

Even with the advertisements, finances proved a major problem, and any impact they might have had was blunted by their scarcity. On June 17, the Campaign for Military Service mailed a fund-raising letter telling potential donors that it hoped to "raise a minimum of $1,765,000 by June 28"—just eleven days later—in order to air the ad campaign nationwide. But because even the ban's critics conceded that the debate was essentially over by the time they received the letter, recipients were reluctant to give generously. The letter brought in only a fraction of what the group had hoped.

The advertising and fund-raising debacles raised a larger point. After spending the 1980s as critics of Republican administrations, the gay political groups were unprepared to work inside the political system. With the exception of Mixner, whose mounting criticism of Clinton's retreat from gay causes endangered his role as unofficial adviser on gay issues, they had few channels to the White House and even fewer beyond all but the most liberal members of Congress. Most of the groups' mainstream political experience had been limited to working with Massachusetts senator Ted Kennedy and other dyed-in-the-wool liberal Democratic and a few moderate Republican lawmakers on AIDS legislation or in fending off a regular barrage of antigay amendments sponsored by Sen. Jesse Helms, the North Carolina Republican, and Rep. William Dannemeyer, the Republican from Orange County, California, who had made a career out of verbal gay-bashing before his Senate-primary defeat in 1992.

Antiban groups also played out their inexperience at the political helm in bouts of noncooperation. Even after it was up and running, the Campaign for Military Service suffered infighting among its member groups, each of which was eager to claim credit for its few successes and cash in on the unparalleled fund-raising opportunities the fight furnished in its early days. The groups never generated more than a paltry thirty-five thousand calls at any one juncture in the debate. The infighting among the gay leadership underscored the disarray within the organizations themselves. The Task Force's new executive director, Torie Osborn, who had headed the Los Angeles Community Services Center, did not assume her post until March, when the fight was well under way. Osborn, who spent most of her tenure playing catch-up, would resign just six months later, complaining bitterly about ideological clashes with an unsupportive board and an uncooperative staff.

In some ways, the Campaign invited the criticism it would come to incur. Lawyers unschooled in politics dominated its leadership. Among its top officials were Chai Feldblum and Bill Rubenstein, brilliant civil rights attorneys whose backgrounds were long on law and short on the fine art of political persuasion. Its executive director, Tom Stoddard, the former head of Lambda, who had been instrumental in creating the country's gay legal movement, had never run a Washington-based political organization. Citing stress from long work hours and AIDS-related health concerns, Stoddard had resigned his post at Lambda in 1992. But the stress at Lambda would pale in comparison to running the Campaign for Military Service. At Lambda, at least, he could point to a string of victorious litigation. The Campaign faced only one bitter setback after another.

~ While the Campaign for Military Service scrambled to get its act together, the religious right was flooding Congress with pro-ban phone calls and using them to generate ever-broader resentment against Clinton. By relying on its well-developed grassroots network, the right's campaign produced ten letters and calls for every one produced by the gay lobby groups. "We're the ones that shut down the phone lines at the Capitol," the Reverend Louis Sheldon, chairman of the Traditional Values Coalition, bragged at a late-January press conference.

For all of his rhetorical excess, and perhaps because of it, Sheldon had reason to brag. On January 27, as President Clinton was dodging his campaign pledge, the congressional switchboard logged 434,104 calls, dwarfing the daily average of approximately 80,000. According to members of Congress, more than 90 percent of the callers opposed lifting the ban, often in extreme terms. It was the highest volume of calls since the contentious 1991 nomination of Clarence Thomas to the U.S. Supreme Court, during which calls were more evenly split.

Protesting efforts to lift the ban quickly supplanted abortion as the chief organizing and fund-raising tool for more than a dozen groups on the right. Randall Terry, who had focused almost exclusively on abortion as the founder of the militant Operation Rescue, viewed the gays-in-the-military debate as an opportunity to take back ground lost in the abortion debate. "We're avalanching Congress with phone calls and letters," he said. According to Terry, his group was leading a "rebellion against President Clinton because sodomy is against God's law, just like baby-killing is against God's law."

The fact that the issue helped fill Operation Rescue's cash-strapped coffers, drained by civil suits from abortion clinics, didn't hurt either. Gays in the military had a Midas-like effect, producing handsome dividends to almost any fund-raisers who invoked it, no matter how far from the actual battle they might be. On January 8, 1992, for instance, convicted Iran-contra figure Oliver North mailed hundreds of thousands of appeals requesting "special contributions" to help the Freedom Alliance, his lobby group, to campaign against lifting the ban. The lucrative mailing list North thus developed would later boost the fortunes of his U.S. Senate bid against Virginia senator Chuck Robb, a Vietnam veteran and outspoken opponent of the ban. Though it's impossible to estimate exactly how much money the religious right's gays-in-the-military marketing campaign raised, it coincided with huge increases in the groups' budgets and membership. From 1992 to 1993, for instance, the Christian Coalition reported a 20 percent increase in both areas. Much of the increase can be traced to the adversarial role such groups assumed with the newly ensconced administration: more than any other issue, gays in the military epitomized that acrimony.

The religious right's success in seizing control of the debate quickly began to register in public opinion polls. An NBC News–The Wall Street Journal poll conducted in December of 1992 found the public closely divided on the issue with 46 percent for lifting the ban and 49 percent against. By late January, less than two months later, opinion had tilted to 50–41 in favor of retaining the ban. The numbers continued to climb in the religious right's direction as the debate progressed into the spring.

⟿ The stunning success of the pro-ban forces emboldened the religious right not only to press ahead with ever more inflammatory antigay and anti-Clinton arguments (Sheldon labeled Clinton the "gay-agenda president"), but also to shift the very terms of the political discourse. Religious-right rhetoric soon came to disregard the established parameters of the military-ban debate, which had evolved since the ban was first imposed in 1943 and codified in 1982 by the Reagan administration. Instead, religious conservatives and their more secular allies repeatedly invoked discredited arguments such as the security rationale and conspiracy theories about Clinton, gays, and the "new world order."

In his book *Military Necessity and Homosexuality*, a 126-page screed that pretends to supply the military rationale for the religious right's support for the ban, author Ronald D. Ray makes only passing reference to the military's abandonment of the security rationale. Indeed, Ray, a retired Marine colonel, suggests that gays and lesbians are inherently prone to subversion. "Even if homosexuals are not 'turned' by foreign agents, evidence exists that homosexuals, as a group or subculture, can and do turn against their country simply on account of the nature of homosexuality and its hostile attitude toward the existing moral order," he writes. Ray also asserts that the "homosexual movement" is a "domestic enemy" that "will kill America's soul and destroy the legacy of our founders" if it succeeds. Instead of grappling with the complexity of the debate as it existed in 1993 when the book was published, Ray simply returns to the McCarthyite 1950s, when *homosexuality* and *traitor* were used virtually as synonyms.

Other pro-ban writers with a broader audience than Ray demonstrated their dependence on out-of-date arguments even more starkly. In her 1993 book, *Exclusion: Homosexuals and the Right to Serve,* Melissa Wells-Petry, a major in the Army's Judge Advocate General's Corps who served on the Pentagon's Military

Working Group, describes herself as the "military's expert on the current ban against homosexuals and all the court cases surrounding the ban that have taken place in the last twenty years." But Wells-Petry's selective interpretation of evidence and insistence on a monolithic view of gays made her appear anything but an expert on the issue. After reading gay activist Larry Kramer's famous diatribe against gay promiscuity in his novel *Faggots*, which was published in 1978, Wells-Petry concludes that most homosexuals have "rejected the concept of monogamy" and are therefore a threat to the health of other military personnel. Actually, the views expressed in Kramer's novel are evidence that homosexuals, like heterosexuals, often disagree about sexual mores.

The 1991 Pentagon report debunking the security rationale seems never to have crossed Wells-Petry's path either. Though she couches her antigay arguments in legalistic language, citing court precedents liberally, she ultimately relies on thoroughly discredited research provided by antigay activist Judith Reisman, whose claim to fame is a massive study comparing classified sex ads in *The Advocate* with those culled from straight publications. At one point, Wells-Petry blithely suggests that if gays were allowed to serve in the military, "gay bowel syndrome," a disease concocted by antigay researchers, would strain the military's medical resources. At another, she suggests that gays are inherently prone to alcoholism, based on 1970s-era studies conducted outside gay bars.

Others wove the president's attempt to lift the ban into elaborate anti-Clinton conspiracy theories. *The Clinton Chronicles*, a book that originally appeared in video form, promises to "follow the trails of deception, lies, corruption, and mysterious deaths that keep leading back to Clinton's 'circle of power.'" The sensationalistic tome portrays the president as a draft-dodging, gay-loving womanizer profoundly out of touch with Americans' godly values. Hinting darkly that Clinton may even be guilty of having his political opponents murdered, the book charges that Clinton's aborted attempt to lift the ban was actually an attempt to weaken the U.S. government so that foreign powers could overrun the country. "Could Clinton be driven by a more sinister motivation than simply advancing the 'gay rights' agenda?" retired colonel Tom McKenney asks ominously in a chapter titled "Bill Clinton: The Unthinkable Commander-in-Chief." "Military leaders tried to make Clinton understand that full and open inclusion of gays and lesbians in our Armed Forces would surely lead to their weakening and, ultimately, their destruction as effective fighting forces. Could he possibly want that?"

In his conclusions, McKenney echoes Pat Robertson, the Christian Coalition founder and noted conspiracy theorist. He alleges that Clinton is a key supporter of the "new world order," a supposed regime hatched by international bankers and the United Nations to take over the government of the United States. "This world government would control every aspect of the lives of the people; that's what socialism meant in Hitler's Germany and in Stalin's USSR, and that's what it would mean in Bill Clinton's New World Order," he writes. "The traditional churches, the prestigious theological seminaries, the universities, the news media, the public school system and related educational institutions—all of which once were strongholds of American tradition, godly values, moral standards, patriotism and truth—have slowly been converted into fountainheads of revision, relativism, situation ethics, Marxist globalism, and socialist propaganda." Only by upholding the military ban could the country hope to head off this dismal gauntlet of degeneracy, he contends.

Though the book's conclusions seem extreme even by the religious right's standards, a number of pro-ban leaders endorsed it. Published by Jeremiah Books, a religious conservative group in Hemet, California, which produced the antigay video *Gay Rights, Special Rights, The Clinton Chronicles* and its video companion were aggressively promoted by Sheldon and Falwell, among others. Yet the religious right leaders' support for *The Clinton Chronicles* went unchecked until January of 1995, when the Reverend Tony Campolo, a Baptist minister and professor of sociology at Eastern College in St. Davids, Pennsylvania, asked Falwell for equal time on his television show to rebut the video's outlandish charges. "These videos are giving the church a bad name," Campolo said. "We in the Christian community ought not to be spreading rumors if we can't prove they're true, we ought not to be denigrating people. We ought to be talking in ways that are fair, and people should listen to us and say there is a kindness in the way we critique people." (Falwell, of course, rejected Campolo's request.)

Kindness was the last thing on the mind of the pro-ban forces. The paranoid worldview expressed in *The Clinton Chronicles* dovetailed with the antigay ideology of the violent antigovernment militias. In a 1993 interview with the *Detroit Metro Times,* an alternative weekly, George Matousek, a member of the Michigan militia, blasted gays and lesbians as a key element of the "new world order." "The homosexual movement will destroy the military," said Matousek, who sought to harness the passions over the national military-ban dispute into a 1994 antigay initiative in Michigan, which never qualified for the ballot. "Soon half the troops will be gone. They don't want to serve next to the queers. And the half that's left will be useless—women and homos, people who can't fight their way out of a paper bag. When that happens, we'll be doomed. Clinton, or whoever's in office, will turn our troops over to the United Nations. And this country won't exist anymore." Asked how he planned to fight the new world order, Matousek replied, "Armed revolution. I believe we're headed there someday. But right now we have to deal with the military— and take back control. That means stopping the queers."

At the heart of such extreme opposition to allowing open gays in the military was the concomitant presumption that the gay movement had undue influence on the federal government and that the government is determined to foist gays and lesbians on the military. Thus, according to these contentions, gay rights has become a glaring example of government intrusion into the lives of ordinary Americans. And even while he contends that gays and lesbians can't "fight their way out of a paper bag," Matousek imagines that Clinton is nothing more than a puppet on their strings.

But Matousek's nightmare is gay leaders' dream, since they can only wish they had the kind of power he attributes to them. In another example of the depth of the cultural divide between the two sides, gays and lesbians adopted exactly the opposite view, feeling that they were the ones betrayed by *their* president and *their* country. Far from seeing the battering ram that conspiracists like Matousek depicted the president and the government as being, most gays merely saw recognition of their right to serve in the military as a means of extending their already hard-won rights to access to American life and easing gay service members' justifiable fears of mistreatment and retaliation from intolerant military officials.

⟶ The final days of the six-month standoff between Clinton, Congress, and the Pentagon were anticlimactic. In an abrupt about-face that would come to characterize his presidency, Clinton carefully courted the military, praising its leadership and charming the troops at every opportunity. As Clinton's self-imposed July 15 deadline neared, the White House, in leaks to the media, repeatedly detailed Clinton's intention to back off his campaign pledge to unequivocally lift the ban and the president's growing impatience with the issue. Despite their tireless efforts, the gay groups were outside the debate at the end, watching from the sidelines as the heavy hitters—Nunn, Powell, and Aspin—ironed out a settlement behind closed doors.

Once Clinton signaled that they were fighting a losing battle, Mixner and the gay groups violated a fundamental precept of Washington politics: no matter how devastating a defeat, scramble to declare some kind of victory upon which future success might be based. Instead, the groups acted as though the military battle was a one-shot war, an either-or proposition. Some activists, in fact, were so caught up in the symbolism that they demanded that Clinton issue the order anyway, fully aware that Congress would immediately overturn it, possibly even hardening the ban in special legislation. As early as January Mixner had already raised the specter that any compromise with the ban's supporters amounted to a "betrayal" of gays and lesbians by the president. "If there's an executive order at the end of it, it's reasonable," he told the *Wall Street Journal.* "If there's not, it's unreasonable." Similarly, Campaign for Military Service's Stoddard told the *New York Times* in early January, "The issue must be dealt with swiftly, decisively, and

at the highest level. Any instruments that defer or delegate this issue to the military are inherently suspect."

Mixner was apoplectic at the very idea of a compromise. After
first agreeing to support a delay in issuing the executive order, he
turned confrontational. Within weeks of Clinton's waffling,
Mixner was berating Clinton, a man who just months earlier he
had repeatedly and publicly called a personal friend. In a March
speech, Mixner pleaded with Clinton not to "negotiate our freedom away." In the weeks that followed, Mixner's disillusionment
deepened. He upbraided Clinton on *Nightline* and spoke to the
predominantly gay Metropolitan Community Church congregations in Dallas and Phoenix of the deep sense of betrayal he felt.
After the compromise had been hammered out in July, Mixner
was arrested for participating in a civil disobedience outside the
White House. Mixner's predilection for grandstanding and hyperbole got him banished from the inner circles of the White House.
It was access gay activists would never enjoy again. "He unjustly
criticized the president," fumed then–White House political director Rahm Emanuel in an interview published in the *Wall
Street Journal* in June. "If somebody criticizes the president, then
I think he is persona non grata."

Mixner, more than anyone else, personified the gay leaders'
inexperience on the national stage and its consequences of intemperate rhetoric and burnt bridges. In an interview after the compromise was in place, Mixner blamed the defeat on Clinton. "Our
biggest mistake was unconditionally believing in [the administra-
tion], believing that they were really not lying to us, placing too
much power and too much faith in them." As for Clinton, he said,
"We should never have put our fate in one individual's hands, especially in a nongay individual's hands." By placing the onus on
Clinton, Mixner was dodging his own role in the fiasco. Mixner, after all, had been the inside arbiter who had promised that a flourish of the president's hand would banish the ban to the dustbin of
history.

In their anger and despair, the gay groups refused to countenance that Clinton, too, had lost a lot of blood in the battle. Asked
at an August 7 press conference whether the compromise was a

sign of political weakness, Clinton angrily replied, "It may be a sign of madness, sir, but it is not a sign of weakness. When a president takes on tough issues, takes tough stands, tries to get things done in a democracy, he may not get one hundred percent. Was I wrong to get eighty-five? It would have been the great, good fortune of being able to say I am Simon Pure, and the people in the military who are serving well and honorably who happen to be homosexual would not be one step further ahead than when I was elected."

⟶ When hyperbole and high-decibel stereotypes are the terms of debate, diplomats of a moderate voice often get overlooked. In the military debate, Barney Frank was an exception. He brought to the table political pragmatism and savvy, which the movement's leadership lacked. Sensing that the battle was a lost cause, the congressman broached a rough outline of a compromise in early May. Under the proposal, which Frank dubbed "don't ask, don't tell, don't investigate," Pentagon officials would be barred from asking recruits about their sexual orientation, and military personnel would be forbidden to disclose their homosexuality while on duty, but would be free to do so during off-duty hours.

Frank justified the compromise on the grounds that it was the best the antiban forces could expect in the face of such overwhelming opposition. The proposal, he argued, was an improved version of the compromise developed by President Clinton and Nunn in late January. At the time, Frank said he developed the compromise because Congress was likely to codify Nunn's more punitive "don't ask, don't tell," or another even more restrictive policy. As the debate over the ban intensified in late January, he said, it became increasingly clear to him that gay and lesbian groups were losing ground to right-wing political groups and the antigay military officials who would dominate the Senate hearings on the ban.

Frank picked his hour to advance. He waited to announce his proposal until after the April 25 march on Washington, D.C., which drew—depending on the estimate—between 300,000 and 750,000 gay rights supporters to the city for the largest gay rally in history. A central theme was intensifying pressure on Congress to lift the ban. Though the vast majority of marchers were unified in placing the military at the top of their political priorities, few turned up to lobby their representatives and senators on Capitol Hill in visits coordinated by the national gay groups. March organizers had drawn up a bizarre list, later revised, of demands ranging from the lifting of the U.S. embargo on Cuba to expressing solidarity with the disability rights movement, thus diluting the event's potential impact. Though the march received considerable positive press coverage, it never translated into public demand for lifting the ban. As hundreds of thousands of gay men, lesbians, and their supporters headed home from festivities on the Washington Mall, political victory was falling further and further out of reach.

Frank's compromise earned him nothing but grief from gay activists. The Campaign for Military Service, the National Gay and Lesbian Task Force, and the Human Rights Campaign Fund denounced him as vigorously as they later denounced the president for adopting much of it. He even drew a sharp rebuke from his normally mild-mannered House counterpart, Studds. "I have faith that the American people will ultimately perceive the fundamental justice of our case," Studds said in a prepared statement after Frank announced his compromise. "Our country is only now beginning to understand what is really at stake here." Stoddard charged that Frank's stance undercut the Campaign for Military Service's fund-raising ability and slowed momentum the gay groups were supposedly beginning to generate. "Barney has created the impression on the part of gay people that we can't possibly get what we want on the issue anymore, and that leads to a sense of despair," Stoddard said.

What Frank lost in support among gays and lesbians, he gained in the gratitude of his party's leadership, which was thankful for the cover his compromise provided them. President Clinton even made a late-night call to Frank's home to thank him personally. Shortly after the Republican landslide in the 1994 congressional election, Frank, who had earned a reputation as a party loyalist, took on an informal role as the leader of debates on the House floor at the urging of minority whip David Bonior. Known for his lacerating wit (he once said that for antiabortion conservatives, many of whom oppose government aid to poor children, "life begins at conception and ends at birth") and his command of legislative maneuvering, Frank saw the offer as an opportunity to put behind him once and for all a widely publicized 1989 sex scandal, in which he acknowledged hiring a male prostitute as a companion.

Frank's ability to perceive political reality more accurately than his gay activist counterparts evolved not just from his long experience as a congressman. Unlike the politics of many gay leaders, his were not formed in the 1960s left, which viewed America through the prism of Southern racism, opposition to the Vietnam War, and U.S. imperialism. As journalist John Judis has pointed out in *GQ* magazine, Frank was influenced more by 1950s liberalism, which was less inclined to see America as intrinsically corrupt. Frank was deeply influenced by Allard Lowenstein, another liberal political pragmatist who believed strongly in reforming the system from within. As Lowenstein was before his death, Frank has been sharply critical of what he sees as the left's—particularly the gay left's—tendency to equate compromise and negotiation with a complete abdication of principle.

Still, Frank's faith in the system may have led him to underestimate his opponents' resolve. After signing off on the compromise, noting that congressional supporters of the ban had conceded considerable ground in the debate, Frank insisted that the seeds of change had been sown in the loss. Indeed, Sen. Dan Coats, the Indiana Republican who led the fight to protect the ban, admitted that "gays are not cowards in numbers higher than the rest of us. They are no longer security risks." But in the 1994 Republican congressional landslide, dozens of antiban Democrats were swept aside, replaced with a conservative majority whose members were more likely to align themselves with Gary Bauer's brand of fundamentalist politics than the more restrained conservatism of Senator Coats. The large, self-styled "revolutionary" contingent of the newly configured Congress, led by firebrand Speaker Newt Gingrich and several Republican presidential hopefuls, were already angling to eliminate the compromise, which they felt was a giveaway to the gay rights movement, and to codify the most restrictive ban ever. The seeds of change would have to lie fallow for a long, long time.

CHAPTER 6

Brushfires

DESPITE THE SHELLACKING THAT GAY ACTIVISTS took throughout the spring of 1993, they were able to console themselves with a few advances. After a bruising Senate debate, Roberta Achtenberg was confirmed to a position in the Department of Housing and Urban Development, making her the highest-ranking openly gay or lesbian appointee to serve in a presidential administration. In Minnesota, Gov. Arne Carlson, a Republican, signed a statewide nondiscrimination bill, making the state the eighth to enact such legislation. Those victories were outweighed by a growing backlash at the local level, however. Emboldened by their ability to stop Clinton's plans dead in their tracks, conservatives set out to consolidate their gains. What followed was a continuation of the national campaign against gay rights.

Three places in particular saw ostensibly local skirmishes that had national repercussions. In Cincinnati, where religious conservatives prided themselves on their stringent stand against anything that remotely resembled pornography, a long-simmering debate on gay-themed art paved the way for a referendum on the

city's gay rights bill. In Cobb County, Georgia, one politician decided to make a statement about gays in the military by demanding that local arts groups adhere to "community standards" in
their choice of material. And in Williamson County, Texas, the
county commission decided to vote against tax breaks for a building complex proposed by Apple, the computer company, because
of a corporate policy providing domestic-partnership benefits to
gay couples.

Nowhere was that battle fiercer than in Cincinnati. The crusade against gay rights there had its roots in the 1970s, when Simon Leis, the Hamilton County prosecutor, went on an
antipornography tear that was still being felt almost two decades
later. Leis shut down adult bookstores, massage parlors, and porn
movie theaters and prosecuted *Hustler* publisher Larry Flynt.
The city became the headquarters for the National Coalition
Against Pornography, run by the Reverend Jerry Kirk. The result-
ing atmosphere was so restrictive that in the middle of the 1993
battle, policemen were monitoring a local theater group to make
sure that a gay-themed play was not obscene. It was just as repressive against individuals as well. In 1990, two men were arrested for "creating a physically offensive condition." Their crime:
holding hands. The pair were found innocent at a trial.

Leis would later say that he saw no difference between his
campaign against pornography and the campaign against gay
rights that followed. "It all goes hand in hand, those areas of
pornography and gay rights," he told the *Cincinnati Post* in 1994.
Certainly, Phil Burress would agree. Burress, who had run his
own irrigation firm and managed a golf course, was the leader of
the antigay effort in Cincinnati. As president of Citizens for Community Values, Burress was the most visible and vocal opponent
of gay rights in the city. Moreover, he had come to his calling
through his fascination with heterosexual pornography, which
Burress later labeled an addiction. The problem was so severe,
Burress said, that it threatened his second marriage.

In the early 1980s, however, Burress began to mend his ways.
He became involved in Citizens for Community Values, founded
by a local minister to promote conservative standards. More im-

portant, in 1983 he attended an antiporn conference in Phoenix that featured finance executive and would-be moralist Charles Keating. Keating, a former Cincinnatan, was a fervent opponent of pornography and founded Citizens for Decency through Law to carry out his crusade. In his Phoenix speech, he told the audience that he suspected that *Hustler* was the catalyst for a rapist who had attacked a family member in Cincinnati. Like Leis, Keating could not distinguish between homosexuality and pornography. He once urged Ohio politicians to "put homosexuals and pornographers in jail" (which was where Keating himself ended up nine years later after he was convicted of selling $250 million in worthless bonds to investors in his Lincoln Savings). Electrified by Keating's address, Burress threw himself into Citizens for Community Values, eventually giving up his irrigation business to devote himself to it full-time. Burress justified his efforts to restrict access to everything from *Playboy* to *The Advocate* as a kind of public health project. "Right to read? It's a bunch of hogwash," he told the *Cincinnati Post*. "You don't have the right to read anything you want. We have to protect each other from dangerous material." Unconcerned about the First Amendment, Burress gladly appointed himself to the position of protector.

Burress's disapproval of pornography and homosexuality dovetailed in 1990, when the Cincinnati Contemporary Arts Center showed an exhibit of photographs by Robert Mapplethorpe, who had died from AIDS the year before. Many of Mapplethorpe's images had a gay, and more specifically sadomasochistic, theme; one of his most notorious photographs showed him with a bullwhip protruding from his rectum. Burress and the Reverend Jerry Kirk led the Citizens for Community Values' charge against the exhibit, mailing out eighteen thousand letters condemning it and asking for financial help in fighting it. They had a valuable and sympathetic ally in Leis, who obtained grand jury indictments of obscenity against the gallery and its director, Dennis Barrie. "If [Mapplethorpe's photography] is art," Leis declared, "this country is running downhill to mediocrity so fast, you can't stop it." Barrie was acquitted by a jury, but not before Cincinnati took a drubbing in the national media as the censorship capital of the country.

~ The Mapplethorpe controversy was the most visible eruption of a long-standing crusade by conservative Christians against forms of expression that they considered immoral or blasphemous. At the time of the Mapplethorpe trial, the religious right was in the midst of an assault on the National Endowment for the Arts for funding projects, several of which were by gay artists, that they found offensive, even sacrilegious. The targets were easy enough, particularly in the case of Andres Serrano's *Piss Christ,* a crucifix immersed in a jar of the artist's urine. (Serrano was not gay, but such distinctions seemed to get lost in the debate.) Mapplethorpe never received money from the Endowment, but the tour of his work was partially funded by a grant from the agency. In 1989, Congress voted to cut $45,000 in funding, the cost of the tour, from the agency's budget as a sign of its displeasure. It was the opening salvo in a war against the Endowment that has yet to cease, even though the agency has been harder to kill outright than conservatives anticipated.

The nature of some of the artworks funded by the Endowment provided a field day for the religious right. In one newsletter, Pat Robertson described the controversy in typically apocalyptic terms: "It is as if a portion of the art community of the western world is rapidly being transformed into a giant moral cesspool in which those in creative authority are stumbling over one another in their attempts to conjure up even more bizarre blasphemy, perversion, and sado-masochistic brutality." The chief architect of the assault on "permissive" art was the Reverend Donald Wildmon, head of the American Family Association in Tupelo, Mississippi. Wildmon was, in essence, the religious right's head censor, determining what was acceptable and what was not. A United Methodist minister, Wildmon had founded the National Federation for Decency in 1977, but the group began to peter out in the 1980s. Wildmon reorganized under the American Family Association, which had a more evangelical bent than its predecessor. It was, Wildmon told the *Wall Street Journal,* "a sound business decision."

Wildmon's pet bugaboo was network television. He pressured

CBS to drop a sex scene from a 1979 made-for-television movie, *Flesh and Blood,* and with Jerry Falwell's Moral Majority, he threatened a boycott against an unnamed major television advertiser in 1981. Spooked by the threat, Procter and Gamble pulled its ads from fifty shows on the grounds that they were too violent, sexual, or profane—exactly the criteria that Wildmon used to determine the acceptability of programs. Wildmon and Falwell withdrew the threat of the boycott immediately afterward, claiming they had "been able to achieve nearly everything we set out to achieve."

The boycott was not the favorite tool of Wildmon alone. Gay activists had used the same tactic over the years against Coors, Miller Brewing, Marlboro, and other businesses that had supported antigay policies either directly or indirectly, to say nothing of the boycott against Colorado. Wildmon, of course, belittled the gay boycotts; in one issue of *The American Family Association Journal,* he approvingly ran an article by syndicated columnist William Murchison that called the Colorado boycott "bigotry on the hoof." Wildmon clearly felt immune to comparable criticism. At various times, the minister led boycotts against Clorox, Pfizer, S.C. Johnson, RCA, K Mart, Levi Strauss, and Holiday Inn, while threatening boycotts against Burger King and Pepsi, because they somehow subsidized or permitted "antifamily" entertainment.

The problem for advertisers, however, was that Wildmon found virtually anything offensive. He had complained about everything from Johnny Carson's *Tonight* show to *Murder, She Wrote,* as well as programs that most parents considered suitable for their children, such as *Highway to Heaven* and *The Magical World of Disney.*° He called the innocuous *Growing Pains* "per-

---

° It was inevitable that Wildmon's sweeping crusade would eventually focus on the paradigm of family entertainment, the Walt Disney Co. After the company extended domestic-partnership benefits to its gay employees in the fall of 1995—by then a standard perk in the film industry—Wildmon launched a boycott against Disney. Given Disney's monopoly on high-quality entertainment, along with its well-established goodwill among consumers, the boycott unsurprisingly had no effect on its target.

verted 'family' entertainment" and once insisted that an episode of *Mighty Mouse* showed the cartoon hero snorting cocaine. Despite the bizarre nature of Wildmon's complaints, he was able to wring concessions from advertisers terrified of being seen as pro-violence or pro-sex. In 1990, Clorox officials met with representatives of Wildmon's television watchdog group and reassured them that they would steer clear of controversial television shows. In return, Wildmon called off his boycott.

Nothing set Wildmon off like homosexuality. *The American Family Association Journal* was a compendium of antigay arguments. The newsletter complained that the "homosexual thought police" muzzled *60 Minutes* commentator Andy Rooney because Rooney made antigay remarks; in fact, Rooney was temporarily suspended from the show by CBS when he made racially insensitive remarks to *The Advocate* while trying to extricate himself from his first statement, leaving gay activists to conclude that racial insensitivity was more important to the network. The *Journal* also included the standard defamatory arguments against homosexuality as the equivalent of pedophilia and the source of a public health threat.

Wildmon's activities inevitably led him into local electoral battles. When Tampa passed a nondiscrimination ordinance in 1992, the Florida chapter of the American Family Association, headed by David Caton, another reformed porn addict, became the principal proponent for a referendum. Under the banner of a group called Take Back Tampa, Caton and his followers circulated the same kinds of material that flooded Oregon and Colorado, proclaiming that "sodomy is not a civil right." The ordinance was repealed, but the victory was a short one; a court ultimately voided the vote. (In contrast to Wildmon's boycott-happy tactics, gay activists in Tampa came up with a more intelligent and positive response to the repeal: a "buycott," which consisted of a list of pro-gay businesses that people could patronize. This tactic seemed far less censorious and threatening.) Caton also tried to mount a statewide initiative in 1994, but the measure was disqualified from the ballot on the grounds that it was confusing and misleading. Still, Caton was a determined soldier. According to

Mother Jones magazine, at an American Family Association conference in 1992, he told the audience, "Go after them tooth and nail with every power you have. Intimidation, that's the bottom line."

Caton received legal advice from the American Family Association Law Center, Wildmon's own entry in the growing field of Christian legal aid. The Law Center was not involved exclusively in gay issues; it brought suit against a textbook curriculum in Sacramento on the grounds that the books, written by such authors as Dr. Seuss, C. S. Lewis, and Rudyard Kipling, promoted witchcraft. But the Center had more than its share of antigay attacks, including a losing effort to petition the Kentucky state supreme court to uphold the state's sodomy law. The Center's general counsel was Benjamin Bull, who had worked in Citizens for Decency through Law, the anti-obscenity group founded by Charles Keating, the man who had electrified Phil Burress. It was no surprise that when Burress named his campaign against the Cincinnati nondiscrimination ordinance, he borrowed from the American Family Association's Tampa effort. Thus was born Take Back Cincinnati.

⌐ The opposition to the ordinance in Cincinnati began months before the measure was passed in November 1992. Among the earliest opponents were members of the clergy. Roman Catholic archbishop Daniel Pilarczyk wrote the city council two days before the measure was introduced in June that it would "seriously undermine the stability of the family and the moral education and values of our youth." The Baptist Ministers Conference came out against the measure, as did several black conservative groups. When the measure passed the city council 7–2 in November, Charles Winburn, a black minister who headed the coalition against the measure, called the new law "a sex manual" that was "antifamily, antibusiness, and . . . definitely anti-God" and promised a petition drive against the ordinance.

Still, the drive did not get under way until the following spring. That was when Phil Burress attended a seminar in Colorado Springs sponsored by Colorado for Family Values, the group behind Colorado's antigay amendment. In the wake of its success, Colorado for Family Values had taken to running conferences for Christian political activists who wanted to specialize in fighting gay rights. The group also offered a $49.95 mail-order kit with a position paper outlining its successful 1992 strategy and a copy of *Legislating Immorality: The Homosexual Movement Comes Out of the Closet* by George Grant and Mark Horne, which purported to "portray the forces arrayed against the family and the stability of our civilization." The seminar that Burress attended not only provided the spark for the petition drive, it also proved to be the start of an important relationship between Burress and Colorado for Family Values. The Colorado group provided Burress with strategic information based on its experience.

A few weeks later, Burress made it clear how much he had come to accept Colorado for Family Values' emphasis on the gay menace. "Anyone who's opposed to the militant homosexual agenda can see this is going to be the issue of the nineties," he said in one interview. "I wouldn't be surprised if it surpasses abortion." Even without help from Colorado, Burress had a substantial arsenal at hand. His group, Citizens for Community Values, claimed to have grown to have sixteen thousand families as members, with a database of five thousand volunteers, four paid staffers, and a projected annual budget of $320,000. "It's a cultural war, no question about it," said Burress. "Homosexuals stand for everything the pro-family movement is opposed to." Such take-no-prisoners rhetoric pitted the two sides against each other as combatants to the finish, as if one side or the other could be eliminated from society altogether.

There was little doubt that Take Back Cincinnati would be able to collect the 9,900 signatures necessary to qualify the ordinance for the ballot. Yet the time before the group turned in the signatures was relatively quiet. Take Back Cincinnati did not take its arguments against the measure public, concentrating instead on collecting signatures from its base of support. Gay activists formed a Bigot Buster hot line and circulated flyers that read, "Never another Colorado, not even in Cincinnati." Stonewall Cincinnati, the local gay political group, led the formation of

Equality Cincinnati, headed by lesbian activist Betsy Gressler, to fight the ballot measure. The unassuming and good-natured Gressler, a past president of Stonewall, had been instrumental in the passage of the ordinance in the first place. Eventually, Nancy Minson, former chair of the Cincinnati Women's Political Caucus, was hired as campaign manager.

The campaign did not get under way until the end of August, when Take Back Cincinnati turned in seventeen thousand signatures, but it began with a bang. On the last day for qualifying measures for the November ballot, Take Back Cincinnati issued an opinion paper calling on candidates to declare whether they were straight or gay. "Since the homosexuals and City Council have made this private issue of sexual orientation a public debate, and have chosen to pass laws based on sexual orientation, perhaps each City Council candidate should state his/her own orientation during his/her political advertisements," the paper stated. Burress said that it was simply to inform the public what stake, if any, candidates had in the issue, much as they would release financial statements: "Since they're passing laws based on sexual orientation, then shouldn't City Council say what their interests are—just like in any other debate [where] they have a personal interest in the issue?" Of course, the real issue was the candidate's positions and not their personal lives; to pretend otherwise was to raise the already intrusive rules for politics to ridiculous levels. Nobody took the bait, but the issue would return after the election.

Issue 3, as the referendum became known, was attacked by a wide range of people and groups, most notably Archbishop Pilarczyk, who had apparently had a change of heart from the year before. "I believe that our city would be best served if the proposed amendment were rejected," he said. "Apparently, the proposed amendment would make it possible to discriminate freely against persons of homosexual orientation in such matters as housing, employment, and public accommodation." Of course, that is exactly what would have been prevented by the measure Pilarczyk originally opposed. Take Back Cincinnati, which eventually changed its name to Equal Rights, Not Special Rights, was able to answer such condemnations of Issue 3 with a powerful counterpunch—black clergy, and in particular Charles Winburn and the Reverend K. Z. Smith. Smith was not only pastor of the Corinthian Baptist Church, he was also president of the mostly black Baptist Ministers Conference. A respected figure in Cincinnati, Smith sprang from the tradition of politically involved black ministers dating back to the earliest days of the black civil rights movement. He spoke at Martin Luther King Jr. celebrations and embraced the African-American festival of Kwanza as an important part of black heritage. When William Seitz, vice president of the city Board of Education, suggested in a letter that black students had higher rates of suspension because their parents were less well behaved than whites, Smith led the effort to recall him.

When Smith became the spokesperson for Equal Rights, Not Special Rights, he gave credibility to the argument that gays and lesbians were well-educated, well-paid people trying to undercut the protections of "legitimate" minorities. This was a key to the religious right's leaders' argument against gay rights, and one reason why they were so happy with Gen. Colin Powell's stand against gays in the military. The argument was also an important reason why conservative Christian leaders were aggressively courting blacks, even though many of the leaders, such as Jerry Falwell and the Reverend Lou Sheldon, had been opposed to many of the civil rights gains blacks had made in the 1960s. That history was papered over by their new outreach efforts. The cohost of Pat Robertson's *700 Club* was a black man, Ben Kinchlow, while Tony Evans, founder of the Urban Alternative ministry, spoke at the dedication ceremony for Focus on the Family's new office complex in November 1993. The Rutherford Institute provided legal counsel to the Reverend Eugene Lumpkin when he was fired from the San Francisco City Human Rights Commission after calling homosexuality "an abomination against God" and suggesting that he agreed with biblical commands to stone gays. Colorado for Family Values flyers pictured African-Americans who supported Amendment 2, along with a quote from an unidentified black pastor in Kansas City, who proclaimed that "the Freedom Bus that went to Selma was never meant to go on to Sodom." (Right-wing representative Robert Dornan was to use that exact same phrase in 1995 during his quixotic quest for the Republican presidential nomination.)

While a significant number of black clergy supported gay rights, the ranks of conservative African-American ministers were a fertile ground for the religious right. While some religious right leaders had a spotty record on civil rights, condemnation of homosexuality was something both sides could agree upon. Some black clergy expressed the extreme views of the far right; in Tampa, the home of the American Family Association's antigay initiative, the Reverend James Sykes of the St. James A.M.E. Church went so far as to say that he would join a "peaceful" Ku Klux Klan rally against gay rights. "For all the bad the Klan does, they are right about gays," he declared. Other ministers were not as radical, but still antigay. In Cleveland, a group that christened itself the Black Church declared homosexuality as "contrary to the teachings of the Bible" and expressed the belief that orientation "can be changed or given up."

Such tenets echoed the positions of conservative white Christians, and the Reverend Lou Sheldon of the Traditional Values Coalition was quick to exploit that sympathy. Sheldon produced an antigay video titled *Gay Rights, Special Rights* that appealed to African-Americans' irritation at claims equating the gay rights movement with the black civil rights movement. The forty-five-minute video featured clips from Martin Luther King Jr.'s "I Have a Dream Speech," contrasting it to the 1993 Gay and Lesbian March on Washington by interviewing only white participants. The video drives its point home by having a black minister telling a cheering crowd that "we will not allow the civil rights movement to be hijacked by a group of people who want to give moral credence to their immoral lifestyle." It was a far cry from the speeches supporting gay rights that the Reverend Jesse Jackson gave to black and white audiences during his 1988 presidential campaign. Among the white speakers featured in the video were former education secretary William Bennett, Mississippi senator Trent Lott, and Donald Wildmon. At $19.95 a video, Sheldon estimated that he had sold almost forty-five thousand by January 1994. "The blacks, who cannot change their skin color, are offended that the gays are seeking protection for behavior they can change," Sheldon told the *San Francisco Chronicle*. The video was distributed throughout Cincinnati during the campaign. Given the growing hostility to civil rights legislation of all kinds, it was not surprising that some African-Americans would feel threatened by gays and lesbians, who were garnering more attention than their own beleaguered community.

~· Equal Rights, Not Special Rights bolstered its arguments by citing the same statistics that had been used in Oregon and Colorado: gay men earn on average $55,420 annually, as opposed to $32,286 for the average American. By contrast, according to government statistics, African-Americans earned only $12,166. The idea that gay men and, to a lesser extent, lesbians were well-to-do came from marketing surveys conducted for gay publications in an effort to convince potential advertisers of the power of the gay market. How representative of the gay community the surveys were was impossible to tell. For one, no magazine's readership, whether *The Advocate* or *The New Yorker*, could be construed as representative of an entire community. For another, closeted gays and lesbians were less likely to respond to any kind of survey for fear of their orientation somehow becoming known. Yet that did not stop the religious right, with its mostly white leadership, from misrepresenting the survey as hard fact and the gay community as white and middle class.

Yet the misleading information was powerful nonetheless, making the issue look like a black-white fight. Black lesbian and gay activists such as Mandy Carter of the Human Rights Campaign Fund and Phill Wilson tried to counter the damaging arguments through outreach to black ministers and organizing efforts for African-American gays. After the lessons of Cincinnati, they would form the National Black Gay and Lesbian Leadership Forum to increase visibility and awareness of African-American gays and lesbians. But they faced an uphill battle. Not only were some segments of the black community hostile to gays. Blacks, as well as Asians and Latinos, felt that the gay community did not always welcome them with open arms either. Indeed, all of them felt that they suffered the same invisibility within the gay community that gay activists readily complained about with the heterosexual population. "When the gay community was formed and became political, the leaders were white men, and they brought their prejudices with them," Perry Watkins, who had been frozen out of the debate on the gays in the military, told the *New York Times*. The tensions within the gay community only made responding to the false accusations of white privilege that much more difficult.

⟋ Betsy Gressler and other officials at Equality Cincinnati were confident that Issue 3 was a losing proposition. "No one thinks it can pass," Gressler said when the referendum qualified in August. "I don't think Cincinnati is as conservative as it is polite and discreet. The hints we're getting is that this might be a very low-key campaign, with Equal Rights, Not Special Rights just going to churches and talking to supporters." It was not low-key from Equality Cincinnati's point of view. Gilbert Bettman, president of the group, declared Issue 3 "un-American." In a letter signed by retired Episcopal bishop William Black, honorary cochair of the campaign, the group linked Equal Rights, Not Special Rights' drive with a national attempt to "foster intolerance, deny human and civil rights, and bend governmental and social institutions to serve the right-wing/fundamentalist agenda of control and repression." The letter opened with the famous quote from Martin Niemoeller: "In Germany, the Nazis came for the Communists and I didn't speak up because I was not a Communist. Then they came for the Jews and I didn't speak up because I was not a Jew. Then they came for the Trade Unionists and I didn't speak up because I wasn't a Trade Unionist. Then they came for the Catholics and I was a Protestant so I didn't speak up. Then they came for me . . . by that time there was no one to speak up for anyone." Contributions would go toward "hard-hitting and compelling TV/radio advertisements," the letter promised.

In keeping with the Nazi imagery raised in the fund-raising letter, the ads were indeed hard-hitting, too much so. The television ad began with a shot of Hitler, cut to a shot of a hooded

Klansman, and then to a shot of the late senator Joseph McCarthy. Print ads and flyers featured the same unholy trio. The tag line came from the Jewish promise about the Holocaust: "Never again." The ads were an accurate representation of just how threatened gays and lesbians felt by the referendum, but they also presented practical problems. How many viewers in Ohio could recognize the unidentified McCarthy, a senator from Wisconsin forty years ago? More important, however, the ads were viewed by many people as incredibly offensive. Jews objected to the premise that repealing gay rights was at all comparable to the genocide of World War II. People trying to make up their minds about the issue could hardly have appreciated being told that they were Nazis or white supremacists if they voted to repeal the nondiscrimination measure. One Midwest gay activist was told by a relative who favored gay rights that he was inclined to vote for Issue 3 just to register his disgust with the ads. Although some activists from outside Cincinnati privately expressed dismay at the tone of the campaign, no one ever did so publicly.

For its campaign, Equal Rights, Not Special Rights relied on many of the same "statistics" and arguments as had appeared in Colorado. Based on the phony research of Paul Cameron, the antigay forces argued that gay men and lesbians died on average in their forties. It presented gay men as promiscuous and a health threat. It raised the specter of pedophilia. None of that was new. What caught Gressler, Minson, and other No on 3 officials off guard was the final onslaught. In the last few weeks of the election, Equal Rights, Not Special Rights flooded the media with its message. Minson later said that every section of the newspaper seemed to have some ad in favor of Issue 3. The blitz was obviously expensive, but no one could tell where the money came from, because it was not included in the last financial disclosure report filed before the election. Short of money, No on 3 could do nothing except watch the tide wash over it. Issue 3 passed, 62 percent to 38 percent. In predominantly black wards, the margin was only slightly smaller, 56–44. The Reverend K. Z. Smith declared himself justified: "We believed all along that the majority did not want homosexuals and bisexuals to have protected rights. The

whole issue wasn't about discrimination; it was about morality"—
as if the two were not somehow related. On the same night,
Smith's fellow minister Charles Winburn, endorsed by the American Family Association, was elected to the city council.

It took several days for the truth to come out about Equal
Rights, Not Special Rights' funding. In the last weeks of the campaign, Colorado for Family Values had poured $390,000 into the
campaign's coffers, nearly four times as much as the rest of
the group's contributions combined. (By contrast, No on 3 raised
$226,000, which included a $75,000 bank loan.) The connection
that Burress had forged in April had proved invaluable. "We were
shocked also that when we kept asking for money, they kept giving
it," Burress told the *Cincinnati Post*. "It's pretty obscene that that
much money would come into our community from outside, to a
group that claimed to be local," said Barry Grossheim, cochair of
Stonewall Cincinnati. Some of the criticism had to be sour grapes;
when thousands of dollars of outside money was raised for the
battle in Oregon in 1992, gay activists did not object to the same
principle.

The real issue was that Colorado for Family Values would not
release a donor list to account for its contribution. "We feel that
because we receive funds from out of state from people concerned on this issue, it's up to us to expend them on that issue
wherever it is," Will Perkins declared. But without a list of contributors, it was entirely possible that Colorado for Family Values,
acting like a political action committee, had skirted state election
laws. Despite such complaints, Ohio officials had no authority
over Colorado for Family Values and could not force them to disclose anything. For its part, the Colorado group could boast that it
had exported the formula for success against gay activists, a claim
it badly needed to save face when a Colorado court threw out
Amendment 2 in December 1993.

⟶ With the passage of Issue 3, Cincinnati saw the same kind of
legal fallout as Colorado had, with some of the same players.
Within two weeks of the election, U.S. district court judge
S. Arthur Spiegel enjoined the repeal from taking effect, setting

the stage for a court battle. Robert Skolrood, an attorney at the National Legal Foundation who had provided legal counsel to Colorado for Family Values during the challenge to Amendment 2, acted as attorney for Equal Rights, Not Special Rights. When the injunction was handed down, Skolrood solemnly stated that "today was a sad day for democracy—not only in Cincinnati but in America."

Skolrood used the Cincinnati case, along with Colorado, heavily in his fund-raising appeals. Indeed, Skolrood was often quite bald in exploiting gay rights in his begging. "Please continue to pray and please send your very best gift today," he said in one letter. "It is a costly business to stop the homosexual agenda." In an issue of *Minuteman,* the Foundation's newsletter, he declared the fight against "the radical homosexual agenda" to be "the battle of the decade," a description, of course, that further legitimized the urgency of his fund-raising appeals. Indeed, Skolrood pulled out all the stops in his condemnation of gays and lesbians. "Groups such as Act Up, Queer Nation, the Lesbian Avengers, and NAMBLA stage pornographic parades, intimidate people on the streets, and recruit children outside," he declared.

While the legal wrangling went on, Cincinnati lost several conventions to a boycott, including those of the American Historical Association and the American Library Association. Within nine months, the Convention and Visitors Bureau estimated that the city lost $20 million because of the boycott. But by far the oddest sideshow involved mayor-elect Roxanne Qualls. As a member of the city council, Qualls had supported the original ordinance and opposed its repeal. With her election, she became the target of an outing campaign led by angry conservative Christians. During an appearance on a radio talk show two days after the election, Qualls was flooded with questions about her sexual orientation. "Did I or did I not vote for a lesbian?" a caller named Betty demanded to know. Qualls refused to answer the question because it was "a matter of privacy." At her inauguration in December, protesters showed up carrying signs bearing such messages as "How can we trust a mayor who isn't straight with us?" "Many Cincinnatians, including myself, are thinking, 'How is that radical homosexual agenda going on in council?'" protester Jennifer Thomas said. "We have our answer now. It's because she is pushing it, because she has a personal investment in it. And she's not going to be able to serve objectively as mayor if she is, in fact, a lesbian and pushing their agenda." Apparently, it never occurred to Thomas and the other protesters that they were demanding of Qualls the very thing they repeatedly criticized gays and lesbians for doing: making a public statement about sexual orientation. Qualls's insistence that her private life was nobody's business was, under other circumstances, the very thing that conservative Christians insisted upon for gays and lesbians.

Emboldened by their success in Cincinnati, Burress and his allies tried to come up with new ways to capitalize on it. In February 1994, under the umbrella of the Ohio Pro-Family Forum, twenty-three groups met to consider a statewide antigay measure. "I can say this: We're not meeting to waste our time," Burress promised. "We're going to discuss all the issues and look at our options." In the light of the negative rulings on Colorado and the ongoing battle over Issue 3, the idea was eventually dropped. But in April, the state chapter of the American Family Association came up with Project Spotlight, its four-step plan to "educate voters about every candidate who is pro-homosexual." Among the actions the plan advocated was the purchase of sixty thousand copies of Lou Sheldon's *Gay Rights, Special Rights* video, to be resold at "a modest profit."

The court case against Issue 3 was put on a fast track in federal district court, with the trial beginning in June 1994. During the trial, Alphonse Gerhardstein, a civil rights attorney, ACLU attorney Scott Greenwood, and Pat Logue, an attorney for Lambda Legal Defense and Education Fund, got expert witnesses for Equal Rights, Not Special Rights to concede fundamental flaws in their reasoning. Under questioning from Logue, Hadley Arkes, a political science professor at Amherst, conceded that his standard of societal "aversion" to gay rights once applied to interracial marriages and women lawyers. Gerhardstein forced Clemson University political science professor David Woodard to acknowledge that the marketing study he used to prove the economic clout of gays applied only to readers of *The Advocate.* According to *The Washington Blade,* Gerhardstein noted that the average income of readers of *Cincinnati* magazine was $90,000. "Would you conclude from this that the average person in Cincinnati earns ninety thousand dollars?" Gerhardstein asked Woodard. "Not at all," the professor allowed. In August, Judge S. Arthur Spiegel struck down the referendum on the grounds that it "effectively places the government's imprimatur on those acts of private bias carried out pursuant to Issue 3's unmistakable mission."

Spiegel's ruling was especially important as the first federal decision on the antigay initiatives and as one of the most pro-gay federal decisions ever. But a month later, Equal Rights, Not Special Rights was able to bring in its own heavy artillery. Robert Bork, the former U.S. solicitor general and failed U.S. Supreme Court nominee, agreed to act as counsel to the group in their appeal of Spiegel's decision. While serving on the U.S. Court of Appeals, Bork had ruled against a gay naval officer challenging the Pentagon's policy on gays in the military, writing in a unanimous opinion that "private, consensual homosexual conduct is not constitutionally protected." Visiting Idaho earlier that year as the state geared up for an antigay initiative campaign, Bork declared that communities had the right "not to have a different morality thrust on people," as if the majority held the right to wipe out the rights of everyone else. Bork was not the only big-name conservative that Burress was able to bring to his camp; former attorney general Edwin Meese III, who shared Burress's abhorrence of pornography and was featured in the *Gay Rights, Special Rights* video, was a speaker at a fund-raiser for Equal Rights, Not Special Rights in October 1994.

The presence of Bork and Meese, to say nothing of the influence of Wildmon (who would serve as co-chair of Pat Buchanan's 1996 presidential campaign), Robertson, and other religious right leaders, underscored the national importance that Cincinnati came to have for conservatives. A three-judge panel of the U.S. District Court of Appeals ruled unanimously in May 1995 that the Cincinnati measure was constitutional, the first decision ever to uphold an antigay measure. The court relied on the 1986 U.S. Supreme Court decision in the *Bowers v. Hardwick* case to conclude that gays and lesbians "are entitled to no special constitutional protection . . . because the conduct that places them in that class is not constitutionally protected." By the time the ruling was handed down, stunning gay activists, the law that had caused all the uproar had been changed by a backpedaling city council to omit sexual orientation from the list of protected characteristics. There was little left for gays and lesbians to do but appeal to the U.S. Supreme Court, a risky throw of the dice.

⤳ While Take Back Cincinnati was gathering signatures for its referendum drive, another battle was brewing in Cobb County, Georgia, a suburb of Atlanta, again because of the arts. During the 1992–93 season, Theater in the Square in Marietta staged two plays that had been hits in New York. *M. Butterfly,* based on the true story of a French diplomat who gullibly believed a female impersonator who was his lover was actually a woman, had won numerous awards while on Broadway and eventually became a movie starring Jeremy Irons. *Lips Together, Teeth Apart,* by Terrence McNally, was about two heterosexual couples vacationing in the Fire Island house that one of the women had inherited from a brother who had died from AIDS complications. The plays were exactly what Cobb County theatergoers seemed to want—popular works from New York imported to the area while they were still fresh. *Lips Together, Teeth Apart* was voted favorite play by the theater's subscribers.

Not everyone liked the plays' gay motifs, however. One theatergoer complained about the McNally production. More important, Bill Byrne, chairman of the Cobb County Commission, was not pleased about *M. Butterfly.* "My wife and I had season tickets to Theater in the Square, and I was pretty shocked by that play," he said. "We hit the road." Another commissioner, Gordon Wysong, was also offended, even though he had not seen either of the plays. "I am not an aficionado of theater," Wysong told the *Washington Post.* He was particularly upset that Theater in the Square received a modest grant from the county as part of its arts funding and decided to do something about it. In July 1993, Wysong announced that he would introduce a resolution before the commission to make a statement about the plays. Echoing the rhetoric of the Republican presidential convention in Houston, the resolution declared its support for "the traditional family structure," condemned "gay lifestyle units" as "directly contrary to state [sodomy] laws," and pledged "not to fund those activities which seek to contravene these existing community standards."

If such a resolution was to succeed anywhere, it would seem to be Cobb County. The county was far more conservative than neighboring Atlanta. Seventy percent of the county was represented by Rep. Newt Gingrich, the conservative firebrand and future Speaker of the House. Prior to Gingrich, the county had been represented in Congress by Larry McDonald, a member of the John Birch Society, who had been killed when the Soviets downed a Korean airliner in 1983. In 1915, it had earned a dark place in the history of anti-Semitism as the county where Leo Frank, a Jewish factory owner, was lynched after being falsely convicted of murder. Like other areas in the Sunbelt, it had seen an enormous change in just a few years. From a population of under two hundred thousand in 1970, it had grown to more than half a million people, making it one of the fastest-growing counties in the nation.

Wysong, who was elected to the county commission in 1992, was a blend of New South and Old South. Born in Atlanta, he graduated from the Georgia Institute of Technology and was the owner of Southern Porcelain, a company that manufactured computer and electronics materials. He lived in an affluent section of Cobb County with his wife, who was his high school sweetheart. Wysong came by his political stance naturally; his mother was active in the John Birch Society and had worked on Phyllis Schlafly's pet cause, the defeat of the Equal Rights Amendment. But Wysong denied that he was motivated by the aims of any religious right groups, even though the Christian Coalition had held a leadership forum in Marietta, which is in Cobb County, just weeks before Wysong came up with his proposal. "I'm not much of a joiner," he said in one interview. "I have always disliked the idea of a group or organization speaking for me." Yet Wysong did not object to being adopted by the religious right, either. "I don't have any particular problem with that," he told the *Atlanta Constitution.* "The fact that we happen to agree is almost a coincidence. This cuts across all political lines." Wysong availed himself of whatever help he could from the religious right. He later described the *Gay Rights, Special Rights* video as "the single most useful resource I have seen on this issue." Although nominally Catholic, Wysong also consulted with the Reverend Nelson Price, head of the Rosewell Street Baptist Church, before introducing his resolution. "What we've tried to do is keep this from appearing to be a religious issue," Price later bragged to *The Christian Index,* a Baptist publication.

Just as Cincinnati's Issue 3 had been an extension of the religious right's condemnation of gays in the arts, the Cobb County Commission's actions spoke volumes about national politics as well. Wysong freely admitted that he wanted to make a statement about the place of gays in society, citing in particular the debate over gays in the military. "I think the outcry from the people from across this country said we do not want the military used for that purpose," Wysong said. "Someone has to articulate it. It was an appropriate way for us to send a message from the citizens." Wysong also tried to relate the resolution to national politics by praising Georgia senator Sam Nunn, who had led the defense of the Pentagon ban. "His courage and correctness should be endorsed by this community, which shares his views," Wysong told the *Atlanta Constitution.* Bill Byrne expressed similar views, somehow laying the responsibility for Wysong's actions at President Clinton's door. "Unfortunately we have elected a president who has raised the issue of alternate lifestyles to a national debate," he declared. "It will have a trickle-down effect on every local and state government."

The response to the proposed resolution was swift. One of the more measured responses came from actress Joanne Woodward, a native of Marietta, who issued a statement saying that she was "extremely disturbed that the Cobb County Commission would attempt to dictate family values; family values that should originate in the home." Other reactions were more heated. Cherry Spencer-Stark, board chairwoman of Theater in the Square, said that the measure "really smacks of Nazism." David Henry Hwang, author of *M. Butterfly*, said in an op-ed piece for the *Marietta Daily Journal* that "Nazis and Communists ruthlessly persecuted both gays and subversive artists, and their societies were none the better for their prejudices."

Unlike Atlanta, Cobb County was hardly known as a haven for gays and lesbians. Yet there was still a sizable gay population in the county who liked it for the same reasons that other county residents did—its peacefulness, quality of life, vigorous economy, and security. An informal group had formed for potlucks in 1990, eventually totaling 175. But the group fell apart. The resolution changed that lack of organization. The chief gay spokesman to emerge was Jon Greaves, who had moved to the county in 1982. Greaves had grown up in Oklahoma and had turned down an appointment to West Point to attend Wabash College, one of the few remaining men's colleges in the country. A credit analyst, Greaves had moved to the Atlanta area to be closer to his brother and also to come out. In 1986, he met David Greer, a native of the county, and the pair settled down together.

Greaves formed Cobb Citizens Coalition, whose goal was to help people have a better understanding of their gay neighbors. "In Cobb, we've been showing them what we look like and letting them hear our voices speaking about ourselves instead of letting other people talk for us and about us, and we've been trying to represent ourselves in a nonantagonistic and nonthreatening way," he told the *Constitution*. "People who are scared are not usually real receptive." Wearing a suit and tie during his public appearances, Greaves went out of his way to look like any other respectable businessman. The visibility of Greaves and other local gays and lesbians made many Cobb citizens aware for the first time of a gay presence in their county, challenging the assumption that homosexuals preferred to live in the gay ghetto of Atlanta. But the gay group lacked the enormous advantages that conservative Christians had—weekly meetings at services, the institutional support of their churches, the financial power of congregations, as well as the ability to rely upon a deeply ingrained stereotype of the gay "threat."

The furor that Wysong's resolution unleashed came to overwhelm all other issues in the county. A few voices, including Greaves, tried to argue that the real problems facing Cobb County had to do with road repairs and trash disposal, mundane issues, but ones that the rapidly growing county badly needed to address and quickly. One local businessman even hired a plane to trail a banner reading, "It's taxes, stupid." G. Conley Ingram, a former state supreme court justice, told the *Daily Journal* that the commission had "more significant things they need to be doing. I get my moral direction from my preacher and my Lord, not the government." Gays and lesbians found an unlikely ally in Otis Brumby Jr., publisher of the *Daily Journal,* whose editorials blasted the commission and whose headlines bluntly labeled Wysong's resolution "antigay." Brumby may have been motivated more by love of Cobb County than by tolerance for homosexuality, but he was obviously appalled at the image of intolerance that the county was acquiring nationally. "Did Cobb County need a self-inflicted black eye?" one editorial asked. "Does it have any business meddling in a matter in which it has no jurisdiction? . . . It likely would take millions of dollars' worth of advertising to reverse the negative impression the country has gotten of Cobb in the past week or so."

That kind of common sense was lost in the bitterness of the controversy. On August 10, the night that the commission voted 3–1 to support the resolution, conservative Christian activists, some with their children, wearing yellow tags reading SUPPORT COMMUNITY STANDARDS, flooded the commission chambers at the urging of their pastors the previous Sunday. Outside the chambers, one man carried a sign that read PRAISE GOD FOR AIDS. Wysong opened the session with a sweeping condemnation of homosexuality and a justification for his resolution. In addition to gays in the military, he cited a push for domestic-partnership benefits in Atlanta and the governor's invitation for the Gay Games to host its 1998 gathering in Atlanta. "It is imperative that we as a board renounce this kind of activity because it threatens the safety, health, and welfare of the community," Wysong thundered. "It is mind-boggling to imagine what activities constitute 'gay games.'" In fact, the Games are an athletic competition that feature the usual events, such as swimming, track and field, and skating, differing only from other competitions by such additions as same-sex skating pairs. The 1994 Games, held in New York City, resulted in the establishment of several new world and national athletic records.

The focus of the hearings was clearly anything but the two plays that had started the ruckus, despite the attempts of a few arts supporters to mount a defense. Instead, the session became a platform for speakers to attack homosexuality. The opening speaker at the hearings was state representative Billy McKinney, whose district included all of six hundred Cobb residents. "We have watched for a long time as our community standards have gone down, gone down," McKinney said to applause. "I'm not a bigot, but I do believe that as the conduct of citizens is degraded, we at some point have to stand up and say what our community values are." Dr. Randell Mickler, minister of Mount Bethel United Methodist Church, told the commission, "I deeply resent one dollar of my taxes going to support a lifestyle my faith considers an abomination." Only commissioner Bill Cooper voted against the resolution. "I have no intention of using my office as a bully pulpit to challenge any group," he said. The vote set the stage for another hearing two weeks later to revoke all funding for the arts, including three children's theaters. Byrne made it clear that the move was punitive: "When the entire arts community turns on us the way they did—calling us Nazis, bigots, and censors—and then turn around and want money from us, that's crazy as hell."

In the intervening weeks, a torrent of antigay sentiment flooded the county. The *Daily Journal* saw more letters on the issue than on any other in three decades. Many of the opinions were viciously antigay. One writer decried gays as "confessed criminals" who had been "hiding their crime and their sin against God!" Even some of the letters that purported to be charitable were unwittingly harsh. "We need to have understanding and compassion for those trapped in the bondage of homosexuality," wrote another reader, as if describing the lives of gays and lesbians as "bondage" was not demeaning. Greaves and the Cobb Citizens Coalition tried to counter the attacks by holding a rally in downtown Marietta. "Maybe this will educate people," said Greaves. "I hope so." It was a sensible, valiant effort. But the counterprotesters at the rally seemed uninterested in Greaves's mission to introduce them to their neighbors. The demonstrators carried signs such as SODOMITE PERVERSION A THREAT TO CHILDREN and HOW MANY QUEERS ARE IN THE WHITE HOUSE? Some protesters wore latex gloves for protection, as one demonstrator put it, "in case one of them touches me or I have to touch one of them." As speakers for the Coalition addressed the crowd of five hundred, hecklers shouted, "You make me want to puke!"

One week later, gay and lesbian activists from Atlanta trekked out to Cobb County for a Queer Family Picnic, which attracted twice as many people and three bomb scares. Conservative Christians held a Prayer and Praise Rally after the picnic, singing hymns and promising to offer help to gays and lesbians who wanted to "change" to heterosexuality. Not all the commentary was as well-intentioned; former governor Lester Maddox, notorious for his segregationist views during the 1960s and now a resident of Cobb County, took the opportunity to blast gays and lesbians in crude terms. "The queers up here have done messed up their lives," he said. "I'm gonna pray for them. Even four-legged animals know better than that. It's contrary to God's will. It's unnatural, nasty, filthy, and sinful."

At no point did Wysong or Byrne ever condemn such bigotry. If anything, the August 24 commission meeting to cut off arts funding was even more of an antigay rally than the August 10 session. In his Sunday bulletin, the Reverend Nelson Price urged his Baptist congregation to turn out for the vote. If Price believed that the issue should not appear religious, his own actions indicated that it plainly was religious, of a particular nature. Members of the Liberty Baptist Church chanted, "Victory is ours," after the unanimous vote. Even the county's chapter of the Aryan Resistance League, a white supremacist group, announced itself pleased. "I'm glad that Cobb County took a stand against this perversion," member John Edwards said. It was a sign of how sorry the debate had become that there was virtually no difference between the rhetoric of neo-Nazi groups and conservative Christians. Gay activists were not without their own unenlightening exaggerations. While Greaves and the Coalition avoided hyperbole, a few others felt no such restraint. Signs renamed Wysong and company the Kobb Kounty Kommission, equating the commission with the Ku Klux Klan.

After the commission voted unanimously to eliminate all local arts funding and spend the $110,000 earmarked for it on police dogs and video cameras for patrol cars, Wysong congratulated himself on his handiwork. "Frankly, this is a model of how to deal with an issue," he boasted to the *Constitution*. Other conservatives agreed, and Wysong was soon inundated with offers from the lecture circuit. "It's nonstop," Wysong marveled. "I'm getting calls from everywhere." Altogether the commissioners received some four thousand phone calls, many of them supportive, in the month after the controversy began.

The repercussions began almost as soon as the measures were passed. Greaves had threatened the possibility of boycott, but Wysong dismissed the prospect. "The idea that some flyspeck of an economic boycott is going to affect the county is ridiculous," he told the *New York Times*. "It didn't work in Colorado and it won't work here." Of course, Colorado lost tens of millions of dollars in convention business, and Cobb County had just opened its own lavish convention center, making it an obvious target. Within weeks, two trade shows estimated to bring in over $1 million to the county were canceled. The county was also trying to attract businesses to relocate to the area, but at least one, a collection agency, said that the votes made it look elsewhere. Home Depot, the hardware chain with headquarters in the county, also expressed its discomfort at the resolutions and eventually announced plans to move to a new location in the Atlanta area. (The company's stance earned it the epithet Homo Depot from some conservatives.) Moreover, despite Wysong's sense of victory, the rest of the country thought the whole episode was a waste of time.

A *Constitution* poll found that 54 percent of Cobb County residents surveyed thought that the original resolution condemning homosexuality reflected the "organized activity of a few people." A *Daily Journal* poll found that 53 percent of those asked believed the controversy hurt Cobb County's image, even though most respondents believed that the county should not be funding the arts at all.

The polls proved to be little solace to gays and lesbians in Cobb County. Greaves, with his high visibility, suffered the most. In October, he decided to leave the area because of the threats he had received. One caller had promised to "make the streets run red" with Greaves's blood. "I thought by expecting it, I could control how I felt about it," Greaves said. "But I couldn't. It bothered me. I couldn't sleep at night. My family could no longer stay where we were living."

⮑ The uproar in Cobb County died down for a while, but it began to bubble again in January of 1994. Jon Ivan Weaver, a gay activist in Atlanta, was watching television coverage about the arrival of the Olympics in Atlanta in 1996 and was appalled to learn that the volleyball event was to be held at the Cobb Galleria Sports Centre. In response, Weaver helped form Olympics Out of Cobb County to pressure the Atlanta Committee for the Olympic Games to pull the volleyball tournament from Cobb County if the commission did not rescind its antigay resolution. The idea quickly became a gay cause célèbre; the Human Rights Campaign Fund and the National Gay and Lesbian Task Force joined in the call to move the event. (As if the prospect of a massive demonstration in Atlanta during the Olympics was not enough, the Gay and Lesbian Alliance Against Defamation rashly threatened a boycott against Coca-Cola, by virtue of its being headquartered in Atlanta.) Olympic gold medal diver Greg Louganis lent his name to the effort as well.

For a while, at least, the county commission seemed able to avoid the matter. Commissioner Byrne said that the Galleria would "provide the best in hospitality, facilities, and amenities for all athletes and all visitors from all participating countries, without

discrimination or hesitation." This grudging tolerance was a significant change from his brimstone condemnation of gays and lesbians just a few months before. Byrne also told the *Constitution*
that "gays have always been welcome in Cobb County. They've always been here," but could not stop himself from adding, "They
will always be with us, just like the hate groups." If anyone should
have known better, it was Byrne, who in June of 1994 was stung by
the same charge of hypocrisy that had hurt Phyllis Schlafly in
1992. Upset at her father's position on the issue, Byrne's daughter
Shannon announced that she was a lesbian. "I'm sorry for what my
dad has done," Shannon Byrne told the *Southern Voice*, a gay
newspaper in Atlanta. "My dad and the commissioners . . . have
absolutely no right to condemn us." Byrne was left to scramble for
an explanation. "I'm not going to damn her because of it or close
her out of my life because of it, but the gay lifestyle as a lifestyle,
I cannot, will not, and do not condone." His response was far different from the resolution he had so wholeheartedly supported,
which pointedly and harshly described his daughter's sexual orientation as against the laws of the state.

The possibility that the Atlanta Committee for the Olympic
Games might relocate the volleyball event also brought Rep.
Newt Gingrich into the debate. Describing the boycott threat as
"emotional blackmail," Gingrich described Cobb County as "a
dramatically freer and more decent place than some of the countries that participate in the Olympics." While that was true, it belittled the importance of the antigay resolution to the gays and
lesbians in the county. Cobb County might not be North Korea,
but that still did not let it off the hook.

As the spring of 1994 progressed, pressure built to repeal the
resolution that was the wellspring of the controversy. More than
three dozen clergy called on the commission to undo the vote,
prompting Wysong to respond, "I don't typically think religion be-
longs in politics, so their position on religion is not an issue"—an
astonishing statement from someone who consulted a Baptist
minister before introducing his measure. Nor did his position
seem to apply to his allies in the clergy, let alone himself. Re-

sponding to the first group of clergy, 250 local ministers endorsed the original resolution. One minister from that group declared, "What we're battling against is a dark and fallen foe. Anyplace we can go toe-to-toe with Satan is a good place to wage that battle." National leaders of the religious right also rallied to Cobb County's support. Pat Robertson held a Christian Coalition fundraiser in June. "It's mom and dad and apple pie," Pat Gartland, president of the state chapter of the Christian Coalition, said. "They made a resolution that this is a family-oriented county, and all of a sudden it's blown all out of proportion." Curiously, the speaker for the event was Dick Cheney, the former secretary of defense. Given that Wysong's original impetus was to make a statement about gays in the military, it was ironic to say the least that the Coalition's speaker would be the man who once dismissed the security rationale for the ban as an "old chestnut" and who had had an allegedly gay man as a chief aide from his days in Congress through to his stint at the Pentagon.

The Atlanta Committee for the Olympic Games reacted to the pressure by trying to elicit a compromise from the county commission, but the commission was unresponsive, voting against a proposal to water down the original measure. "Basically, I don't think there is any compromise on this issue," Wysong said. "I was comfortable with the original resolution, and I didn't see that this would accomplish anything." Byrne said that he was resentful of the pressure and that, if it wanted to, the commission could "withdraw the proposal and tell the Atlanta Committee to find another place." For many Cobb County residents, this was putting a questionable principle above civic interests, contributing to the growing disdain for politics that Americans everywhere felt. When the Olympic organizers finally announced in August 1994 that they would relocate the volleyball event, residents reacted bitterly. "Forever and always Cobb County and the Cobb Galleria Centre will be recognized as the community that had a chance to participate in the Olympics and threw it away," said Tad Leithead, chairman of the local chamber of commerce. "It's a travesty. It makes you want to cry." For his part, Wysong seemed not to care at all. "My view is they ought to do whatever's best for the Olympics," he said blandly.

⟶ The single greatest example of politicians willing to make a statement at the expense of taxpayers occurred in Williamson County, Texas, just months after Wysong introduced his resolution in Cobb County. For years, Texas officials had been luring high-tech firms from Silicon Valley with the promise of lower taxes and operating costs. By the fall of 1993, Williamson County was on the verge of becoming one of the biggest beneficiaries of the courtship. Apple Computer decided to build an $80 million complex in the county, which was just outside Austin. The 130-acre campus would originally employ seven hundred people full-time, but a county study estimated that the eventual ripple effect from the relocation could be as many as forty-five hundred jobs pouring $300 million into the local economy. It was a prospect that would set most politicians salivating. Not in Williamson County. Two county commissioners announced in October that they were not willing to grant Apple the $750,000 tax break that it had asked for because the company offered domestic-partnership benefits to gays and lesbians. Commissioner Jerry Mehevec said he opposed such policies "because those companies are destroying the family as we know them in America." Commissioner Greg Boatright echoed the sentiment, saying domestic partnership benefits are "detrimental to the family and what Williamson County stands for." That losing hundreds of good-paying, reliable jobs in an expanding industry was truly detrimental to local families never seemed to have entered Mehevec's or Boatright's minds.

Domestic-partnership benefits were hardly the rage in corporate America. While they often applied equally to gay and straight couples, it was the gay benefits that attracted the most attention and criticism. Only a handful of companies offered them, and many of those were Silicon Valley firms who had a high number of openly gay employees. Software giant Lotus started the trend in 1991, and it quickly became recognized as the next step beyond a nondiscrimination policy. Employers from Microsoft to Yale University to Levi Strauss had adopted the benefit plan on the principle that equal work deserved equal compensation, including equal benefits. For gays and lesbians, domestic-partnership benefits were a statement that they were more than just tolerated by their employers; they were fully accepted and their relationships were given equal weight to those of their heterosexual coworkers. For corporations, the policies were relatively low-cost ways of trying to attract talented workers; since both partners in gay relationships often received insurance coverage from their respective employers, the policy was used by at most a handful of employees. In the high-tech industry, where competition for skilled workers was fierce and turnover high, domestic partnership was one more lure to reel in potential employees.

The religious right did not see it that way, of course, viewing it as simply the first step toward gay marriage. Robert Knight, the director of cultural studies at the Family Research Council, Gary Bauer's Washington-based think tank affiliated with Focus on the Family, described domestic partnership benefits, along with gay marriages, as "really wedges designed to overturn traditional sexual morality." Knight listed seven reasons for opposing the benefits, on the grounds that they "deny the procreative imperative," "injure the crucial kinship structure," somehow "breed cynicism," and pave the way for gay adoption "despite the clear danger this poses to children's development of healthy sexual identities." Knight insisted that "cities, corporations and universities are being lobbied or intimidated into conferring marital benefits on same-sex couples." (*Intimidation* was a code word the religious right used against gays and lesbians to describe the kind of powers of persuasion that conservative Christians employed as well; Knight and his allies could not even concede gays the right to the same kind of tactics that they themselves employed.) The benefits were far more circumscribed than Knight would allow; what they amounted to was the right of an employee's proven domestic partner to the same benefits a married spouse would have. Generally, that meant health insurance at an additional charge, along with bereavement leave.

Knight's boss, Gary Bauer, seemed less willing to define the trend as the result of unspecified "intimidation." Rather, he pinned the blame on the companies themselves. "A lot of the leftist effort to redefine what a family is by extending benefits to same-sex partners or to advance the multicultural agenda with its insistence on quotas of all sorts is actively being embraced by large companies," he told *Fortune* magazine. As for the culture war, Bauer declared, "Business isn't going to be able to stay neutral in this fight, any more than someone could in 1773 as the American Revolution began to build." As *Fortune* pointed out, the religious right had a deep distrust of the *Fortune* 500 and other big firms, seeing in corporate America a weak ally at best, despite its Republican leanings. As the Christian Coalition's Ralph Reed put it, "You just can't focus on economic arguments and ignore family values."

That was the contention of the Williamson County commissioners. Indeed, they seemed to go Reed one better; they were willing to ignore economic arguments in favor of family values. On November 30, the commission voted 3–2 to deny Apple a tax break, even though Apple had made it clear that it would take the complex—and the jobs—elsewhere if the commission turned its request down. The meeting was occasionally raucous, with some people shouting that America was "not founded on same-sex lovers and live-in lovers." The vote was a reversal of past policy; the commission had in the past routinely approved the abatements for Dell Computer and five other companies. This time, however, religious conservatives phoned the commission to make their dissatisfaction clear. David Hays, the commission's swing vote, reported getting one hundred phone calls from people who saw Apple's presence leading to an influx of gays and lesbians. "They think supporting a company that has that policy is a blow against family values," said Hays, who defended his stand by saying that he could not bring himself to side with Apple. "If I had voted yes, I would have had to walk into my church with people saying, 'There is the man who brought homosexuality to Williamson County,'" he rationalized—as if gays needed his permission to move to the county or did not already live there in the first place. In fact, throughout the controversy, almost all of the gay presence came from outside Williamson County, reinforcing that stereotype.

Some politicians felt that the commission was meddling where it had no right to be. "I don't agree with the idea of same-sex marriages, but government needs to stay out of business," said Charlie Culpepper, mayor of Round Rock. "Families need jobs." This had been the traditional Republican attitude about corporate enterprise, but Christian activists were advocating a much more intrusive approach. "I just believe if you got moral convictions, there's a time to exercise them or do away with the convictions," said Commissioner Mehevec. The standard applied not only to business; conservative Christians had taken control of the county school board and ousted the school superintendent for not allowing prayer at high school football games, even though he had presided over a rise in students' test scores.

In the face of pressure from Gov. Ann Richards, the commission, and in particular Hays, eventually relented. On December 8, they voted 3–2 for a modified tax break for Apple that provided abatements to the computer giant in return for allowing the county to have rights-of-way on roads in the complex. Hays tried to explain his flip-flop by saying that this time he was not directly voting for a tax break for Apple, so he was not using "taxpayer dollars to subsidize, and therefore, tacitly endorse a benefits policy with which I disagree." Despite the vote, Hays did not back down from the novel belief that politicians should involve themselves in corporate human-resources policies and even reject companies based on those internal policies. On that point, at least, he remained in agreement with Christian activists. The litmus test on gay rights that had once applied only to politicians now applied to business as well.

～ The battle in Williamson County was not solely about national corporate decisions. It was also about a local decision, in nearby Austin, known as the most liberal city in Texas. In September, the month before Mehevec and Boatright made their opposition to Apple known, the Austin city council passed a domestic-partnership policy for city employees, at the urging of gay activists. As had happened so often before, the vote prompted a backlash and the promise of a referendum. Under the banner Concerned Texans Inc., led by the Reverend Charles Bullock of the Christ Memorial Independent Baptist Church, conservative Christians quickly gathered the necessary signatures to put the policy on the May 1994 ballot as Proposition 22.

Bullock had been involved in other antigay crusades, having taken it upon himself to lead other clergy in a campaign against homosexuality in 1992, after a lesbian couple's wedding announcement ran in the *Austin American-Statesman.* He tried to coach his opposition to the city's domestic-partnership policy in economic terms. "We think it's irresponsible spending by the city in light of all the other problems we have," he said in April. But the economic argument made little sense. Even as Bullock spoke, the city had spent only $104,000 on the policy, which was used over three times more often by heterosexual couples than same-sex pairs. The real heart of Bullock's argument was that the policy was, in his words, "morally wrong," the first of three reasons cited in a full-page newspaper ad placed by Concerned Texans. Other supporters reinforced the religious argument driving the political debate. One local church had a sign declaring before the election GOD VOTED FOR PROP. 22 (presumably by absentee ballot). While Concerned Texans denied any outside funding, they did get a boost from a familiar source: Kevin Tebedo of Colorado for Family Values, who made an appearance in Austin to promote the antigay cause.

The campaign that followed fit the same pattern that other referenda did. Gays and lesbians organized a campaign under the title Mainstream Austin Coalition, whose primary campaign argument was that the policy was about the right to health care. But voters were more concerned that it was their money being spent, not what it was being spent on, and on that point at least, the campaign was never able to come up with a good response. Instead, it chose to characterize Concerned Texans Inc. as nothing more than, in the words of campaign manager Mark Yznaga, "the radical right," which may have been what the group was, but which still did not get at taxpayers' qualms. Although national gay groups did provide the campaign advice and, in the case of the Human Rights Campaign Fund, personnel, the domestic-partnership policy was repealed by an overwhelming 62 percent to 38 percent. As Dianne Hardy-Garcia, executive director of the Lesbian and Gay Rights Lobby of Texas, noted, the gay community simply did not have the structures in place to provide what the campaign needed most: money. Without some kind of national organization that could channel money to each site of the antigay battles, every campaign was forced to start its fund-raising from scratch, with all the attending problems.

As much of a setback as the Austin vote was, it dimmed in comparison to the legacy of gay-bashing to which the antigay rhetoric in Texas contributed. On the same night that the Williamson County commission voted down Apple's tax break, three young men in Tyler came across Nick West, an openly gay medical clerk, in a local park. The men took West to a gravel pit ten miles outside of town and held him hostage for several hours, terrorizing him. Finally, they shot him at least nine times with a shotgun and two .357 magnum revolvers. Before the arrest of the trio, the first in the state for an antigay hate crime, one of the group boasted that he enjoyed "fag-bashing."

Hardy-Garcia saw the death of West as the inevitable result of teaching hatred against homosexuals and organized a rally in Tyler to underscore the point. "We will not be silent about this hate crime," she promised. Indeed, Texas had seen a virtual epidemic of antigay murders in the past several years, nauseating in their viciousness. In one case, a gay man had his hands bound behind his back while he was repeatedly stabbed, his throat slit, and his genitals cut off. In another, a gay man was stabbed and thrown through a plate-glass window. Although prosecutors vigorously pursued the West case, law enforcement officials, judges, and juries were not always so concerned about serving justice. A man who impaled a gay man on a tree limb and left him for dead got probation. In the most notorious incident, Dallas judge Jack Hampton went easy on an eighteen-year-old who with a pal had shot to death two gay men on the grounds that "prostitutes and gays [are] at about the same level. . . . I'd be hard put to give somebody life for killing a prostitute."

Conservative Christians denied that their rhetoric had anything to do with violence against gays. "The people who did those murders had hate in their hearts," said Kirk Ingels, chairman of the Christian Coalition's Austin chapter. "No true Christian would ever do anything like that, even though we are adamantly opposed to the homosexual agenda and its spread." But the religious right's condemnation of homosexuality was often so harsh that it was hard to separate it from a condemnation of gays and lesbians, no matter what the disclaimers might be. And the distinction between sin and sinner, between homosexuality and gays and lesbians, that the religious right made was an abstraction that was easy to disregard. If the sinner embodied the sin, it wasn't hard to hate the person as well. In fact, the person was in a real sense the personification of the sin. An outburst of antigay rhetoric invariably led to a rise in antigay threats and attacks, as had happened with Jon Greaves in Cobb County, and in Oregon and Colorado. Gay-bashers in Texas and elsewhere may have had hate in their hearts, but hate had already been on the lips of others before the assaults ever began. The constant attacks on gays and lesbians by politicians and religious right activists throughout the country only brought the rhetoric that much closer to ugly reality.

CHAPTER 7

Family Values

B Y THE TIME SHE REACHED THE AGE OF THIRTY in 1990, Ninia Baehr felt that something was missing in her life. A feminist with a master's degree in women's studies, she had participated in her share of radical politics. She had spent the last couple of years traveling the women's music festival circuit, eking out a modest living selling sex toys to lesbians. "I would think to myself, 'Wow, I've met thousands of lesbians and there isn't one for me,'" she said in a 1994 interview. "I was just lonely, thinking I was going to be alone for the rest of my life." After Baehr moved back to Hawaii in 1990, Baehr's mother set her up on a blind date with another young woman, Genora Dancel. It was love at first sight. After just a few dates, the two realized that they wanted to spend the rest of their lives together. Unbeknownst to the happy young couple at the time, their meeting would be the genesis of a gay marriage movement heard round the world.

In September 1990, Baehr and Dancel joined another lesbian couple, Tammy Rodriguez and Antoinette Pregil, and a gay male couple, Pat Lagon and Joseph Melillo, in applying for marriage licenses from the state of Hawaii. Across the country, the scene had been repeated with increasing frequency since the early 1970s. Like a growing number of gays and lesbians, the couples felt that with the exception of legal sanction, their relationships represented a lifetime commitment to one another that was equivalent to any traditional heterosexual marriage. Baehr and Dancel's love for each other only intensified their anger when, as expected, the state denied their application. Given their intense devotion and careful courtship, and with so many unprepared opposite-sex couples diving headlong into matrimony, they could see no reason why they were denied equal access to the institution. Planning for their future together meant struggling with many of the issues married couples took for granted: the right to visit a sick spouse or child in the hospital; joint tax returns; spousal health and social security benefits; and inheritance rights, to name just a few.

Ignoring repeated warnings that they were more likely to be struck by lightning than to succeed, the six filed suit against the state of Hawaii, seeking a permanent end to the ban on same-sex marriage. But in the mainland, many veteran gay activists showed considerably less enthusiasm for the couples' cause. Convinced that it was not only a losing legal battle, but a public relations disaster, national gay and lesbian organizations discouraged them from pursuing the case. Based on the bleak history of such challenges, the activists were sure the challenge would go down in flames. Furthermore, they worried that efforts to secure gay marriage rights seemed to legitimize the claims of gay rights foes, whose allegations that antidiscrimination protections inevitably led to same-sex marriage had been dismissed as canards by national leaders. To them, the couples looked like renegades with their own agenda. Moreover, the activists, many of whom had gotten their start in the sexual liberationist 1960s and 1970s, were inclined to see marriage as a vestige of patriarchy. They feared that by seeking the right to marriage, gays and lesbians would merely be legitimizing a repressive institution.

At first the prognosis of the gay groups was confirmed. A state court rejected the lawsuit on the grounds that the ban on gay marriage is "obviously designed to promote the general welfare interests of the community by sanctioning traditional man-woman family units and procreation. But what happened next struck the couples and the nation like a clap of thunder. In May 1993, the Hawaii Supreme Court, relying on an obscure footnote in the plaintiffs' court papers, declared that the denial of the couples' marriage license applications appeared to violate the equal-protection clause of the state constitution, which prohibits gender-based discrimination.

The case, *Baehr v. Lewin,* was remanded to a lower court for a trial, in which the state would be forced to prove that the marriage ban is justified by "compelling interest," the highest possible burden of proof the state could be required to meet. The court warned the state to avoid the usual assortment of "unreliable data, irrational misconceptions, and insupportable misrepresentations about homosexuals. . . . Constitutional law may mandate, like it or not, that customs change with an evolving social order." After several delays—and barely controlled fury among religious conservatives—the case was scheduled for trial in July 1996, smack in the middle of the presidential election.

Immediately after the Hawaii court ruling in 1993, shock waves began to ripple outward. State legislatures, many dominated by right-wing Republicans who had ridden the 1994 GOP riptide into office, began considering proposals to supersede their constitutions' "full faith and credit" provisions, which require states to honor one another's contracts, in regards to prospective gay marriage licenses granted in Hawaii. The issue even contributed to Arizona's Democratic gubernatorial candidate Eddie Basha's defeat; after suggesting he supported the probable pro-gay outcome of the Hawaii case—and was lambasted for it by his Republican opponent—his poll numbers dropped precipitously. Much like the gays-in-the-military debacle, another backlash seemed poised to break loose.

The Hawaii case was only the most visible outgrowth of an even larger movement among gays and lesbians to form families and raise children with full legal sanction. For years, gays and lesbians had been having their relationships blessed by spiritual authorities. The Reverend Troy Perry, for instance, had performed same-sex commitment ceremonies at the predominantly gay Metropolitan Community Church since its founding in 1968 in the minister's living room, using his coffee table as an altar. At the 1993 Gay and Lesbian March on Washington, D.C., Perry performed a mass wedding of hundreds of same-sex couples dressed in tuxedos and wedding gowns. Other gays looked to sympathetic Unitarian Universalist ministers to conduct ceremonies, taking advantage of the association's tradition of inclusive doctrine. The embrace of home and hearth was taking on increasing political overtones, catapulting demands for gay marriage, domestic-partnership benefits, and parenting, adoption, and custody rights to the top of the nation's gay rights agenda and becoming part and parcel of arguments to strike down discrimination.

The seeming cruelty of antigay court rulings contributed to the urgency of the cause. In September 1993, for instance, Sharon Bottoms became a symbol for the plight of gay parents everywhere when a Virginia court, citing the "moral climate" of the home, stripped her of custody of her two-year-old son, Tyler, because she is lesbian. The Bottoms case made national headlines, but for years gays and lesbians had quietly suffered a series of stunning personal losses that underlined the need for legal protections. Lesbians were particularly hard hit by custody cases in which homophobic court rulings stripped them of their biological children, born from failed heterosexual marriages. Gays and lesbians were not only losing their children. In 1983, Karen Thompson was barred from seeing her partner, Sharon Kowalski, after Kowalski was paralyzed and brain damaged in an automobile accident. Because their long-term relationship lacked legal standing, Thompson could only watch with horror as Kowalski's antigay parents, who had never approved of the relationship, were awarded sole guardianship. (In 1991, a state court overturned the decision, awarding Thompson guardianship.)

For gay men, AIDS stripped away most vestiges of economic and social privilege they might have had in comparison to lesbians. Many lost the apartments they had shared, sometimes for decades, with their deceased male partners after nursing them through long, painful illnesses and the throes of death. Many saw the families of their partners descend on their homes shortly after his death to claim possessions, even though the families had harshly rejected their son because of his homosexuality during his life.

The effort to win recognition for gay and lesbian families represented a major shift from the 1960s and 1970s. In those early decades, the movement, then led by a small group of left-wing activists, was dominated by demands for sexual liberation and radical social change. As the movement expanded to include a larger and ideologically more diverse mix of activists, the liberationist rhetoric fell out of vogue, and the movement began to mirror consciousness of AIDS and the more conservative mores of the 1980s and 1990s. Before the 1980s, when AIDS and increasing acceptance collaborated to bring gays and lesbians out of the closet in huge numbers, few homosexuals believed they had the option of raising children while being open about their sexual orientation. Many gays and lesbians simply moved to big cities, leaving family ties scattered across the country. Those lesbian or gay parents who remained in more rural areas often sought to cloak their relationships in what they believed to be a thick, protective coat of privacy, only to face intrusive, often bigoted interventions by neighbors, family members, or covetous ex-spouses. By the 1980s and 1990s, however, gays and lesbians were increasingly accepted by and integrated into their biological families, which could help support their relationships and offspring. Sex was out and family—with its attendant commitments—was in. The fierce, long-simmering debate among the community's intellectual leaders over assimilation—whether gays were just another ethnic group to be absorbed by America's melting pot or a distinct subculture, like black nationalists, that desires no part of the larger, corrupt society—sounded increasingly outdated because it ignored the new reality of how gays and lesbians were living their lives.

The outpouring of support among the gay rank and file for marriage and adoption rights made it clear that the community was already integrating into the larger culture and invoking its most cherished values in heretical ways. The majority of homosexuals, who live outside the big cities, were already assimilated through family ties, work, church, and community. While sexual culture, even in the midst of the century's worst epidemic, and radical politics, even in the midst of conservative backlash, both continued to flourish, more and more gays were choosing to settle down, form relationships, and raise children.

The emphasis on family matters put gays and lesbians on a collision course with the religious right's own family-values campaign, which sought to define *family* in strict, traditional patriarchal terms. The new playing field presented thorny new problems for both sides of the debate. For the good part of its political history, the gay community's rhetoric conceded the institution of family to the religious right. Now the emerging portrait of homosexuals as responsible, hardworking family men and women was far more likely to win the sympathy of most Americans. Yet the religious right, hell-bent on depicting gays as threats to the heterosexual family, refused to recognize that many gays and lesbians maintained stable, loving relationships that are virtually identical to those of heterosexuals in substance, if not in form.

In its passionate demand for marriage and family rights, however, gays and lesbians may have failed fully to comprehend the issue's enormous potential for backlash. Most Americans were willing to tolerate homosexuals as long as they were relegated to invisibility and second-class status, and conservative legislators are gearing up to enshrine opposition to gay marriage into law. Normally supportive heterosexuals were asking themselves if they should accept gay marriage when they were only beginning to come around on job discrimination, which doesn't challenge cherished social structures. Coming off the gays-in-the-military fight, it was not surprising that the remaining American institution that formally discriminated against gays and lesbians would become the next major battleground. But as with the military debate, the movement never conducted a public conversation that would allow it to weigh the tension between the moral attractiveness of the issue and its political expediency.

~~ Nowhere was the ideological clash more evident than in Hawaii. With its small gay community and placid but liberal-leaning political environment, it was an unlikely place for a national gay marriage debate to originate. It took three dedicated gay couples with little political experience and a straight attorney to bring the issue to the forefront of the gay rights debate.

Convinced that the case was a surefire loser, neither the American Civil Liberties Union of Hawaii nor the Lambda Legal Defense and Education Fund, the country's largest gay legal group, based in New York City, would touch the case. So Bill Woods, a veteran gay activist and founder of Hawaii's Gay Marriage Project, recruited his old friend Dan Foley, the former legal director of the ACLU, who was then in private practice. Laid-back, but with a fierce commitment to civil rights, Foley agreed to represent the couples despite the long odds because he saw marriage laws as fundamentally unjust to homosexuals. To him, gay marriage bans were comparable to miscegenation laws, prohibiting interracial marriage, which the U.S. Supreme Court eventually struck down in 1967.

A San Francisco native, Foley grew up with a keen awareness of antigay discrimination. His beloved uncle, who opened one of the first gay bars in Marin County in the 1950s, suffered greatly at the hands of his rigid Irish Catholic family. As a sociology major at the University of San Francisco in 1969, Foley, with his uncle's coaching, wrote his senior thesis on the treatment of sexual minorities in America. By the time he took on the case, Foley was extremely well versed on gay rights issues. At the ACLU in 1985, he successfully sued the island of Maui when the mayor, under pressure from the religious right, revoked a park permit for the Miss Gay Molokai Pageant, an annual drag carnival. In 1988, he persuaded a state court to overturn an antiporn statute on the grounds that it violated the right to privacy of consumers.

But Foley had another motive for his work. A devout Buddhist, Foley worried about what he saw as the religious right's tendency to articulate moral values that represented the views of only a fraction of religious believers. In their quest for a more "Christian" nation, Foley felt that the religious right posed as much of a threat to religious minorities as to sexual ones. Researching homosexuality at his local Buddhist temple, Foley discovered that his faith did not distinguish between sexual orientations. What mattered in the Buddhist tradition was individual sexual responsibility, not identity. In the three gay couples, as committed and loving as any heterosexual pairs, Foley knew he had stumbled upon ideal clients. This was one case in which the religious right, try as they might, would be hard-pressed to depict gays as sex-crazed child molesters. While his clients in the two previous cases—drag queens and porn consumers—were as deserving of legal protection as anyone else, they reinforced, rather than broke down, a conservative public's stereotyped understanding of sexual minorities.

Foley warned the enthusiastic couples that the odds were long. Courts in Kentucky, Minnesota, and Washington State had rejected 1970s-era legal challenges out of hand. As recently as 1993, a District of Columbia judge dismissed a challenge to the city's ban on same-sex marriage on the grounds that the Ten Commandments and the biblical book of Genesis defined marriage as a heterosexual institution—and this in perhaps the nation's most liberal political bastion. "If homosexual marriage was anathema to [early] Christian dogma and morally repugnant," D.C. superior court judge Shellie Bowers wrote in his angry ruling, "it would still be so."

At the same time, Foley knew he was holding some trump cards. With its liberal judiciary, long tradition of tolerance for diversity, and native culture of flourishing same-sex relationships, Hawaii, where flouting mainland taboos could be a virtue rather than a vice, was perhaps the best state in the country in which to mount a challenge to marriage laws. The first state in the country to legalize abortion, in 1970, and to ratify the Equal Rights Amendment, Hawaii boasted of a model universal health-care program and of a social climate where mixed-race marriages were practically the norm. The state's large minority population, into which the religious right had made few advances, made it sympathetic to civil rights claims. Japanese-Americans alone composed more than one-quarter of the islands' population. Drawing explicit comparisons between the treatment of gays and their own internment during World War II, the Japanese-American Citizens League—after a bloody internecine battle—voted to endorse the court decision.

Foley also knew that local activists could be mobilized to oppose the influence of the same out-of-state religious right groups that had aided the antigay cause so effectively in Oregon and Colorado. In 1981, when Jerry Falwell and his Moral Majority were at their zenith, the televangelist traveled to Hawaii on a mission to "save the fiftieth state," as *Out* magazine has reported. Alerted by news reports of Falwell's upcoming visit, Woods and a group of local activists prepared to send him back to his Lynchburg home. Because Falwell had yet to incorporate a Moral Majority chapter in the state, the group was able to register the name for themselves. The upstarts took out ads in local papers announcing that the Moral Majority of Hawaii stood for a variety of liberal causes, including abortion rights, gay rights, and the separation of church and state. When Falwell finally appeared, he was met by close to three thousand protesters and a summons from a local sheriff, who informed him that the newly formed group was suing him for copyright infringement. Falwell left the islands with his tail between his legs.

Still, in its opposition to gay marriage, the religious right had many allies. Even liberals otherwise sympathetic to gay rights draw the line at same-sex unions. Former Hawaii governor John Waihee, who signed the statewide gay rights bill in 1991, balked at the idea of gay marriage, and so did enough lawmakers that a bill expressly banning gay marriages zipped through the legislature. "The state's responsibility in marriages has to do with upholding historical and traditional values in the man-and-woman relationship and the family," Waihee told the *Honolulu Star-Bulletin* in 1993. In a state heavily reliant on its image to attract visitors, tourism officials were mortified at the possibility of Hawaii becoming the same-sex wedding capital of the United States, despite at least one study indicating the state would reap billions of additional tourist dollars, most of them gay, were the state to become a popular destination for gay marriages.

Waihee's opposition was blunted by the election of his successor, Ben Cayetano, a Democrat who bucked the conservative trend of the 1994 election and who was outspoken in his support for gay marriage. And even the state's conservative politicians showed an unusual sensitivity to the gay cause. Though polls showed that Hawaiians opposed the court decision by a two-to-one margin, opposition to the decision was surprisingly tepid. Throughout the arguments before the court, the Waihee administration refused to make what it termed "homophobic arguments" that gay marriage is immoral. The strategy was in sharp contrast to Colorado, where the state went so far as to elicit testimony from antigay researcher Paul Cameron to make its case. The most aggressive opposition came from the Mormon Church, which attempted to make the antigay arguments that the state was avoiding. But the church's notorious, if now repudiated, support for unusual marital arrangements—such as polygamy—made it look hypocritical. To many Hawaiians, especially women, the practice of men taking more than one wife seemed at least as offensive as homosexuality.

Conservative members of the state legislature fared little better. Despite passage of a bill defining marriage as the exclusive domain of opposite-sex couples, Democratic lawmakers, who outnumbered Republicans decisively, managed to kill an amendment declaring that the purpose of marriage was procreation. Since gays don't reproduce, the bill declared, they should be banned from marriage. Liberal lawmakers correctly pointed out that gays do in fact raise children—plaintiffs Tammy Rodriguez and Antoinette Pregil had raised several foster children and a daughter of their own—and that the bill would exclude heterosexuals who did not have children. The idea that marriage was exclusively for procreation had overtones of an "earlier time when women were viewed as chattel and property" and "was a slap in the face for people who chose not to have children, people who are older and get married, people who are disabled and get married," argued Rosalyn Baker, a member of the Senate Judiciary Committee. Even the bill's supporters apologized for their stance. "I was seen as the bad guy, antigay, and that was not my intent," said Terrance Tom, chairman of the House Judiciary Committee.

Since the court had already ruled that the marriage ban was constitutionally suspect, the bill, which was amended to delete the procreation argument, was superfluous. In an effort to mollify gays and lesbians as well as the high court, moderate legislators introduced far-reaching domestic partnership legislation that offered nearly all the legal rights of marriage. The bill never made it out of committee. In the end, the best lawmakers could do was to create a commission to study the issue in more depth. Meanwhile, the fateful trial date drew ever nearer.

Religious conservatives inside the state showed no such respect for their opposition. Already organized after a bitter battle over a statewide antidiscrimination law in the spring of 1991, which Governor Waihee signed into law, they wrote a line in the sand that read *gay marriage*. "The institution of marriage will be further undermined by the state and evil will triumph," warned the *Wanderer*, a conservative Catholic tabloid. The gays-as-Satan imagery did little to dispel claims by gay activists that a far more dangerous and ambitious movement was afoot among the marriage ban's defenders. Gay marriage provided Mike Gabbard, head of Stop Promoting Homosexuality and Common Sense Now, two religious conservative groups based in Honolulu, with the fodder he needed to fill his monthly newsletter, *Stop Promoting Homosexuality*, and weekly radio talk show, *Let's Talk Straight, Hawaii*.

Having gotten his start in antigay activism as an aide to state senator Rick Reed, who advocated concentration camps for everyone who tests HIV-positive, Gabbard had earned credibility with religious conservatives. Yet neither Gabbard's unusual religious and family background nor his race fit the profile of the typical antigay religious fundamentalist. A dedicated Hare Krishna, Gabbard grew up in a prominent family on the island of Samoa. Even from that distance, Gabbard was not immune to one of the worst embarrassments of the religious right. Not long after he began his antigay crusade, one of his cousins appeared on the cover of *Island Lifestyles,* a Honolulu gay weekly, declaring his homosexuality.

In February 1992, Gabbard's animosity toward gays hardened into an abiding personal hatred that made Paul Cameron look like a shrinking violet. After months of picketing by Woods and a small group of gay activists, Gabbard was forced to close his small restaurant, The Natural Deli. Though the business was already teetering on the verge of financial collapse, Gabbard blamed gays for his loss and turned his attention full-time to producing a steady stream of antigay literature. In one edition of his newsletter, he speculated wildly about the private thoughts of gays and lesbians: "What homosexuals haven't realized is that they can't kill God. . . . But in the solitude of their homes late at night with the curtains drawn, when the false mask of being 'gay' is taken off, when the feelings of guilt and shame surface, when the emptiness, loneliness and pain set in, these so called 'homosexuals' cannot hide from the Truth." The "Truth," according to Gabbard, is that God is "providing encouragement to get back on the right track." Yet for Baehr and Dancel—and increasing numbers of gays and lesbians across the country—it was their relationship that had put them on the right track and the ban on same-sex marriages that threatened to derail them.

In the Hawaii marriage debate, national religious right groups saw the beginning of a movement whose advent they had long anticipated with dread. "This is a front-burner issue, because if you destroy the heterosexual ethic, then you are destroying a major pillar of Western civilization," said the Reverend Lou Sheldon, president of the Traditional Values Coalition, based in Anaheim, California. "I don't think Hawaii wants to be known in a pejorative way as favoring homosexual marriage. It's too much of a family resort place."

Ignoring the hard lessons Jerry Falwell had learned in the state more than a decade earlier, religious right groups flocked to the state to get a piece of the marriage action. The Rutherford Institute, a national Christian legal group based in Charlottesville, Virginia, asked the state supreme court to reject the marriage suit on the grounds that it would provide "special status" to violence-prone, mentally ill homosexuals. Rutherford had gained a foothold in the state in 1991 by challenging the state's gay rights act on the grounds that it violated the First Amendment rights of religious institutions. Noting that the bill, like similar ones across the country, specifically exempts religious institutions from its reach—and that no religious group in the state had ever complained that it had been applied to them—a federal court judge dismissed the suit as frivolous. Rutherford's legal strategy, which they tried in several states, proved a disaster. In rejecting a Rutherford Institute suit against New Jersey's gay rights bill, which also includes a strong religious exemption, U.S. district court judge William Bassler put it even more strongly: "There is a clear conclusion that the statute is not intended to apply to the exercise of religion. There is no way on God's earth that this statute would ever be applied to church services."

Like other religious right groups, Rutherford argued that antidiscrimination protections for homosexuals violated the free speech and association rights of Christians who believe homosexuality is a sin. "The problem is that once homosexuals are given special civil rights—above and beyond those you and I enjoy—religious persons, ministries, and churches will be forced to accept the homosexual lifestyle in our workplaces, privately owned businesses, public schools, and even in our local churches," the group warned ominously in a 1993 fund-raising letter. Even by the low standard of accuracy established by fund-raising letters, the Institute's missive was disingenuous. Not only do antidiscrimination bills uniformly contain exemptions for religious institutions, they also routinely include religion in their list of protected categories. The bills did not, as the Rutherford Institute suggests, provide gays and lesbians rights "beyond" those of religious believers. Indeed, they treated religion and sexual orientation in precisely the same manner. People who face discrimination—whether it be on the grounds of religion or sexual orientation—in housing, employment, or public accommodations have the right to file suit under the same provision of the law. And with religion already protected at the federal level under the 1964 Civil Rights Act, people of faith could avail themselves of a uniform national protection that gays conspicuously lacked.

In the gay marriage case, the Rutherford Institute's tendency to exaggerate its claims may have come back to haunt it. When the case reached the state supreme court, the group submitted a two-hundred-page brief replete with sexually explicit descriptions culled from gay porn magazines and demonstrably false statistics quoted directly from antigay literature. According to those close to the case, Associate Justice Steven Levinson, the Jewish author of the plurality opinion, was reportedly struck by the similarities between the group's antigay diatribes and classic anti-Semitic arguments.

Founded by attorney John Whitehead, a former agnostic who was "born again" in 1974 after reading a book on biblical prophecy, the Rutherford Institute is on the leading edge of the religious right's legal movement that encompasses such groups as the National Legal Foundation, which drafted Colorado's antigay initiative, and Pat Robertson's American Center for Law and Justice. Samuel Rutherford, after whom the Institute was named, was an obscure seventeenth-century Scottish theologian who argued in his book *Law and the Prince* that the Bible should form the basis for constitutional law. Similarly, Whitehead believes that the traditional separation of church and state is a liberal conspiracy to eviscerate Christianity in America. The antiestablishment clause of the First Amendment, Whitehead argues, was intended by the founders to prevent the federal government from instituting a national church, not ban the state from supporting Christian doctrine. (Pat Robertson has alternately called church-state separation a "lie of the left" and a "Soviet concept.")

Whitehead often refers to Rutherford as the American Civil Liberties Union of the religious right. But Rutherford lacks the ACLU's bipartisan spirit and meticulous attention to precedent. The civil liberties group routinely defends anyone—liberal or conservative, straight or gay—whose constitutional rights have been trampled upon. Whitehead has attempted to make a similar claim. In his publication, *Rutherford* for instance, Whitehead brags of defending Herbert Hall, an AIDS educator at He Intends Victory, a Christian AIDS ministry in Irvine, California. But Hall describes himself as an ex-homosexual who was born again when he learned that he had tested HIV-positive. (Rutherford sued the American Red Cross for religious-based discrimination, charging that the organization violated Hall's rights by denying him certification as an AIDS educator because of his fundamentalist beliefs.)

In his 1994 book, *Religious Apartheid: The Separation of Religion From American Public Life,* Whitehead argues that the discrimination inflicted on fundamentalist Christians by the separation of church and state in the United States is analogous to the effect of apartheid on South African blacks. "From the removal of crosses and nativity scenes in public places to the prohibition of individual prayer in the schools, examples of this apartheid are occurring daily (sometimes hourly) throughout the country," he wrote. But Whitehead's analogy is no more illuminating than the gays-as-Holocaust-victims analogy. While he can point, with some justification, to scores of instances in which fundamentalist Christians are ridiculed for their ideas, he trivializes the horror of apartheid—which contributes to the oppression on an entire race and which devolved from a long history of such oppression—to equate it to the plight of evangelical Christians in America. Evangelicals have shown how false the point is by their use of one of the fundamental rights of citizenship South African blacks were routinely denied: the right to vote. Just because a group could—and had never been denied the right to—vote did not mean it was free from genuine oppression, as is the case with gays and lesbians. Nonetheless, such exaggerations threatened to undermine efforts by Rutherford and other religious right groups to appeal to people of color, many of whom manifest a robust suspicion of the groups' political priorities and a well-founded distrust of the lack of diversity in their leadership ranks. While categorizing fundamentalist Christians as a persecuted class, a common classification claimed by gays and lesbians as well, Whitehead posits homosexuals as the moral equivalent of the

South African white-minority ruling class, subjecting others to their values by legal coercion. "The family, once the bedrock of society, is under siege from state agencies and culture at large," he explained in *Religious Apartheid*. "As new forms of family, such as homosexual liaisons, gain more acceptance, the traditional family is losing its authority."

In a 1990 interview with *Church & State,* a publication of the liberal lobby group Americans United for the Separation of Church and State, Whitehead declared that the fear among civil libertarians that the religious right will one day impose Christianity on the nation is "absurd. . . . Anyone who comes to me and tells me the church is going to take over the government, that to me is a totally laughing matter." While he might not have desired a nation run by the church, Whitehead clearly wanted biblical values—right-wing biblical values—to hold greater weight than secular ones. Because he believed that Christian arguments are inviolable, Whitehead failed to countenance that opposing perspectives merit careful consideration or even that the separation of church and state actually helped insure religious liberty and limit religious tyranny. Under Whitehead's philosophy, his own organization might suffer as much as gay ones. If church-state separation withered and died, many Christian right groups would lose the tax exemptions that have allowed private religious institutions to flourish unencumbered by standard state regulation.

～ At the outset of the marriage battle, Foley and his gay clients received little assistance from the national gay groups. It was only as the case advanced—and the odds of winning improved—that the gay leadership decided to adopt the issue themselves. "The politically savvy thought we were nuts and didn't really want to touch us," complained Baehr. To their credit, the gay lawyers worried that in their eagerness to gain marriage rights, gays and lesbians were marching lemminglike into the sea. In testing gay marriage at the state level they saw the potential for dozens of mini *Bowers v. Hardwick,* the devastating 1986 U.S. Supreme Court ruling upholding sodomy statutes. Antigay courts were not the only thing worrying gay activists. Polls have consistently shown that only a small minority of Americans support legalizing same-sex marriages, and the gay leadership realized that gay marriage is an issue far ahead of what the overwhelming majority of citizens are willing to accept. Only recently, in fact, have surveys shown a majority of the public opposing workplace discrimination against gays, a far less challenging position.

At the same time, many influential activists had a deep-seated philosophical antipathy to the institution of marriage that had little to do with the merits of the case. Before signing on to the Hawaii case, instead of laying the groundwork for the inevitable battle, the gay leadership devoted much of its time to esoteric arguments about whether mimicry of the traditionally straight institution of marriage was damaging the gay *liberation* movement. The parameters of the debate were illustrated in the fall 1989 edition of *Out/Look,* an academic gay quarterly that ceased publication in 1993. Squaring off were the two top attorneys at Lambda—Tom Stoddard, its executive director, and Paula Ettelbrick, its legal director. Even Stoddard, who supported gay marriage rights, apologized in the article for his support for the "oppressive" institution of marriage. But by gaining the legal right to marry, he argued, gays and lesbians would transform the institution by "abolishing the traditional gender requirements of marriage. . . . [Gay marriage] can be one of the means, perhaps the principal one, through which the institution divests itself of the sexist trappings of the past." Stoddard explained somewhat defensively that he himself would be unlikely to marry "even though I share a household with another man who is exceedingly dear to me." Stoddard concluded his essay, which was written before the Hawaii legal challenge was filed, by predicting that gays and lesbians would "earn the right for themselves sooner than most of us imagine."*

Ettelbrick, however, saw the gay marriage movement as in-

---

* As the marriage debate took off, however, Stoddard, like many gay leaders, would warm up to the idea. In 1994, Stoddard "married" his partner in a commitment ceremony.

herently assimilationist and thus corrupt. "The thought of emphasizing our sameness to married heterosexuals in order to obtain this 'right' terrifies me," she wrote in the *Out/Look* article. "It rips away at the very heart and soul of what I believe it is to be a lesbian in this world. It robs me of the opportunity to make a difference." As an alternative, Ettelbrick proposed pursuing domestic-partnership legislation, which she said liberates relationships from society's narrow definition of them. Only that way, she said, will gays and lesbians remain committed to "pushing the parameters of sex, sexuality, family, and in the process transforming the very fabric of society." Ettelbrick's sentiments were noble, but only a small fraction of gays and lesbians have shown the desire or the ability to live their lives as political dissidents. And, in an age when AIDS has made serious, perhaps irrevocable encroachments on society's sense of sexual exploration, marriage and monogamy have come to symbolize safety and accountability, not enslavement. In Hawaii, for instance, many gays and lesbians viewed the activist cross fire over marriage as a purely esoteric exercise undertaken primarily for the gratification of gay intellectuals on the mainland. Many local gays and lesbians saw same-sex marriage as a logical outgrowth of the tolerance and deep-rooted history of gay archetypes within the indigenous culture, wherein their relationships were accepted without question.

As was the case in the military battle, many in the gay leadership and in the rank and file whose funds kept it afloat were out of sync. A 1994 survey by *The Advocate* of gay men found that 85 percent of respondents said they would marry a same-sex partner if they were legally able to do so. Even more relevant, the poll indicated that gay men identified marriage as a higher priority than even the military ban or a national nondiscrimination bill. While it was wise to advise caution on such a volatile issue—something gay leaders had failed to do in other cases—the activists underestimated just how traditional, perhaps even "assimilationist," many gays and lesbians actually were. Gay couples didn't just want commitment ceremonies, but legally sanctioned marriages in ritual church ceremonies. They wanted, in short, to be just like everyone else.

⟶ Evan Wolfson understood the wellsprings of the drive to create gay and lesbian families. From his many years of gay rights litigation, he also understood the ferocity of the opposition. A pugnacious former Brooklyn district attorney who had cut his teeth as a junior prosecutor in the Iran-contra hearings, Wolfson prevailed upon the Lambda Legal Defense and Education Fund to create a marriage project in 1994, which he would direct from the group's New York City headquarters. From this perch, Wolfson, who served as cocounsel for *Baehr v. Lewin,* would travel the country preparing gays and lesbians for the battle to come, becoming what he would later dub the "Paul Revere" of same-sex marriage. Wolfson was exactly what the gay movement lacked in so many instances—a skilled organizer who had the foresight to anticipate the rough waters ahead. Alternately shunned and attacked by gay activists for his role in promoting gay marriage, especially in the aftermath of the GOP takeover of Congress when many fellow activists considered his exhortations futile, Wolfson feared that the movement was ill equipped for the political backlash likely to follow a legal victory in the case. Already, there were ominous signs.

Wolfson fretted that gays and lesbians from the mainland would travel to Hawaii for a marriage license and then return home expecting to enjoy the legal recognition of marriage. Beginning in the spring of 1995, close to a dozen state legislatures across the country moved to preempt the possibility that they might become complicit in lending credence to Hawaii's law under the U.S. Constitution's "full faith and credit" clause. A flurry of state-by-state legislation and litigation, Wolfson knew, was likely to follow the decision. Moreover, congressional conservatives and right-wing pressure groups were eagerly drawing up federal legislation that would define marriage in traditional heterosexual and thus exclusive terms. Even the state of Hawaii was already threatening to appeal any decision granting marriage rights to gays and lesbians to the U.S. Supreme Court, which was unlikely to sympathize with the Hawaii court's unique logic in the case. "Preparing to win the right to marry, then, does not mean spending the next year and a half planning honeymoon or marriage trips to Hawaii," Wolfson warned in a July 1994 column in *The Advocate*. "Wherever you live, marriage is coming; there will be a tidal wave out of Hawaii that will reach every corner of the country and affect every gay issue. If we are to defend this victory against the inevitable backlash of the bigots and build on it in every state, our organizations, our allies, and each one of us must prepare for battle now."

But not everyone welcomed Wolfson's message about the importance of gay marriage, at least in the terms he defined it. Many activists were already knee deep in issues ranging from hate-crimes to AIDS legislation, and could ill afford to drop everything for the inevitable marriage fight. By hammering away on the issue, Wolfson was indeed the Paul Revere of gay marriage. The problem for the gay movement was, however, that it was not just that the British were coming; any number of well-armed foes were already well entrenched.

 ⟶[Gay and lesbian relationships were increasingly resembling straight relationships in another key respect: children. Through artificial insemination, adoption, and surrogate moms, same-sex couples, and even single gays and lesbians, created families. Both gays and lesbians have had children through heterosexual marriages before they acknowledged their homosexuality and often bring these offspring into subsequent same-sex relationships. Indeed, it was these children who were an essential driving force behind the gay marriage movement. As gays and lesbians formed families, they needed legal recognition for their relationships to help provide for and protect their children, in part from the incursions of antigay activists who would use the state to interfere in those intimate relationships.]

The trend toward gay parenthood, in turn, helped break down the well-worn stereotypes of gays and lesbians as destructive pleasure seekers and child molesters. In the minds of many

Americans, the old images of single gay men cruising the streets—
never an accurate representation—were being replaced by far
less threatening images of happy gay couples and their healthy
children next door. The new image strikes at the heart of the religious right's antigay campaign. If gay marriage infuriated religious
conservatives, gay marriage with children sent them into orbit.
Much of the religious right's conception of gays relied on the
notion that homosexuals, supposedly deprived of procreative
powers, need to "recruit" children, a thinly veiled reference to
pedophilia.

For years one of the religious right's favorite tricks was to link
all gays and lesbians to the agenda of the North American Man-
Boy Love Association, a tiny organization that advocates not only
the abolition of age of consent laws, but also intergenerational sex
between men and boys. In its guide to antigay initiatives, Colorado for Family Values contended that "73 percent of homosexuals incorporate children into their sexual practices." Noting that
NAMBLA was a "regular participant in homosexual marches,"
John Whitehead wrote in *Religious Apartheid* that "the logical im-
plication of American acceptance of homosexuality is the acceptance of pedophilia as simply another form of sexual orientation."
Yet Whitehead and his allies should have known full well that laws
prohibiting discrimination based on sexual orientation routinely
define it as "homosexual," "heterosexual," or "bisexual," and reit-
erate, rather than undermine, the validity of sexual misconduct
laws. Whitehead also conveniently ignored the fact that gays and
lesbians found NAMBLA as distasteful as did heterosexuals. Organizers of gay pride parades admitted NAMBLA only reluctantly, and some have yanked up the welcome mat entirely. Most
national gay groups, at the prompting of the Log Cabin Republicans, a gay Republican group, had passed resolutions condemning
NAMBLA. What little support the group retains in the gay community is derived primarily from sympathy for its mere right to associate and speak freely, not the content of its agenda.

Still, some gay activists played into the religious right's hands
by equivocating in their position toward NAMBLA. Influenced by
the sexual liberationist mores of the early days of the movement,

many thoughtful activists who opposed NAMBLA's goals could not escape the suspicion that to denounce the organization would be to mimic society's condemnation of their own sexual orientation. The highly charged political atmosphere surrounding NAMBLA made it all but impossible to have an intelligent discussion of the group or its agenda. While advocacy of pedophilia obviously had no place in respectable discourse, there was nothing inherently wrong in debating the appropriate age for consent laws. (In states where the age of consent is eighteen, for instance, a nineteen-year-old can be charged with statutory rape for consensual sex with a seventeen-year-old, regardless of the sex of either partner.) But because NAMBLA had become just another game piece in the good-gay/bad-gay ploy, both inside and outside the gay community, such substantive issues were obscured almost entirely.

But while agitators inside the gay movement had urged official condemnation of NAMBLA for years, it took North Carolina senator Jesse Helms to finally convince the gay organizations to put their opposition to NAMBLA on public display. In January 1994, Helms led the successful effort to have the United Nations cut all ties to the Brussels-based International Lesbian and Gay Association because NAMBLA is a member of the group. (Helms learned of the U.N.-NAMBLA connection from *The Lambda Report*, a religious right publication devoted exclusively to "monitoring the gay rights agenda.") In the wake of the incident, every major gay organization issued a press release excoriating NAMBLA. "NAMBLA is not a gay organization," a spokesman for the Human Rights Campaign Fund declared bluntly.

The Boy Scouts ban on openly gay scouts and scoutmasters has played much the same role as NAMBLA in the gay rights debate. Religious right groups portrayed gay protests against the exclusionary policy as tantamount to advocating an opportunity to "recruit." While the stereotype of the leering homosexual scoutmaster continued to play a prominent role in the religious right's fund-raising materials, several recent cases have begun to break it down in the public eye. In 1990, James Dale, a Matawan, New

Jersey, Eagle Scout had his membership terminated by the Scouts after officials learned that he was gay. When he was dismissed, Dale, whose clean-cut, all-American appearance and Eagle Scout background made him the antithesis of the stereotype, was only twenty. (In October 1995, a New Jersey state judge cited the biblical story of Sodom in rejecting Dale's claim that the Scouts had violated the state's ban on antigay discrimination.)

~ In the opportunities it provided for "recruitment," the religious right had long viewed public schools as simply a larger version of the Boy Scouts. In 1978, California voters defeated the Briggs Initiative, backed by the religious right, which would have banned openly gay teachers from the public school, providing a crucial blow to Anita Bryant's still-thriving Save Our Children campaign. With the increasing visibility of gay and lesbian parents—many with children enrolled in school districts—the battle shifted to sex education curricula, which religious right leaders also saw as another avenue for homosexual indoctrination. Even minor, seemingly innocuous references to gays and lesbians have incurred the wrath of the religious right. For instance, only 2 of the 443 pages in *Children of the Rainbow*, a New York City multicultural curriculum adopted in 1990, even mentioned gays and lesbians. Yet the fracas over the curriculum centered almost exclusively on those two pages. Among the passages that have drawn fire are an instruction that educators "be aware of the changing concept of *family* in today's society" and notations that "children of gay/lesbian parents may have limited experience with male/female parental situations; if there is no representation of their lives in the classroom, they may suddenly be made to feel different" and that "educators have the potential to help increase the tolerance and acceptance of the lesbian/gay community and to decrease the staggering number of hate crimes perpetrated against them." Even stronger criticism has been hurled at the school system's decision to include in *Children of the Rainbow*'s bibliography three books that are intended to promote respect for gay and lesbian parents. The books—*Daddy's Roommate, Heather Has Two Mommies,* and

Gloria Goes to Gay Pride—have been widely praised by educators, but Mary Cummins, president of a Queens school board, said they must be excluded from the bibliography because "we will not accept two people of the same sex engaged in deviant sex practices as a 'family.'"

In New York, the Archdiocese of New York formed a powerful union with the New York chapter of Pat Robertson's Christian Coalition to oust *Children of the Rainbow* from city classrooms. Nationally, the strategy of using sex-education and family-life curricula mentioning gays as a means of mobilizing antigay conservatives contributed to the election of hundreds of right-wing Christians to local school boards. The strategy was masterminded by Robert Simonds, the executive director of Citizens for Excellence in Education, a political group based in Costa Mesa, California, which claims to have elected more than two thousand of its members to school boards. By 1992, after high-profile campaigns focusing in part on the districts' sex education programs, religious conservatives controlled at least three school boards in San Diego alone—those of the Vista, Cajon Valley, and Escondido school systems. In a 1992 fund-raising letter, Simonds alleged that schools routinely encourage students to experiment with gay sex. "Children are taught that one in ten children born are genetically and irreversibly homosexual," Simonds wrote. "On this presumption, homosexuals are allowed to enter the class-rooms and describe their life-styles to innocent children [and] then hand out hot-line phone numbers to call for help in enjoying their new life-styles. This is open recruitment."

Actually, few schools allowed gay and lesbian activists to address students, and in those that did, the hot-line numbers to which Simonds referred almost invariably belonged to suicide-prevention groups that provided support for gay teens, who, according to studies, inflict violence on themselves at rates dramatically higher than their nongay peers. In fact, many more school districts had adopted curricula advocated by Simonds rather than gay-positive ones. Such curricula were developed under the Adolescent Family Life Act, which was signed into law by

President Reagan in 1982. The two most popular programs, *Teen-Aid* and *Sex Respect,* link gay sex uncritically to AIDS. *Sex Respect* contends that AIDS is nature's way of "making some kind of comment on sexual behavior."

Yet in challenging Simonds and other foes of inclusive sex education curricula, gay activists would have had more success if they had bothered to establish a credible record of long-term participation within school districts. Too many activists, with no children in the schools, have showed up at the hour of a school board vote on a gay- or AIDS-related curriculum issue, made a lot of noise, and returned home, never to be seen again. That kind of ephemeral single-issue activism with little electoral focus played directly into the hands of the religious right's claim that the gay movement's chief interest in schools is "recruitment" and has left little incentive for more evenhanded board members to challenge the religious right vociferously. With gays as virtual strangers, parents had no reason to question the religious right's depiction of them as deviants and recruiters. A growing number of gay and lesbian teacher and parent groups, such as the Gay, Lesbian and Straight Teachers Network, tried to change the situation.

According to some estimates, one-third of all adolescent suicides could be attributed to teenagers struggling with society's condemnation of their burgeoning homosexuality. As many adult gays and lesbians attested, support programs, both inside and outside the schools, were the only reason they survived their adolescence. Religious conservatives like Simonds contributed to the distressingly high suicide rates among gay teens by fostering an atmosphere of intolerance. By insisting that gay teens were purely the product of "recruitment," they could turn a blind eye to the overwhelming evidence of the reality of gay and lesbian youths and the life-threatening hostility many were needlessly forced to endure. It was hard enough to come to terms with being a gay teen without receiving the relentless message from some adults that you were depraved.

Homosexual youths were not the only ones affected by the antigay climate in public schools. Simonds might recall the story of Jimmy Baines of Bangor, Maine. As a fourteen-year-old, Baines and two other youths taunted Charlie Howard, a twenty-three-year-old gay man, with antigay epithets and threw him over a bridge into a river, where he drowned. Since his release from prison in 1992, Baines has devoted himself to fighting antigay violence and says that at the time of the murder he thought he was fulfilling God's will by killing a "queer."

The extraordinarily complicated relationships between curricula, sexuality, and suicide had been obscured by the political cross fire over the high suicide rates for gay teens. Because most of the studies were based on small samples of adolescents who happened to have contacted social service agencies, religious conservatives claimed the problem was greatly exaggerated, yet they took no steps to address the problem itself and continued to deplore both gays and homosexuality. Gay activists, meanwhile, often bandied the numbers about uncritically to make points in curricula battles. Lost in the middle of the fight were the fates of gay and lesbian youths themselves.

⌒ From the 1970s to the 1990s, as the battleground shifted from gay teachers to gay families and gay-inclusive curricula, antigay conservatives faced an increasingly uphill battle. The gays-as-pedophiles argument successfully played on parents' fear of the threat strangers posed to their children. But aside from this contention, increasingly risky with the discrediting of antigay researchers like Paul Cameron, the religious right was left arguing that homosexuality makes parents unfit, a far more difficult point to make to Americans inherently suspicious of outsiders dictating who should raise kids and how it should be done.

Instead, the religious right turned to the argument that gay parenting is itself a form of recruitment. If homosexuals can't recruit the children of heterosexual parents, the reasoning goes, they will recruit their own children. As same-sex parents, they will inevitably disrupt the highly restrictive, dualistic notions of gender that religious right activists often hold dear, rearing kids so confused about proper sex roles that they will be more likely to become gay. "How is a child to behave with two male or female parents?" asked Roger Magnuson, author of *Informed Answers to*

Gay Rights Questions, published in 1988. "How is he to understand true femininity or true masculinity when his most significant role models are homosexual parents?"

Adherence to such views spawned state bans on gay foster parenting and adopting and, in some cases, even the extreme measure of taking biological children away from their gay parents. "Is [stripping gay parents of custody] discrimination based on sexual orientation, or is it child protection based on the mother's sexual behavior?" asked Anne Kincaid, a spokeswoman for the Family Association, a religious right group in Virginia. "It looks like there would be compelling state interest to protect the child." But here the religious right butted up against research indicating that children growing up in lesbian and gay families were just as well-adjusted as those raised by their heterosexual counterparts—and no more likely to be gay. A summary of the findings of thirty studies of the children of gay and lesbian parents dating back to the 1970s published in the October 1992 edition of the psychological journal *Child Development* concluded that the studies were nearly unanimous in their findings that the children had developed in a healthy fashion.

Religious right groups, however, dismissed the summary because it was prepared by University of Virginia psychology professor Charlotte Patterson, who was openly lesbian. Instead, they preferred to cite the findings of 1983 and 1994 studies conducted by Cameron's Family Research Institute. Of 5,162 respondents, only 17 reported having had a homosexual parent. Of those, 11 "explicitly attributed their sexual orientation, in part at least, to parental homosexuality." Typical of Cameron's slipshod research, the study's sample size—17—was far too small and the questions far too biased to be of any scientific value.

〜 In part to avoid the ugly legal situation surrounding gay foster parenting, in part availing themselves of advances in reproductive technology, never-married lesbians began in the 1980s to raise their own biological children through artificial insemination. In many ways, Sharon Bottoms, who was the first parent to draw the attention of mainstream America to the plight of gay and lesbian parents, was a throwback to the earlier era in gay history when gays and lesbians had children through heterosexual unions. In April 1995, after a contentious four-year custody battle with her mother, Kay Bottoms, the Virginia Supreme Court stripped Sharon of custody of her five-year-old son, Tyler Doustou. In a bitterly divided 4–3 decision that ignored the sociological evidence on gay parenting, Justice A. Christian Compton declared that "living under conditions stemming from active lesbianism practiced in the home may impose a burden on the child by reason of the 'social condemnation' attached to such an arrangement, which will inevitably affect the child's relationship with its peers and with the community." As in Colonel Peck's famous justification for excluding his own son, Scott, from the armed forces (he feared for his safety), the court's acknowledgment of pervasive antigay hostility could just as easily have been the linchpin for a ruling steadfastly establishing gay rights. The court failed to note that a child could just as easily be condemned for having a single mother or even a weight problem.

Bottoms's custody battle with her mother, Kay Bottoms, began in 1992 when Sharon tried to limit her mother's visits to Tyler. Bottoms had received a divorce from her husband, Dennis Doustou, an unemployed construction worker, before the child's birth. Bottoms accused her mother's live-in boyfriend of seventeen years of sexually abusing her between the ages of twelve and eighteen. Kay Bottoms accused her daughter of neglecting Tyler. Kay Bottoms sued, and in September 1992, Henrico County circuit court judge Buford M. Parsons Jr. awarded her custody. Parsons based his ruling both on Virginia's sodomy law, which he said made Bottoms a criminal, and *Roe v. Roe,* a 1985 state supreme court ruling that found that gays and lesbians are by definition unfit parents because children are damaged by their exposure to their sexual orientation. "In the opinion of this court, her conduct is immoral," Parsons said of Bottoms.

Bottoms, whose simple, straightforward style served her well during the media blitz surrounding the case, only wanted to live a quiet life with her partner; suddenly she found herself thrust into the role of a national activist. A high school dropout, Bottoms worked as a clerk at a K Mart in Richmond, Virginia, as the case wound its way through the courts. In 1994, Bottoms and her girl-friend, April Wade, who was a chef at a Red Lobster restaurant, exchanged vows in a commitment ceremony at a Richmond church. If their relationship had been legally sanctioned, Bottoms would surely have retained custody of Tyler.

⌐ With her long history of drug and alcohol abuse, arrest record, ⸱ and by some accounts, lesbian background, divorced mother Megan Lucas was an unlikely candidate for poster girl of the religious right's antigay-parenting campaign. But because the twenty-two-year-old Lucas, suddenly appearing in conservative dresses as her star began to rise, took on a gay couple in a much publicized custody case, she became a darling of the religious right.

The battle began in early 1993 when Ross and Luis Lopton, a Seattle gay couple who had taken the same surname to symbolize their commitment to each other, were notified by the Washington State Division of Children and Family Services that a foster child named Gailen was available for adoption. The couple was over-joyed when they learned that Gailen's Scandinavian–Puerto Rican ancestry matched their own perfectly. After undergoing four years of training and counseling to become foster and, later, adoptive parents, the couple felt they were equipped to deal with the spe-cial needs of the four-year-old Gailen, who had been diagnosed with attention deficit disorder, a behavioral problem common among children who have been in foster care. The state selected the Loptons from twelve families that were being considered as adoptive parents.

Lucas, who bore the child as an unmarried teenager, had sur-rendered her parental rights in 1992. But as the Loptons were preparing to take Gailen home for good, Lucas had a sudden change of heart. Informed that Gailen would be adopted by a gay couple, Lucas sued for her parenting rights, claiming she had been coerced by social workers into giving up the boy. Again in-voking the social stigma argument about children of gay parents, she said in court papers that the thought of the boy living with a gay couple was "her worst nightmare." "He will be ridiculed for having a father and a father," she explained in the *New York Times*. In 1993, Lucas, who had by then married the boy's father, explained that she had undergone a religious conversion and was better prepared to raise the child. "We haven't always been the best place for him, but we are now," she insisted. "Our house is a normal loving household."

The conservative groups could not have picked a worse test case to support its claim that gays are inherently unfit parents. As a teenager, Lucas had been arrested several times on theft and drug charges. When Gailen was five months old, Lucas, overcome by personal problems, left him in the care of her mother and sister. In 1990, the state took custody and placed him in a series of foster homes. But the early evidence that she was an unfit parent didn't stop the religious right from jumping on Lucas's bandwagon. John Whitehead's Rutherford Institute provided Lucas with financial support and legal research. The Washington Citizens Alliance, an offshoot of Lon Mabon's antigay Oregon Citizens Alliance, began collecting signatures for a statewide initiative, which ultimately failed to qualify for the ballot, that would ban gay adoptions and prohibit positive depictions of homosexuals in the public schools.

That religious right groups would support a parent who, by their own supposedly strict moral standards, lacked even the most basic parenting ability and good judgment was not as surprising as it might have looked at first glance. The religious right had long welcomed sinners into the born-again fold as long as they were willing to renounce their past and pledge eternal fidelity to Christ. The problem was that would-be paragons often returned to their past behavior. It didn't take long for Lucas to do just that. Though Lucas obtained a temporary restraining order keeping Gailen away from the Loptons, she quickly ran into a series of legal setbacks as her personal problems reemerged. Lucas had filed for custody one day after her parental rights had expired under Washington law. As a result, the state received a stay of the restraining order, keeping the child in the Loptons' custody until the courts had a chance to decide the issue. Meanwhile, Lucas would make the court's decision an easy one. For the religious right, the most damning charge, denied by Lucas, came from a former lesbian female friend who claimed the two had had a sexual liaison. "Megan and I had a sexual relationship on numerous occasions during a seven-month period," said the friend, Marcy Kokinda. "It was not so much a romantic relationship as a sexual relationship that eventually ran its course." (The charge was substantiated by affidavits signed by three mutual friends and a social worker.)

While Lucas, who by this time was pregnant again, was suing the Loptons, her new marriage hit the rocks. The boy's father, Wade Lucas, filed for divorce and sued for custody of her unborn child, claiming Megan Lucas was an unfit mother. In testimony that even Megan Lucas's attorney conceded was damning, a court-appointed social worker determined that she was an unfit mother. Megan Lucas has "a long and significant history of drug and alcohol abuse that remains both a threat to her own health and safety as well as that of her children," the social worker said. In a defense that could not have pleased Rutherford lawyers, Lucas claimed that another man, not Wade, might actually have been the father of the child.

But the worst was yet to come. In February 1994, Lucas received a suspended one-year sentence for stealing a vacuum cleaner from a former employer. Depressed from the arrest and the fierce custody battles, Lucas attempted suicide twice by taking overdoses of four medications. In explaining the suicide attempts, Lucas told the same social worker that she would rather "die and take the unborn baby with me than risk Mr. Lucas gaining custody of it." What little was left of her credibility—and the suit against the Loptons—was destroyed with that statement.

The buttoned-down, respectable Loptons made as ideal an example of gay parenting as Lucas did a poor one for the religious right. While Lucas hit the national talk-show circuit to make her case, the Loptons stayed home with Gailen, politely declining all interview requests. While Lucas's checkered past made her the epitome of an unreliable parent, the Loptons offered the stable, loving home that Gailen had lacked throughout his young life.

Lucas quickly became the religious right's Tawana Brawley. Antigay conservatives, who continued to support Lucas throughout her self-inflicted ordeal, did not allow the reality of the case to interfere with their principles. In their 1994 book, *A Nation Without a Conscience*, for instance, prominent religious right leaders Tim and Beverly LaHaye approvingly quoted Lucas's desire for her son to live in a "traditional family," never mentioning her troubled past as a mother. In essence, the right was saying that one bad heterosexual parent is better than two good gay ones. In the fight over family values, the needs of the children mattered less than the politics of the parents.

CHAPTER 8

Running on Religion

THE 1994 REPUBLICAN ELECTORAL REVOLUTION was the partial realization of Pat Robertson's dream of mainstream political access when he formed the Christian Coalition in 1989. Of the
freshman class of eighty-seven, rivaling even the watershed 1992
elections in turnover, seventy-four were Republicans. Close to 60
percent of the victorious congressional candidates had received
Christian Coalition backing. It was the Christian Coalition's executive director, Ralph Reed Jr., during a preelection appearance on
Robertson's Christian Broadcasting Network, who most accurately predicted the size of the landslide. Reed could predict what
was happening because the Christian Coalition was making it happen. The victory, bragged *Christian American,* the Coalition's
newsletter, was "propelled by the largest surge of religious voters
in history," exceeding even the fabled 1980 outpouring that swept
Ronald Reagan to power.

Indeed, the extent of religious right clout in the wake of the
1994 GOP sweeps, which reached into state legislatures and gov-
ernors' mansions, made even the oasis of the early Reagan administration look like a drought. As Robertson had meticulously

planned, the Christian right would no longer be forced to go begging in Congress; it was now one step closer to dictating the terms of the debate. The Christian Coalition had positioned itself as the flagship of the religious right, working its magic by painstakingly cultivating a massive grassroots constituency, based primarily on the thousands of evangelical churches across the country. Half a decade of fierce pitched local battles—like those fought over gay-related issues from Cobb County, Georgia, to Portland, Oregon— had finally translated into the national electoral leverage religious right leaders had predicted it would. From Robertson's mailing list, the fruit of his failed 1988 presidential campaign, and a relatively small initial investment, the Coalition had become one of the country's most powerful lobby groups, with more than 1 million members and a $25 million annual budget, dwarfing the combined resources of the national gay lobby groups.

Vowing to press a conservative social agenda with gay rights figuring to land high on their hit list, Christian conservatives were preparing their own versions of House Speaker Newt Gingrich's Contract with America, the ten-point Republican campaign platform produced in the fall of 1994, to press more specifically for antigay legislation and cuts in AIDS funding. The Christian Action Network, a Lynchburg, Virginia–based lobby group headed by former Jerry Falwell aide Martin Mawyer, saw the election as a perfect opportunity to push an antigay agenda at the federal level, distributing a Pro-Family Contract with America that called for further tightening the military ban on gay and lesbian service personnel and "de-funding the homosexual agenda," which it never bothered to define. But fault lines on the religious right were also beginning to emerge. The Christian Coalition, following executive director Ralph Reed's pledge to broaden its base beyond divisive social issues, proposed a Contract with the American Family that made only passing mention of homosexuality, though its fund-raising missives continued to harp on the threat gays and lesbians supposedly posed to families and Christian values.

Despite its contribution to the Republican landslide, the Christian right would continue to fight for its agenda with the party leadership, which remained wary of charges of extremism, which would scare voters and hurt its prospects in national elections. Nor did the Christian right get everything it wanted in the November election. While the majority of candidates it endorsed were victorious, two of the high-profile candidates it could call its own were trounced: Iran-contra figure Oliver North, in his bid for the U.S. Senate from Virginia; and Allen Quist, in his race for the Minnesota governorship. The only winner the Christian Coalition could claim had actually risen from its ranks was Terry Beasley, a Christian conservative in South Carolina who was elected governor of the state.

In the cases of North and Quist, both of whom were deeply flawed candidates, their tendency to make extreme pronouncements haunted them throughout their campaigns. Quist, who aired blistering attacks on his Republican opponent, Arne Carlson, for his gay rights support, got into trouble by contending that men have a "genetic predisposition" to head families. (The anti-abortion Quist was also hurt by the revelation that his wife had had an abortion in the 1970s.) A regular contributor to *Christian American,* North made the support of his opponent, incumbent Chuck Robb, for lifting the military ban one of the central themes of his own campaign. Hinting broadly that the White House was overrun by gay activists, he charged that the president's staff was "teeming with twenty-something kids with an earring and an ax to grind." But many voters knew that North had his own ax to grind against the very institution he sought to enter and to which he had lied under oath in the late 1980s. The message voters sent in rejecting the two was that, while they might be sympathetic with the Christian right on many issues, they objected to candidates too closely aligned with it. This tension would later play a central role in the 1996 Republican presidential primaries.

⌐ Pat Robertson's dream was the gay movement's nightmare. The Republican takeover of Congress, as well as a host of governorships and state legislatures, ended the hard-won access gay rights lobbyists had developed with lawmakers under Democratic rule. The Democratic coalition politics upon which the national gay rights groups had relied to press for and sustain support on

legislation ranging from AIDS research to hate-crimes statistics
had gone the way of House Speaker Tom Foley's gavel, trans-
ferred to the hands of the pugnacious Newt Gingrich. Not only
were the gay groups now facing incumbent Republicans whom
they had thought they had the luxury to ignore, they also had to
contend with a freshman class filled with firebrands bent on a far-
reaching conservative revolution that would roll back a decade of
gains made by AIDS and gay rights advocates. With no connections to the elected officials and with overtures from them hardly
forthcoming, gay groups were reduced to trotting out relatives—
some not particularly close—of right-wing politicians to draw attention to the hypocrisy of their antigay views.

The single ally upon whom the gay groups once thought they
could depend, President Clinton, had, in attempting to underscore his newly rediscovered centrism, been fleeing from association with them since the gays-in-the-military debacle. Shortly
before the 1994 election, the Justice Department scuttled the appointment of Tom Potter, the former Portland, Oregon, police
chief, when it learned that he had been an especially hated target
of the Oregon Citizens Alliance for his pro-gay stands and lesbian
daughter. Religious conservatives inside and outside the state
complained bitterly about his aggressive support for the inclusion
of sexual orientation in hate-crimes and civil rights legislation.
Not long after the midterm election, Clinton ousted Surgeon
General Joycelyn Elders, the administration's most outspoken, if
not always most informed, advocate for gay causes after she had
become a lightning rod for the religious right. In just two years,
gay lobbyists went from pariahs to consummate insiders and finally back to pariahs once again. As the presidential election
neared, Clinton would undertake another about-face by making
a series of low-profile overtures to gays and lesbians. But in the
aftermath of the Republican congressional landslide, the gay
movement was left, in the words of Steve Morin, a longtime gay
aide to California Democratic representative Nancy Pelosi, with
"nowhere to turn."

Yet the nation's changing political alignment had little impact on the National Gay and Lesbian Task Force, the country's

second-largest gay political organization. Shortly before the election the group tapped for its top post Melinda Paras, a former Marxist guerrilla in the Philippines who had been accused of financial mismanagement at the Shanti Project, a San Francisco AIDS organization where she had worked until 1993. Though Paras was not the group's first choice, critics privately complained that turning to her in the new political environment was installing an isolationist to lead a besieged nation in the midst of a war. While Paras was by many accounts a skilled organizer and a talented administrator, only in the unreality of gay politics would someone whose resumé still had the whiff of 1960s radicalism and the taint of financial mismanagement be invited to lead an organization into the conservative 1990s.

Even without Paras's political baggage, the Task Force was singularly unprepared for the pivotal election year. Having gone through three executive directors since Urvashi Vaid's departure in 1992, the group was adrift. Flat membership levels and lackluster fund-raising forced the D.C.–based organization to slash its $4-million budget by 35 percent. On several occasions, staffers were forced to take unpaid furloughs to allow the group to stay solvent. Tension between the group's board and staff drove several top officials from their posts. Lobbying and organizing efforts languished. Elizabeth Birch, the high-profile chair of the Task Force's board, jumped ship to head the Human Rights Campaign Fund, the nation's largest gay political group and longtime Task Force rival. Upon assuming the Campaign Fund's directorship, Birch promptly proposed folding her old organization into her new one, thereby eliminating the competition between the two and the duplication of tasks. (The proposal was thwarted by Paras and the Task Force's board.)

More important even than the financial problems and internal dissension, twenty-five years after its founding the Task Force still lacked a consistent political direction, with its staffers endlessly replaying old debates about assimilation versus separatism. As had been the case since it moved its offices to Washington, D.C., in 1986, the group still found itself torn between lobbying Congress and devoting its energies to building the movement's untended and overstretched grassroots supporters. In March of 1993, Torie Osborn, the dynamic former director of the Los Angeles Gay and Lesbian Community Services Center, took the reins of the group with great fanfare only to find herself in the midst of internecine warfare over the group's collective decision-making process, a remnant of 1960s-style political organizing. "The organization is riddled with a downwardly mobile activist fear of success and money," Osborn, who had earned a reputation as a high-powered fund-raiser, said in an interview shortly after her departure following just six months on the job. "There would be endless debates about whether we were bringing in too many rich white male donors—like that would be somehow corrupt."

As if to underscore Osborn's assessment, Paras's appointment represented a return to downwardly mobile activism, in which activists spend more time arguing about the political purity of their positions than in the hard work of building a political movement. The movement Paras knew best had built required heavy artillery: at a 1993 Task Force conference, Paras described her experience as a Marxist guerrilla organizing to overthrow the Marcos government in the Philippines in the 1970s. "Our movement," she told the audience, "was about arming the people, guerrilla warfare, going out to the countryside to the small barrios—I know this is not familiar to a lot of you, but for some of us it's almost like old rote—creating mass organizations of millions of people, and basically overthrowing the government."

Paras's political background undercut her credibility and made the Task Force easy prey for congressional conservatives and right-wing pressure groups seeking to portray the gay rights movement as outside the mainstream. But she was hardly the only gay activist still fighting old political battles. The June 1994 commemoration of the twenty-fifth anniversary of the Stonewall riots encapsulated the factionalized politics of the gay movement. The vast majority of the close to 1 million participants were gays and lesbians from across the country who viewed the festivities as an opportunity to enjoy New York in the company of other gays and lesbians. They spent the weekend watching the Gay Games athletic competitions, attending a plethora of colorful parties, and buying souvenir T-shirts, while paying passing homage to the event that had come to symbolize the birth of their freedom movement.

While most gays did not have partisan politicking at the top of their agenda, a small group of gay activists had nothing but this on their minds. At the June 26 march from the United Nations headquarters on Manhattan's East Side to Central Park, groups ranging from the North American Man-Boy Love Association to the Lesbian Avengers vied feverishly to claim the mantle of Stonewall. The proliferation of splinter groups and marches mirrored larger disagreements over the political significance of the Stonewall riots and the general direction of the contemporary gay rights movement. Some said that because the original riots were led by less "respectable" gays and lesbians, their spirit as outcasts should distinguish the gay rights movement. Others argued that the celebration of a fringe status was not suited to contemporary politics, dominated as they were by social conservatives only too eager to exploit and reinforce such marginality. In an article in the June 13 issue of *The New Republic,* gay conservative social critic Bruce Bawer accused activists of mythologizing the riots to further their own sundry left-wing political agendas. The true heroes of the period, he contended, were the more straightlaced members of the Mattachine Society. Gay playwright Tony Kushner, author of *Angels in America,* returned fire in the left-wing *Nation* magazine, denouncing Bawer's arguments as "assimilationist" and calling for gays and lesbians to embrace a radical social agenda sympathetic to the splinter groups.

The squabbling over the legacy of Stonewall reflected the growing political diversity of the gay movement and the rambunctious, pluralistic nature of its politics. But at the same time, the disagreements were merely new manifestations of old divisions that showed no signs of healing, much less of yielding constructive, mutually conciliatory strategies for confronting the movement's foes. In the end, they deprived gays and lesbians of the solidarity they needed to prevail in the political arena, complicating the already difficult work of the national political groups by placing them in the middle of a raging ideological battle within their own ranks.

～ While the Task Force was moving to the left, the Human Rights Campaign Fund, the larger and more politically connected of the two, was attempting to shore up its respectability. The Campaign Fund's board selected Apple Computer executive Elizabeth Birch to replace Tim McFeeley, who ended his stint as the group's head after five years. As Apple's top litigator, Birch had credentials that signified a benchmark for leaders of gay organizations. But while Birch had earned a reputation as a skilled behind-the-scenes organizer as cochair of the Task Force board, she lacked experience in the rough-and-tumble world of Beltway politics.

In July 1995, Birch faxed a letter to Christian Coalition executive director Ralph Reed Jr., requesting his appearance at its Road to Victory '95 Conference in September in order to "establish a dialogue to narrow the gulfs which currently divide us." Just hours after faxing the letter—and getting no response from Reed—Birch leaked the letter to the Associated Press, complaining that the Christian Coalition was unresponsive to concerns about antigay bias at the organization. But the short time between the sending of the letter and the publication of the story allowed Reed, with some justification, to portray Birch's overture as an "act of grandstanding," aimed more at garnering press coverage than at substantive dialogue between the two organizations.

With her tactical blunder, Birch wasted a golden opportunity. The Christian Coalition's antigay crusades—and their devastating impact on the lives of gays and lesbians—have largely gone unnoticed by the media, which has seldom regarded them as newsworthy. Gay groups themselves have called on the religious right to end its verbal gay-bashing by resorting to crude anti-Christian stereotypes, and the groups' failure to provide regular documentation of the pattern has made their responses to the most conspicuous and outrageous instances sound rash and ill-informed. Recognizing that the general public is fed up with the hollowness of the culture wars, Birch's rapprochement with the Christian Coalition struck a much needed tone. In an interview with *The Windy City Times,* a gay weekly in Chicago, Birch was careful to explain that she was not challenging the underlying religious beliefs of the group's members. But, she said, "if there is one central message of the Gospel, it's a message of love. I believe people in the Christian Coalition are very sincere in their beliefs, and what drives and motivates them to take action. But I believe if they're truly confronted with how [Christian Coalition rhetoric] translates into human terms—by, for example, leading gay and lesbian teenagers to prostitution and suicide—they'd be horrified by their actions." Birch placed the emphasis where it should be—on the Coalition's fund-raising letters that depend on defamation of gays for their impact, without attacking the religious beliefs of evangelical Christians. "By singling out a group of Americans—lesbian and gay Americans—to make a lot of money, they don't just drive money into the coffers of their organization; they are really twisting and dehumanizing an entire group of Americans, and that has real, tangible effects," she said. "It translates into violence against gays and lesbians."

Birch elaborated on the theme in an eloquent open letter to participants at the Christian Coalition's Road to Victory '95. While every major Republican presidential candidate was paying homage to the Coalition, Birch read the letter to a small crowd, which included a smattering of religious conservatives, in a nearby ballroom. "I do not know when the first direct-mail letter was issued in your name that defamed gay men and abused gay women, that described us as less than human and certainly unworthy of trust," Birch said. "Neither do I know when people discovered that the richest financial return came from letters that depicted gays and lesbians with intentionally dishonest images. But I do know—and I must believe that you know too—that this is dishonest, this is wrong."

Birch's analysis was a major improvement over the simplistic name-calling that has dominated the gay groups' angry critique of the religious right. For instance, Scot Nakagawa, project director of the National Gay and Lesbian Task Force's Fight the Right

Project, had spoken of the religious right's "infiltration of the Republican Party." (Actually, it had done nothing of the sort. The religious right earned its preeminence in the party in a highly democratic fashion—by fierce and efficient organizing.) After a Campaign Fund poll found that many voters were wary of the religious right's political inroads, the gay groups adopted a strategy of referring to religious conservatives as the "radical right." Conjuring the image of a religious bogeyman trampling on the rights of Americans might be effective, but it did a disservice to civil discourse by failing to convey the diversity of the conservative evangelical movement, the sincerity of their claims, and their right to participate in the political process. A significant number of evangelical Christians, for instance, were registered Democrats. "Radical right" was no more accurate an appellation for religious conservatives than "gay agenda" or "militant homosexuals" accurately portrayed the multifaceted movement for gay rights.

Birch faced formidable obstacles in bringing questions about the Christian Coalition's antigay messages to public consciousness. While the Christian Coalition conference received reams of press coverage, Birch's plea for tolerance was all but ignored. Therein lies one of the gay movement's dilemmas: when the gay groups modified their rhetoric for the good of the debate, they were placed at a real disadvantage in getting their message out in media outlets still attracted to more bellicose rhetoric and wedded to the culture war as a framework of analysis. In an era obsessed with winning and losing, in which split-screened guests of opposite ideologies screamed at each other on talk shows, the language of reconciliation was often lost in the storm. Compounding the challenge facing Birch and the gay movement was the fact that the media, and society, still accorded far more deference to charges of racism, anti-Semitism, and sexism than to antigay prejudice. Birch's protest, for instance, came on the heels of well-publicized allegations of anti-Semitism in Robertson's tome *The New World Order*. In that book Robertson contended that European bankers, many of whom he elsewhere identifies as Jewish, were part of a conspiracy to control the international financial sys-

tem—a belief that had long been a staple of anti-Semitic literature. Much of the coverage focused on a March 2, 1995, letter to
Robertson from Abraham Foxman, national director of the Jewish
Anti-Defamation League, calling on Robertson to repudiate the
book's "message of a worldwide Jewish conspiracy." (In a letter responding to Foxman's, Robertson denied that he was anti-Semitic
on the grounds that he supported the state of Israel, and he dispatched Reed to sweet-talk an audience of Anti-Defamation
League members.) Even though Robertson's antigay appeals
were more contemporary—*The New World Order* was published
in 1991—and less equivocal than his anti-Semitic ones, many
Americans still viewed them as a natural outgrowth of religious
fundamentalism, and not as a calculated device to raise money by
playing on the fears about and ignorance of homosexuals. Anti-
Semitism had become the kiss of death in American politics; homophobia remained an apparently permissible and eminently
effective political tool.

Having the Bible wielded against them was not the only disadvantage faced by the struggling gay organizations. When
matched up against the fund-raising machines and sophisticated
political operations of the religious right, gay groups came up far
short. Combined with approximately sixty staffers, 150,000 members, and annual budgets totaling $12 million, the Task Force and
Campaign Fund have less than half the firepower of the Christian
Coalition alone. While the religious right had a natural constituency in the thousands of evangelical churches across the
country, the gay organizations depended upon a politically divided, geographically diffuse community that is often profoundly
distrustful of electoral politics and national leadership. For gay
groups, even identifying potential donors is a Herculean task,
given the intense veil of privacy, shame, and fear of retaliation in
which many gay people lead their everyday lives.

Despite the giant progress registered since Stonewall, millions of gays and lesbians were still in the closet, and many of
those who were open did not view themselves as part of a mainstream political movement. While there were thousands of

bustling gay bars across the country—and gays still maintained potent power bases in many urban areas where they had established thriving communities—the gay groups justly contended that few of their members and potential enrollees spend nearly as much time and energy on politics as they do on barhopping. As the Stonewall 25 celebration demonstrated, the lack of ideological solidarity among activists and the unwillingness to forge compromises, which political marginality had never prompted them to outgrow, made gay politics a minefield for even the most adept gay leaders.

But gay organizations still had to assume some of the responsibility for the dismal state of gay politics. Gay leaders contributed to the lack of enthusiasm for their cause by failing to evoke a compelling vision of the struggle for gay rights as consonant with the concerns of nongay America and by remaining ideologically out of sync with the more mainstream gay rank and file, from whose experiences a more pressing and resonant set of priorities might be derived. Furthermore, repeated strategic blunders had made big donors wary of contributing to the cause for fear that they were squandering their money. Alternately cheerleaders and crepe-paper hangers, the gay groups undermined their credibility by vacillating between portraying the political environment as unremittingly hostile and making unrealistic claims about their successes. Just one month after the November 1994 Republican revolution left gays and lesbians facing the most hostile political landscape in more than a decade, the Human Rights Campaign Fund's departing executive director, Tim McFeeley, said in a press statement that "1994 may go down in history as one of the most productive years since the beginning of the modern movement for lesbian and gay equal rights."

⚬ At the heart of the gay movement's lack of success in American politics is its failure to understand its opposition. By the start of the 1996 presidential campaign, the gay groups still lacked a research arm that would allow them to monitor the religious right's antigay activity. Gay activists who were interested in the religious right were forced to turn to the libraries of three nongay groups, the B'nai B'rith's Anti-Defamation League, People for the American Way, and Political Research Associates, a Boston-based opposition research entity. When political attacks on abortion rights began to mount in the early 1990s, Planned Parenthood established a library on antiabortion activists and published a newsletter on their activities. With antigay initiatives springing up across the country, the gay groups did nothing in kind.

The most logical place for such an undertaking would be the Gay and Lesbian Alliance Against Defamation, a media watchdog group with its headquarters both in Los Angeles and New York City. But the organization, which has chapters around the country, devoted as much precious time and energy to trivial matters as to the gains of the religious right and the press coverage of its efforts. The organization's main filing system, located in the office of the New York chapter, was so disorganized that even its own staffers had trouble locating crucial documents. While the nation has been embroiled in a series of high-profile gay-related battles in the aftermath of Bill Clinton's election, the New York office spent weeks organizing protests against Marky Mark for allegedly making antigay comments, culminating in a public burning of Calvin Klein underwear, for which the rap star modeled. When the media was exploring allegations of anti-Semitism in Robertson's book, GLAAD concentrated instead on the portrayal of lesbian models in *Vanity Fair* magazine and charges that tiny Bradford College in Massachusetts had discriminated against transvestite activist Leslie Feinberg by canceling her commencement address. Without an accessible pool of detailed and reliable information from which to devise a counterstrategy to the right's, the gay groups were at a distinct disadvantage that reinforced their tendency to lump all Christian right activists together. Despite its lack of focus, GLAAD did have the political sense to create a new organizational structure that copied the Christian Coalition's successful model, establishing local chapters to feed into their national network. The organization dispatched Donna Red Wing, who had been instrumental in the campaign to defeat Oregon's antigay initiatives, to travel the country recruiting members and laying groundwork for national electoral clout.

⟶ Research played a pivotal role in the November 1994 defeat of Measure One, Idaho's far-reaching ballot measure that would have banned gay rights ordinances; prevented public-school teachers from discussing homosexuality as "healthy, approved, or acceptable"; and limited library books about homosexuality to adults only. As the result of both a 1993 state court decision striking down Colorado's antigay initiative and lackluster organizing, Idaho was one of only two states from an original set of ten targeted in 1994 by the religious right to face an antigay referendum on the fall ballot. (The other measure, in Oregon, also went down to defeat.) Conscious of the need to broaden their agenda, religious conservatives put their energy into political candidates instead.

The wound that killed the Idaho initiative—which lost by less than 1 percent—was the revelation that Jeremiah Films, a Hemet, California, religious conservative group that provided the initiative's backers with copies of the antigay video *Gay Rights, Special Rights,* had also produced four anti-Mormon videos. Even though Measure One's opponents had written off the majority of Mormon voters because of the sect's well-known antipathy to homosexuality, heavily Mormon precincts weighed in solidly against the initiative, providing the slim margin of defeat.

The films—*The God Makers, The God Makers II, The Mormon Dilemma,* and *Joseph Smith and the Temple of Doom*—depicted the Church of Jesus Christ of Latter-Day Saints as a satanic cult bent on the destruction of Christianity, not unlike the organization's depiction of the gay movement. After discovering Jeremiah Films' anti-Mormon propaganda through extensive background research on the Idaho Citizens Alliance, the initiative's sponsor, the No on One Coalition released the information to the media just days before the election. This raised serious questions about the credibility of *Gay Rights, Special Rights,* which, like other antigay videos, depicts gay pride parades running amok with bare-breasted lesbians and gay men dressed as nuns. A spokesman for the Mormon Church called the anti-Mormon films "evil piece[s] of mischief, vicious in spirit and false in fact," and conceded that the anti-Mormon videos undermined support for the measure among Mormons.

The research exposed the Achilles' heel of the religious right generally: its tendency to depict in the most far-fetched and demonstrably false manner anyone—not just gays—who does not share its views. Despite the assistance it received from slick national groups like the Christian Coalition and Focus on the Family, the Idaho Citizens Alliance was particularly prone to crude tactics and defamatory characterizations. In part, this was the legacy of Lon Mabon, the founder of the Oregon Citizens Alliance, who had started the Idaho group as an offshoot of his own; Mabon's tactics in the antigay campaigns of Oregon were similarly ham-fisted. A 135-page guide titled *Debating the Gay Rights Issue* and sold to Alliance members as part of the pro-initiative campaign claimed that "promiscuous sodomite activists are the most violent and irrational group of people on earth" and that they have called for the "closing of all churches that oppose them and the total destruction of the family." It also came perilously close to endorsing antigay violence: "One statement that is sure to get an outraged response from sodomites and chuckles from normal onlookers is an innocent observation that 'gays' should enjoy getting beaten up by 'homophobes.'"

As had been the case with the antigay campaigns that came before it, the gay groups in Idaho responded with their own hyperbolic characterizations of the opposition. Mary Rohlfing, cochair of Idaho for Human Dignity, told the *Twin Falls Times-News* that the similarity between "the deceitful rhetoric [in the manual] and what Germans heard about the Jews from the Nazis is uncanny." Kelly Walton, whom Mabon had dispatched to found the Idaho Citizens Alliance, topped off the exchange by complaining that gay activists "called us 'Nazis' and it's so unfair. Everything Hitler stood for I'm one hundred and eighty degrees opposed to." But at the same time, Walton could not stop himself from making the claim that "there's good evidence that Hitler was a homosexual."

Walton's rhetorical excesses and slipshod organizing hurt his cause throughout the campaign. The bungling of the Idaho Citizens Alliance seemed to copy its parent group in Oregon, performing sloppy legal work, falling captive to its opponents' charges of carpetbagging, and turning a tin ear to voter concerns. A father of four, Walton moved his contracting business from Oregon, where he had served as Oregon Citizens Alliance vice president, to the southeast Idaho town of Burley, from which he led the antigay campaign. Walton angered wary taxpayers when he dismissed complaints about the huge cost of possible legal challenges to his proposal with a terse "so be it." He ridiculed Larry EchoHawk, the nation's first Native American state attorney general and a moderate Democrat, by calling him "Harry EchoSquawk" after EchoHawk pressed his opposition to the initiative.

But however unsophisticated Walton had proved, his selection of a successor was all the more inept. In the summer of 1994, Walton stepped aside as director of the Alliance in favor of Boise painting contractor Bill Proctor, who did nothing to elevate the tenor of the debate or improve the reputation of the proposition's sponsors. The revelation that Proctor had a long history of drug use and dealing, culminating in a conviction and a sixteen-month prison term in the early 1980s, along with two failed marriages, made him a less than ideal champion of family values. But Proctor insisted that the black marks only improved his credentials. It was in prison that Proctor said he found God and formed an abiding dislike for homosexuals. "Being [in prison] was a real mind-bender," he told the *Idaho Statesman.* "There was a lot of homosexual rape." Only his imposing physical stature, he added, prevented him from being victimized. If a drug addict like him could be saved, he reasoned, so could homosexuals. "People's lives can be changed and transformed," he said. "I know that since I was saved, my life has changed dramatically, and I'm not the same person I was then."

In making their case for the initiative, Walton and Proctor trotted out the same antigay canards that had played so well in Oregon and Colorado. Without naming their sources, they claimed that gay men—lesbians rarely figured into their thinking—were sex-obsessed pedophiles who die at an early age as a result of the "medical consequences" of gay sex. Dependent on voters' ignorance of homosexuality, they avoided disclosing the inevitable source of the statistics: antigay researcher Paul Cameron. In a rare instance of critical reporting, the *Statesman* quoted a spokesman for the federal Centers for Disease Control and Prevention pointing out that it's impossible to estimate accurately the life expectancy of gay men because "one's sexual orientation is not on a death certificate."

Rohlfing's Nazi analogy was a departure from the generally intelligent tone of the anti-initiative campaign. Learning from mistakes committed by activists in antigay initiative fights in Oregon and Colorado, No on One became a model of pro-gay organizing. Activists based the campaign not only on the goal of defeating the initiative, but on creating the infrastructure for Idaho's first substantial gay movement. Like the religious right, the activists used the initiative as a vehicle for a larger cause. The initiative "is just the beginning," said Brian Bergquist, chairman of the No on One Coalition, during the campaign. "We don't want to get so wrapped up in winning that losing means you stop."

Until the measure was first floated in 1993, gays had done little statewide organizing. Like other antigay measures elsewhere dating back to the 1970s, the 1993 initiative had a galvanizing effect on the state's gay community. It was through the efforts of Bergquist and his partner, John Hummel, an attorney, that the first statewide gay group, Idaho for Human Dignity, got off the ground. A conservative, largely rural state, Idaho was home to a range of white-supremacist groups, from neo-Nazi Richard Butler's Aryan Nation to the Idaho Militia, one of the most radical of the country's militia outfits. It did not offer gays safe meccas like San Francisco or even Portland, where natives and large populations of immigrant gays have settled to form communities that they could truly call their own. The joke at the No on One headquarters was that there were no gay people in Pocatello—or at least none that the group could identify. About a quarter of the state's 1 million inhabitants live in the Boise area, where most gays were integrated into neighborhoods throughout the city, but concentrated on the north side. The rest of the state's population was scattered over a vast area, which complicated the task of statewide organizing. On the other hand, the homogeneity of the gay movement simplified the activists' work. In a state that is over more than 90 percent white, activists had few of the battles over race that had divided their peers in Colorado. Similarly, the fault lines of gender, drag, and transgender issues that have shaken up campaigns against antigay initiatives elsewhere never extended to Idaho. The group won the support of most of the state's top politicians, including a large number of the Republicans, who dominate the state legislature. Spooked by the specter of a potato boycott or a slackening in the resort business around Sun Valley, tourism and business officials threw their support behind the gay cause.

Yet opposition to the Idaho Citizens Alliance proposal was by no means unanimous. In the spring of 1994, Helen Chenoweth, a long-shot candidate for the U.S. House seat from western Idaho, the only one in the state's delegation occupied by a Democrat, announced her support for Measure One, becoming the only major politician in the state to do so. A religious conservative who aggressively courted support from the militia movement, Chenoweth was considered radical even by the state's right-leaning standards, leading many gay activists to discount the threat her campaign posed to their interests. Even though the initiative went down to a narrow defeat in the November election, Chenoweth was elected as part of the Republican electoral revolution that would forever change the climate for gay politics.

Chenoweth's political base was south-central Idaho, which voted overwhelmingly for Measure One. A grandmother of six, Chenoweth portrayed gay rights as one aspect of the vast conspiracy theory known as the "new world order," in which the federal government supposedly inflicts liberal values on unwilling Americans. According to Chenoweth, the federal government's mysterious "black helicopters," used in the state to patrol for fires and wayward wildlife, helped enforce those values. By bringing together diverse aspects of the far right, from anti-environmentalists to gun owners to property-rights advocates, Chenoweth was able to cobble together a narrow majority. Among her staunchest backers was Sam Sherwood, a leader of the United States Militia Association, who considers House Speaker Newt Gingrich a liberal and has threatened to wage guerrilla war against President Clinton.

As Sidney Blumenthal wrote in *The New Yorker* magazine, Chenoweth, a divorced mother, was a late convert to the Christian right. It was not until 1989, when the Washington-based Family Research Council, Gary Bauer's lobbying group, dispatched a lobbyist to Idaho to work on behalf of antiabortion legislation, that Chenoweth came aboard. By the early 1990s, she had become a deacon at a charismatic church that engaged in a ritual known as "laughing" or "laughing therapy," in which members of the congregation engage in ecstatic fits of laughter in order to lose themselves more thoroughly in the Holy Spirit. Though Chenoweth was not motivated primarily by faith, she shared a conservative political philosophy that made her an easy choice for the religious right to get behind.

Chenoweth got her start in national politics in 1980 by working to bring down liberal Senate icon Frank Church, who was narrowly ousted from office in the Republican revolution that put Ronald Reagan in the White House. But like Robertson, Falwell, and other right-wingers who had invested heavily in Reagan's election, Chenoweth came to see the revolution as a wasted opportunity, arguing that the state's conservative movement came to depend too heavily on Washington. The next time around, she vowed, conservatives would be so well organized on the local level that they would write their own ticket for the national level. The Reagan administration "diminished the sagebrush rebellion," she has said, referring to the backlash against federal-lands management in several Western states. "By about three years after Reagan was elected, there was no sagebrush rebellion."

As an antigay rights, antiabortion, antiregulation conservative

strongly backed by the Christian Coalition, Chenoweth represented the new face of the Republican Party. Dozens of hard-line
conservatives like her, many with little patience for the moderate
wing of the party or even for moderate voters, won election to
Congress in 1994. Chenoweth's ability to harness divergent interests of the right without becoming a captive of any one in particular made her an ideal model for Republican candidates in
conservative districts. But whether such a profile translated into
an enduring legislative impact or further triumph in congressional
and national elections was unclear. Angered by Chenoweth's inability to work with the Republican leadership in Congress and by
her staunch defense of the violent militia movement, Republican
officials in Idaho considered mounting a primary challenge to her
1996 reelection bid. Whether the Republicans could win a national election if fringe social issues, like those championed by
Chenoweth, played a central role remains an open question. The
1996 presidential election, in which every major Republican candidate is so far pandering to the religious right, may provide some
answers.

⌒ The role of conservative Christians in the 1994 Republican
landslide was not lost on the 1996 Republican presidential hopefuls. With the exception of Pennsylvania senator Arlen Specter,
every candidate went out of his way either to embrace the religious right or at least accommodate its demands. The white knight
of Houston, Pat Buchanan, quickly found that others were joust-
ing on the same far-right playing field that he had once had to
himself. There was good reason: because of their massive recruitment and political savvy, the religious right wielded enormous influence or exercised outright control in the majority of state
Republican Party machines. Because its leverage within the GOP
had only increased since 1992, religious conservatives, despite
Reed's less strident noises, had no incentive to take a more conciliatory stance on "pro-family" issues, including gay rights, especially since they had clung to the notion that Bush's refusal to
stand by them contributed to his defeat. If only Bush had hammered Clinton relentlessly during the campaign over his pledge to

lift the military ban on gays and lesbians, they argued, the outcome of the election might have been different.

The religious right was determined to translate its electoral success into concrete gains, both in public policy in the new conservative Congress and in the fast-approaching Republican presidential showdown. Indeed, shortly after the 1994 election, Focus on the Family leader James Dobson wrote to Gingrich complaining that the religious right had been relegated to the "back of the bus for too long," once again implying that religious conservatives constituted a discrete minority against whom the political system discriminated. Dobson and Bauer paid visits to leading presidential candidates in which they threatened to withhold their support if the candidates did not toe the family values line. Religious conservatives, it seemed to Dobson, were merely seeking to collect what was rightfully theirs. But in so doing, he and other religious right leaders with an equal sense of entitlement risked turning the 1996 presidential campaign into a replay of the 1992 election, in which the Republican Party, dubbing the Democrats the party of gays and themselves the party of God, met a drubbing at the polls. In four years, the Republicans had failed to learn the lesson of the political price they had paid for an intolerant public image, and the country's debate over the complex interplay of sexuality and religion had failed to advance beyond the rhetoric of crude antigay stereotypes and name-calling, typified by Pat Buchanan's infamous "culture war" speech at the 1992 Republican National Convention in Houston. Those in the party who understood the price to be paid for an extreme image couldn't do anything about it because of the power the religious right exerted over the party apparatus.

Despite their continued lip service to antiabortion measures and cutbacks in public education, antigay posturing became the chief means whereby Republican candidates demonstrated fidelity to religious conservatives. With no openly gay Republican constituency, such attacks had little potential for political harm to them. Bob Dole, who had taken a moderate approach to gay issues in the past, made a garbled attempt to reject any association with gay causes, even Republican gay causes that would benefit his campaign financially. In August 1995, Dole returned a $1,000 check from Log Cabin Republicans, a gay Republican group, which his own staff had solicited, saying that the group's political agenda was "not in line" with his values. The move was a particularly transparent political ploy because Dole continued to accept donations from record and film industry executives whom he had criticized weeks earlier for having "sold [their] souls" and "debas[ed] our nation" by producing gangsta rap and violent movies. Time Warner, the corporation that Dole and former secretary of education William Bennett singled out for scorn, had donated $50,000 to Dole's Better America Foundation in 1993 and 1994. Scrambling to put a fine point on it, a spokesman for Dole explained that Log Cabin promotes a "narrow political agenda at odds" with Dole's campaign, while the entertainment executives and Time Warner push a variety of issues.

Pressure from the religious right made Dole appear downright schizophrenic on the gay issue. In a March 1995 *New York Times* profile, Dole said that "everyone should be treated alike, whether they're black or brown or disabled or homosexual." Admirable sentiments, to be sure. But just two weeks after the *Times* profile appeared, Dole sent a letter to the conservative *Washington Times* backing off his earlier statement. Mimicking the religious right's antigay language, Dole said that he opposed the "special-interest gay agenda that runs from gays in the military and reaches so far as to suggest special status for sexual orientation under federal civil rights statutes." The deliberate obfuscation of gay rights laws for political profit played on. The "gay agenda," if one exists at all, had never called for "special status" under federal civil rights statutes, but only to be included in them, on an equal footing with a long list of protected categories. In fact, in 1994 gay lobbyists agreed to tailor a bill that would protect gays and lesbians from discrimination under federal civil rights laws more narrowly than protections for other minorities, seeking a ban on employment-related bias alone. Calling protections against bias for gays "special rights" simply allowed Republicans like Dole to look the other way from the reality of antigay discrimination, which Senator Dole had already acknowledged in signing a pledge from the Human Rights Campaign Fund the previous year. In that pledge, Dole, along with dozens of other legislators, agreed not to discriminate on the basis of sexual orientation in his own congressional office.

Rich Tafel, executive director of Log Cabin Republicans, was apoplectic after Dole's apparent policy reversal in the summer of 1995. To soothe Tafel, Dole's national finance chairman, John Moran, took Tafel on a personal tour of Dole's Washington, D.C., campaign headquarters to introduce him to the candidate's campaign staff. "I'm taken through the entire campaign and introduced to everyone clearly as a gay person," only to have the check returned shortly thereafter, Tafel complained to *The Advocate*. Moran, however, was seeing green when he rolled out the red carpet for Tafel. Behind the $1,000 donation from Log Cabin, the maximum legal donation from a political action committee, were tens of thousands in potential contributions from wealthy gay Republicans across the country.

Thanks to the inconsistency of his stance, Dole was fast acquiring the political reputation he most wanted to avoid—that of George Bush. In his four years in the White House, Bush managed to antagonize both gays and religious conservatives. Much like Dole's, Bush's outreach efforts to the religious right failed to overcome their basic distrust of a politician whom they saw as the great compromiser. Even the Bush administration's most modest expressions of sympathy for the gay cause, like inviting gay activists to a bill-signing ceremony for hate-crimes legislation in which sexual orientation was included, had been considered a betrayal of the religious conservative cause.

Dole was not the only one who had been put in an awkward position by the ascendancy of the religious right in the Republican Party. The Log Cabin Republicans liked to invoke the moderate, principled party of Abraham Lincoln. But as the religious right gained in power, the centrist wing of the Republican Party, upon which Log Cabin depended for support, all but died. The group was in the embarrassing position of not being able to give its money away to any Republican presidential aspirant with the exception of California governor Pete Wilson and Senator Arlen

Specter, both of whom quickly dropped out of the campaign. (Asked if he would accept a check from Log Cabin, Specter responded, "My name is spelled A-R-L-E-N.")

The Log Cabin's most ideologically sympathetic backer in Congress, Rep. Steve Gunderson, an openly gay Republican from the rich agricultural lands of western Wisconsin, found himself torn between a rock—demands from Speaker Gingrich, with whom he maintained a close working relationship—and a hard place—gay activists, to whom he felt increasingly loyal since coming out publicly in 1994. When House majority whip Dick Armey referred to openly gay representative Barney Frank as "Barney Fag," Gunderson was reluctant to publicly criticize Armey for the remark, partly because he feared that Frank was making political hay out of the comment for the Democrats. Frank promptly accused Gunderson of "shilling for Armey." (In response to Armey's claim that the "Barney Fag" comment was an unintentional slip of the tongue, the ever-witty Frank said, "I turned to my own expert, my mother, who reports that in fifty-nine years of marriage, no one ever introduced her as 'Elsie Fag.'")

Ultimately, Gunderson's sense of solidarity with gays won the day. Dole's decision to return the Log Cabin check infuriated the congressman, who had endorsed Dole's candidacy. In a September 6 letter to Dole, Gunderson asked, would Dole reject the "support of anyone who happens to be gay? If this is so, do you intend to now reject my support and request those on your staff who happen to be gay to resign?" During an appearance on national television two weeks after receiving Gunderson's tongue-lashing, Dole was backpedaling yet again. As rumors circulated that several of his top campaign officials were gay, Dole bragged that his Senate office and campaign had adopted antidiscrimination protections for gays and lesbians, referring to his Human Rights Campaign Fund pledge. Then in October, having already flip-flopped twice, Dole told flabbergasted reporters that the August decision to return the $1,000 was a "mistake," blaming the decision on his staff. Ultimately, the reversals failed to satisfy anyone.

Dole was not the only candidate the religious right succeeded in backing into a corner on the issue of gays. Texas senator Phil

Gramm, who often referred to himself as the only "true conservative" in the race, fared little better. In his March 1995 meeting
with James Dobson of Focus on the Family and Gary Bauer,
Gramm told them that he felt uncomfortable assuming the role of
"political preacher" to win their support. Explaining that a successful national campaign must focus on economic issues, Gramm
added that he would leave the preaching to them. The evangelical
lobbyists came away angry at Gramm, who they felt had betrayed
their support by not speaking out forcefully enough on what they
deemed their issues.

Gramm was speaking not from principle, but from necessity.
He could hardly be accused of being shy to use gay rights as a
wedge issue. In his successful 1984 Senate bid against Democrat
Lloyd Doggett, Gramm gleefully used Doggett's decision to accept contributions raised at a Houston gay strip club against the
Democrat. But later, in an effort to avoid the lion's den into which
too much courting of either the religious right or moderates might
cast him, Gramm simply took refuge in wishful thinking. In an *At-
lantic* magazine profile in early 1995, Gramm told conservative
author David Frum he would attempt to persuade the Christian
right that economic conservatism is indistinguishable from social
conservatism. "If you are talking about values issues," he said,
"what is more value-laden than the welfare system? Aren't we
talking about values when we're talking about stopping the subsi-
dizing of conceiving illegitimate children? Aren't we talking about
values when we're talking about cutting spending and doubling
the dependent exemption for children?"

Through the trappings of his zigzag pursuit of the right, a
more astute and reflective Gramm sometimes came into view. He
rightly complained that the presidency and the pulpit should not
be confused. But when pressured by the Christian right, it didn't
take him long to become a preacher. In a May 1995 commencement address at Jerry Falwell's Liberty University in Lynchburg,
Virginia, Gramm offered an olive branch to religious conservatives. Falwell inserted in programs for the event a warning that
Gramm "remains uncommitted on gays in the military and is said
to favor several pro-choice leaders as vice presidential candi-

dates." As if following a script written by Falwell, Gramm denounced abortion rights and deplored the already restrictive gays-in-the-military policy as "destructive and unworkable." (In a nuance seemingly lost on the gathering that day, the latter epithet could just as easily have sprung from a mildly progressive impulse as from a die-hard right-wing viewpoint.)

Predictably, Gramm's offering failed to satisfy the religious right's ravenous hunger for red meat. "Social conservatives are looking for more than an occasional bone," the Family Research Council's Bauer said of the Lynchburg speech. But Bauer's expressions of ideological and moral purity were highly selective. When *The New Republic* magazine revealed in May 1995 that Gramm had invested $7,500 in *Beauty Queens,* a heterosexual soft-porn movie that was never made, Bauer and other religious conservatives, who had made a living out of complaining about the country's faltering sexual mores, dismissed it as insignificant. Similarly, Bauer scoffed at accusations that married Republican senator Bob Packwood had sexually harassed dozens of women, some of them his own employees, during his long political career. "It may be that . . . there are no penalties required, that you've got a bunch of folks applying 1995 political correctness to 1960 acts by a senator who is boozing it up and just was maybe a little offensive," the normally pious Bauer told the *Washington Times* in August 1995, two weeks before Packwood was ousted from the Senate.

Needing a strong finish in an Iowa straw poll to resuscitate his dormant campaign, Gramm again verbally bashed gays to attract religious conservative voters. In August, Gramm mailed a fundraising letter to six thousand subscribers of *The Report,* an antigay newsletter published by religious conservative Bill Horn. Horn's claim to fame was leading a successful campaign against Jonathan Wilson, a member of the Des Moines school board, because Wilson was gay and supported the inclusion of sexual orientation in the nondiscrimination policy of the city's public schools. "I have been speaking with Bill Horn of *The Report,*" Gramm said in the letter. "He has shared his concerns regarding the threat that certain agendas may have in tearing down the very essence of our nuclear families. Thank God for Bill and the thousands of parents who would not be intimidated by the liberal media or the radical homosexual community."

In his haste to win the religious conservative vote, Gramm overlooked Horn's questionable credentials. Horn moved to Altoona, Iowa, less than a year before embarking on his antigay campaign, to raise money for a Midwestern office of *The Report,* whose headquarters in Lancaster, California, is an offshoot of Springs of Life Ministry. Although he was leading a revolt against any inclusion of homosexuality in the Des Moines school curriculum, Horn neither lived in the district nor enrolled his children in its schools. Wilson, by contrast, had served on the school board for twelve years before announcing that he was gay at a January 1995 board meeting. The debate, fanned by a local right-wing radio talk-show host, became so heated that law enforcement officials provided Wilson—whose daughter, a senior, was his second to attend a Des Moines Public School—with a bulletproof vest to wear to board meetings due to repeated threats to his life.

In the end, Wilson's demonstrable involvement in the school district made little difference. In the September 1995 election, despite an infusion of cash from outside the state, Wilson finished fourth in a field of twelve. The two candidates who were elected to the board had been endorsed by the state Christian Coalition chapter, which poured close to $100,000 into the race. Once again, gay issues provided an effective opening for religious conservatives to make inroads into local politics. Spurred by an influx of conservative voters, the turnout was one of the largest in the history of city school-board elections. Gay activists and their liberal allies were no match for the well-calibrated campaign waged by the right, which used Sunday-school buses to shuttle conservative voters to the polls. As the Iowa presidential primary approached, the Christian Coalition could point to the results of the school-board election and its role in producing them to bring the presidential aspirants into closer rein.

Public statements in the election's aftermath perpetuated the acrimony of the race. In the frustration of the loss, Wilson lost his characteristic cool and overstated the impact of his opponents' triumph. "This election," he said, "sadly represents a loss to every individual who is different in any way." Horn confirmed Wilson's fear that, in the view of many organizers in the religious right, gays and lesbians were not welcome in Des Moines politics. "If Mr. Wilson wants to be a homosexual activist school board member," Horn asserted, "he needs to move to San Francisco."

～ During the first one hundred days of the new Congress, the religious right reluctantly agreed to lie low while the Republican leadership pushed through its Contract with America, which focused almost exclusively on economic issues. In wringing the concession out of the right, Gingrich agreed to allow congressional hearings on the Reverend Lou Sheldon's allegation that gay activists were proselytizing in the nation's public schools. Upon receiving confirmation of the hearings in August 1995, Sheldon, who is president of the Traditional Values Coalition, dashed off a fund-raising letter contending that "people do not want their children brainwashed by teachers or the curriculum promoting homosexuality as 'normal' but that is what is happening!" In the letter's low point, Sheldon quoted the "foremost authority on homosexuality," antigay psychiatrist Charles Socarides, blaming gay adolescents for their own suicides: "Kids are not committing suicide because of actions against homosexuality but because they know within themselves that it is not normal." For a contribution of "$50 or more" Sheldon offered to send donors a new book by Socarides, *A Freedom Too Far.* "This is our golden opportunity!" Sheldon concluded. (Sheldon failed to mention that Dr. Socarides's son, Richard, was a high-ranking openly gay official in the Clinton administration and that Socarides, far from being the "foremost authority on homosexuality," continued to engage in unethical "reparative therapy," which seeks to "convert" gays to heterosexuality. Dr. Socarides, who had been married four times, dedicated his 1968 book, *The Overt Homosexual,* to Richard.)

In addition to fund-raising, Sheldon hoped to use the platform provided by the hearings to generate public support for the reintroduction of a thwarted 1994 measure that would have axed federal funds to schools "encouraging or supporting homo-sexuality." The bill, sponsored in the House by Missouri Republican Mel Hancock and in the Senate by North Carolina Republican Jesse Helms, was derived from a series of unsuccessful Helms-sponsored antigay measures introduced in the late 1980s and early 1990s banning federal funding for everything from sexually explicit AIDS education to sex surveys that included questions about homosexuality. In the Republican-dominated Congress, Helms was even eyeing legislation that would prohibit federal funds from being used to "promote" homosexuality in any way. Like much of the gay rights debate, the congressional battle was bogus; education was traditionally a local concern over which the federal government had little say, a point reiterated on all other fronts by many of the same conservatives who were encouraging Sheldon's hearings. In the peculiar contradiction of the Republican revolution, those who most loudly proclaimed their desire to get rid of big government were most willing to intrude into matters where government had never gone before.

The hearings did little to improve Sheldon's reputation in mainstream political circles. After bragging for months that he had orchestrated the hearings, the committee, headed by Michigan Republican Peter Hoekstra, went to great lengths to distance itself from Sheldon's taint of extremism, relying instead on the more respectable William Bennett, who testified that schools should teach virtues to students, without specifying exactly what such a project entailed. Sheldon's star witness turned out to be Claire Connolly, a lesbian who claimed that gay men were using federal AIDS funding to hold orgies in gay community centers across the country. Hoekstra backed away from Sheldon after lobbyists from Human Rights Campaign, the gay lobby group, detailed his long history of antigay activities in press releases.

Gingrich and Dole did not share Sheldon's enthusiasm for the explosive gays-in-the-schools issue, though not out of any real concern for the plight of vulnerable gay and lesbian youths. Instead, they remained wary of the religious right's obsessive focus on such issues, which would detract from their legislative agenda.

The Republican leadership's concern found a sympathetic ear in the Christian Coalition's Ralph Reed. Unlike his more openly radical counterparts—including his boss, Pat Robertson—Reed made sure that his group's Contract with the American Family mentioned homosexuality only in passing. At the September 1995 Christian Coalition conference, Reed warned speakers like the rabid Sheldon to steer clear of ad hominem attacks on homosexuals. The dictum was consistent with Reed's desire to broaden the Christian Coalition's base beyond the fervent, but sharply confined, antigay and antiabortion constituencies who made up the core of its membership. In a summer 1993 edition of *Policy Review,* a publication of the conservative Heritage Foundation, Reed argued that the "pro-family movement" faces a "communications dilemma.... Though blessed with talented leadership, strong grassroots support, and enormous financial resources, it has not yet completely connected its agenda with average voters."

Reed's own image required some refurbishing as well. In the late 1970s and early 1980s, before taking the helm of the Christian Coalition in 1988, Reed was one of the most vehement of antiabortion protesters, staging mock funerals for fetuses and holding confrontational sidewalk protests outside abortion clinics. As recently as 1991, Reed was employing some of the most extreme of the religious right's rhetoric—rhetoric that helped its political opponents depict the movement as sinister and threatening. "I want to be invisible," he bragged. "I do guerrilla warfare. I paint my face and travel at night. You don't know it's over until you're in a body bag." In another interview, he used the war metaphor for which Robertson has become famous: "It's better to move quietly, with stealth, under the cover of night.... It comes down to whether you want to be the British army in the Revolutionary War or the Viet Cong. History tells us which tactic was more effective."

But as Reed and the Christian Coalition entered the 1996 presidential campaign, his more radical background was all but forgotten. In a summer 1995 issue, featuring a smiling Reed on the cover, *Time* magazine described him as the religious right's "fresh face, the choirboy to the rescue, a born-again Christian

with a fine sense of the secular mechanics of American politics."
In another profile, *People* magazine, ignoring the Christian Coalition's antigay fund-raising letters, proclaimed that Reed "speaks
softly, steering clear of the vitriolic, us-versus-them rhetoric."

Like the GOP power brokers who would later take up his
agenda, Reed failed to see that it was not the religious right's
narrow focus that was its primary problem. As the overwhelmingly negative response to the 1992 Republican convention
demonstrated, mainstream voters were uneasy with the intensity
of the religious right's intransigent reading of personal morality.
The live-and-let-live attitude of many American voters did not
jibe with the evangelicals' strict biblical mandate. Claiming a direct pipeline to God causes people great discomfort; that was
why candidates who were members of the religious right, and
not just allies, had such a hard time winning office. While some
voters, perhaps even a majority, might like the notion of a nation
rooted in "Christian values," their definitions of those values
were far more flexible and less dogmatic than the religious
right's and remain broad enough to encompass not only evangelicals, but liberal mainline Protestant denominations as well as
Reformed Jews.

Americans honor strength of character as readily as depth of
faith. That was why, despite popular sympathy for their values, to
most voters the religious right still smacked of intolerance. Pat
Robertson, for instance, has consistently registered in opinion
polls as one of the least popular figures in American politics.
Reed's dilemma was not so much how to broaden his group's
agenda, but how to shed the Christian Coalition's intolerance
without losing its claim to a fixed morality or its core constituency.
The Coalition's membership, according to a September 1995 poll,
was more united on morality than on economics. Sixty-two percent of the poll's respondents said that "moral decline" was the
most important issue facing the country, while only 9 percent
cited the deficit or taxes. Despite Reed's best efforts to smooth out
his movement's rough edges, the poll results showed a majority of
its members likely to support attempts to repeal or preempt gay

rights, portending more destructive antigay campaigns in the name of combating moral decline.

⟶ One year after Idaho and Oregon voters rejected statewide antigay initiatives, and one year into the Republican takeover of Congress, Maine voters were faced with the first statewide antigay initiative east of the Rockies. Learning crucial lessons from other states' campaigns, gay activists in Maine successfully depicted the measure as an out-of-state effort to dictate a coercive policy contrary to the state's famed independent streak. The ballot measure, which would have barred the state from ever protecting gays and lesbians from discrimination, was defeated 53 percent to 47 percent in November 1995. With the failure, the religious right was forced to discard initiatives as an effective tool, at least for the immediate future.

Led by Carolyn Cosby of Concerned Maine Families, the antigay campaign was hurt by dissension within the ranks of the state's religious right in the state and by the organization's repeated strategic missteps. Following Reed's exhortation to avoid the most blatant antigay pronouncements for fear of a close association with rank bigotry, the Maine chapter of the organization officially refused to back Cosby's work. And though he supported the initiative, Jaspar Wyman, the onetime head of the Christian Civil League, the state's leading group of religious conservatives, warned that the campaign should steer clear of the antigay rhetoric that characterized campaigns in Colorado, Oregon, and Idaho. "This must not become a campaign calculated to arouse hatred or fear of any group of our fellow citizens," he said.

Across the country, antigay ballot measures partly depended for their success on the religious right's ability to falsely equate antidiscrimination protections for gays and lesbians with "special rights." The circumlocution of the ballot language in Maine took the tactic to a new low. As the measure appeared on the ballot, gays, lesbians, or homosexuality were not mentioned. Instead, it proposed to limit the categories of the state's human rights act to those currently in place, thereby barring sexual orientation from ever gaining inclusion. Cosby chose the strategy in an attempt to avoid the appearance of leading an intolerant crusade and to tap into the larger current of opposition to affirmative action in the state. Paul Volle, head of the state Christian Coalition, told Portland's *Community Pride Reporter,* a gay monthly, that he was wary of Cosby's attempt to have it both ways. "If you really stop and think about it, [Concerned Maine Families] have some real ethical problems going on with their finances and how they got the signatures from the standpoint they were trying to tell the general public and the media that it's not a gay rights issue."

Reminded of the boycotts, protests, and lawsuits that followed passage of Colorado's antigay initiative, Maine voters were leery about the involvement of outside interests in the battle, especially from the right. Even though Maine Won't Discriminate, the group leading the effort to turn back the measure, received close to half the $1 million it raised from national gay groups and out-of-state gay donors, it was Concerned Maine Families, which raised only a fraction of its $100,000 budget from outside the state, that was tainted by its association with well-known national antigay activists. Tony Marco, one of the leaders of Colorado for Family Values, made high-profile visits to the state as a paid consultant to Concerned Maine Families. The group also shelled out thousands of dollars in legal fees to Bruce Fein, a conservative lawyer and former Reagan Administration official who served as a legal adviser to antigay campaigns in other states.

Yet it was Cosby herself who inflicted the most damage to her cause. Throughout the campaign, Cosby tried the impossible: to put a happy face on an initiative that would have barred gays and lesbians from antidiscrimination protections forever. Pressed by the Portland *Sunday Telegram,* she admitted that if she had a gay child she would "love" him or her. Indeed, Cosby confessed that she couldn't "imagine being here under these circumstances today and having a child who is homosexual," leaving many voters to wonder how she could justify imposing the initiative on anyone's children.

⁓ The crude and defamatory approach to gay rights that the religious right has championed through the Republican Party lacked an effective counterweight in Clinton and the Democrats, who were struggling with their own lack of identity and political vision after their devastating losses in November 1994. While the religious right gained a stranglehold on the Republican Party, Clinton, fearful of another gays-in-the-military debacle, shunned the movement, save for one important speech in May 1995. The combination of Clinton's inept handling of the military ban and gay groups' complete inability to provide even a semblance of political cover for him left gays and lesbians without a voice at the national level, making them particularly vulnerable to the religious right's attacks. In the six-month period after the Republican takeover of Congress, the White House dismissed its most outspoken champion of gay causes, Surgeon General Joycelyn Elders; refused to file an amicus brief in the Colorado antigay initiative case, the most important gay-related case to reach the U.S. Supreme Court in the 1990s; and watched as Roberta Achtenberg, its highest-ranking gay political appointee, left the administration to run for mayor of San Francisco, without seeking out a suitable gay replacement.

The moves came on top of two years of neglect in the wake of the gays-in-the-military defeat. While Clinton fulfilled his promise to appoint an AIDS czar, his first pick for the job was a politically ineffective former Washington State official, Kristine Gebbie, whom he stationed in a small office over a McDonald's up the street from the White House. Gebbie's successor, Patricia Fleming, was a top aide of Health and Human Services Secretary Donna Shalala, whom the administration kept on a short leash. Clinton's most vocal openly gay official, the flamboyant AIDS activist Bob Hattoy, was shuttled to an obscure position in the Interior Department after he raised difficult questions about Clinton's commitment to gay and AIDS issues. The cumulative effect of the decisions was to distance the White House from gays and lesbians and to appeal to the moderate-to-conservative voters whom Clinton believed were essential to his reelection bid.

Yet at the same time he was appealing to so-called Reagan Democrats, Clinton, perhaps remembering the estimated 3 million gay dollars that poured into the coffers of his 1992 campaign, continued to make overtures to gays and lesbians. In August 1995, he issued an executive order abolishing the federal government's ban on security clearances for gays and lesbians. Though the ban had only rarely been enforced in the last decade, the executive order carried considerable symbolic value for gay activists embittered by Clinton's refusal to embrace their cause. Unlike the botched attempt to eliminate the military ban, Clinton's security-clearance order became effective immediately, leaving little room for divisive political debate. The White House issued the order without comment while Congress was away on its August vacation. The only peep of dissent came from the familiar antigay firebrand Rep. Bob Dornan. The California Republican declared that he "wouldn't trust homosexuals with a five-dollar loan, let alone the nation's secrets." Given Dornan's history of antigay activism, it seemed extremely unlikely that a homosexual looking for a loan would come to him anyway.

Murmurs of dissent upon Congress's return to session in September were squelched by openly gay representative Barney Frank, who repeated his threat to reveal the names of closeted Republican members and their staffs if the GOP pursued repealing the executive order. On the eve of the National Lesbian and Gay Journalists Association conference in September, Clinton announced his endorsement of the Employment Non-Discrimination Act, a proposed federal bill that would extend to gays and lesbians a more limited version of the legal protections that are extended on the basis of race, sex, disability, and national origin. The gesture was mostly symbolic; Clinton had already endorsed a stronger version of the bill during his campaign. It also entailed limited political risk. The legislation was sure to be blocked by the Republican-controlled House, on whose leadership neither gay lobbyists nor the president had any real influence. The bill's many exemptions, including one banning affirmative action based on sexual orientation and another excluding religious institutions from its reach, didn't stop religious conservatives from attacking it. The Clinton administration, declared Robert Knight, director of cultural studies for the Family Research Council, had been "relentlessly pursuing the homosexual agenda within the federal government and the military. This would extend it to the private sector where it would have grave consequences." If Clinton was "relentlessly pursuing the homosexual agenda," Knight was one of the few to recognize it.

In the antigay climate pervading Washington, Clinton could only become effective not by pursuing specific policies, but by elevating the tone of the debate. One month before issuing the executive order on security clearances, Clinton took aim at the "extremism of rhetoric and excessive partisanship" that pervades American politics in general and gay politics in particular. Having repeatedly been savaged, usually in unfair and inaccurate ways, by right-wing talk-show hosts and religious right conspiracy theorists, Clinton could sympathize with gays and lesbians. During an eloquent speech at Georgetown University, Clinton eviscerated Jesse Helms's remarks just weeks earlier contending that federal money should be denied people with AIDS because they contracted the disease through "deliberate, disgusting, revolting conduct."

Reasserting the inclusive national vision he had rarely invoked since the early days of his presidency, Clinton scored much needed points with gays and lesbians. "The gay people who have AIDS are still our sons, our brothers, our cousins, our citizens," Clinton said, noting that even though smoking causes lung cancer, no one was proposing to stop treating the disease or cease searching for a cure. "We need to respect our differences, and hear them. But it means instead of having shrill voices of discord, we need a chorus of harmony. In a chorus of harmony, you know there are lots of differences, but you can hear all the voices." Clinton's words represented a genuine advancement in civil discussion of the issue. In the face of the unrelentingly harsh attacks on gays and lesbians from the religious right, his remarks were nothing short of courageous. But the problem was that as the choirmaster, Clinton had already struck too many wrong chords and changed his tune too many times to call for the harmony that he envisioned. As the presidential election approached, the discord would only grow louder.

From Arms to Armistice

GIVEN THE BITTERNESS AND POLARIZATION of the contemporary gay rights debate, chances for civil discourse and a peaceful resolution appear dim. The extreme way in which religious conservatives and gay activists define one another makes compromise and negotiation nearly impossible. If, in the view of many on the religious right, gays are literally the "spawn of the devil" bent on the destruction of Western civilization, how can Christian conservatives come to accept or even respect gay and lesbian participation in the political system? If gay activists insist on depicting the Christian right as a fascist and even neo-Nazi movement determined to destroy constitutional democracy, how can they come to appreciate more fully and fairly the role of religious Christians in American politics? The culture-war metaphor, made famous by Pat Buchanan at the 1992 Republican National Convention and widely applied by the media in framing the gay rights debate, implies that there can be only one winner. As long as the debate is couched in terms of driving one side out of the political arena, it is likely to remain unproductive.

It is a sign of the dismal nature of the debate that in the midst of the 1996 presidential campaign the country is fighting many of the same battles over gay rights it has been fighting for more than a quarter century. In the late 1980s and early 1990s, Lon Mabon of the Oregon Citizens Alliance rose to prominence by merely mimicking Anita Bryant's antigay crusade of more than a decade earlier, adding his own destructive spin. The fund-raising tactics of the religious right have changed little since master new-right fund-raiser Richard Viguerie figured out in the early 1970s that the regular demonization of homosexuals would rake in millions for Christian and other right-wing groups at the heart of the country's conservative revolution. Indeed, antigay attacks have become such a fixture of the direct-mail fund-raising of conservative groups that to abandon the strategy would be to endanger their very existence. Thus, even as the general public has become more accepting of the gays and lesbians in their midst, the religious right's antigay views have calcified, inhibiting dialogue with gays and lesbians almost completely.

Religious conservative groups are not the only ones to benefit from the culture war. Over the years, gay rights groups have become equally dependent on the religious right's antigay pronouncements for their own growth. Religious right groups portray gays and lesbians as the "most pernicious evil today," in the words of the Reverend Lou Sheldon, the president of the Traditional Values Coalition, a conservative group funded in large part by incendiary antigay appeals. Homosexuality, according to him, must be "stopped before it spreads throughout the nation like a cancer." Gay activists have traditionally responded by mocking the Christian values that Sheldon claims to represent, rather than seeking to redeem these values among gays and lesbians from their association with rank bigotry, or to articulate their own moral standards, which vary little in substance from the religious right's, for average Americans to hear. Gay leaders have adopted an increasingly defensive posture. For instance, in a surreptitious 1994 ambush against an Austin, Texas, church whose minister had made antigay remarks, the Lesbian Avengers dumped piles of manure on the church's steps. The protest may temporarily have satisfied the activists' anger, but it poisoned rather than enlightened the political debate over gay issues in Austin. Predictably, the right used the incident to demonstrate the accuracy of its claim that gays and lesbians are "Christian-bashers."

Perhaps the most notorious example of the way in which both sides confirm each other's worst fears is the cross fire over a nine-year-old essay, by gay activist Michael Swift, in Boston's left-wing *Gay Community News.* "Tremble, Hetero Swine!" Swift sardonically begins his satirical manifesto. "We shall sodomize your sons, emblems of your feeble masculinity, of your shallow dreams and vulgar lives. We will raise vast private armies . . . to defeat . . . the family unit. Perfect boys will be conceived and grown in the genetic laboratory." The article has repeatedly been trumpeted to this day by religious conservatives in organizational newsletters and election-related literature as the definitive proof of the gay community's antifamily agenda, even though the vast majority of gays and lesbians have never heard of it, let alone agree with its sentiments. In fact, the gay community is far too disorganized and politically diverse to agree upon a unified "gay agenda" that the religious right claims to have identified. If Sheldon had any qualms about depicting Swift's essay as representative of the gay community's views, he didn't dare admit them publicly. In the inflammatory video *Gay Rights, Special Rights,* which he sells nationwide as a tax-deductible donation to the Traditional Values Coalition, Sheldon featured excerpts from the essay, replete with ominous background music over scenes of innocent children.

But the religious right's chronic reliance on Swift's essay and other gay-activist propaganda is indicative, if not of willful distortion, then at least of woeful ignorance of the central aims of gay rights supporters. The article is hardly the dire threat the religious right contends. As lesbian social critic Cindy Patton has pointed out, the writer is actually parodying paranoid right-wing conspiracy theories about the gay movement. Conveniently left out of the right's depiction of the essay is its opening line: "This essay is an outré, madness, a tragic, cruel fantasy, an eruption of inner rage, on how the oppressed desperately dream of being the oppressor." Sheldon is not the only one to distort such rhetoric and the flamboyant behavior often displayed at gay pride marches. Gay conservatives have blamed it for providing the religious right with ammunition and for giving gays and lesbians a reputation for irresponsible behavior. While encouraging responsible rhetoric and behavior is admirable, creating good-gay/bad-gay divisions is unlikely to appease the Sheldons of the world and does little to elevate the tenor of the debate. Antigay activists have demonstrated such a determination to depict all gays and lesbians in an unflattering light and to avoid meaningful dialogue with gays that they will fasten onto even the shoddiest evidence to make their case, and failing that, as antigay researcher Paul Cameron has shown over and over again, they will manufacture their own "evidence."

In its most extreme form, the fight produces an almost comical distortion of reality. *The Lambda Report,* a newsletter devoted exclusively to monitoring what it calls the "homosexual agenda" from a conservative Christian perspective, seeks out the most radical gay activists to profile in a sensationalistic manner. This allows its editor, former *Washington Times* reporter Peter LaBarbera, divorced from any obligation to fairness and accuracy, to depict gays and lesbians as dangerous subversives. The January 1994 edition, for instance, features a lengthy exchange between LaBarbera and Ed Hougen, a gay publisher who is an advocate for the North American Man-Boy Love Association, a small group that garners little more sympathy among gays and lesbians than among religious conservatives. The discussion ranges from Pat Califia's *Macho Sluts,* a book that contains explicit lesbian sex scenes, to whether six-year-old boys can be "sexually aggressive." The combatants are more interested in scoring points for their uncompromising positions than in shedding light on how Americans can live together, much less in recognizing individual gays' claims of intolerance and discrimination.

LaBarbera's tactic is as old as the gay rights battle. For years, antigay activists have culled gay bookstores and the gay press for examples of depravity, which they then cite to conscript new foot soldiers and raise money to combat the "gay threat." But the damaging "evidence" is almost invariably based on gays and lesbians speaking frankly about the problems they face in their lives and in their community—problems that are often different only in context from those faced by heterosexuals. In his antigay research for the Pentagon during the gays-in-the-military debate, Lt. Col. Robert Lee Maginnis, who advised a high-level Pentagon task force on the military ban, described with barely concealed glee his frequent trips to Lambda Rising, a gay bookstore in Washington, D.C., where he discovered *Men Who Beat the Men Who Love Them,* a 1991 book that honestly depicted the often-ignored problem of domestic violence among gay men. From this anecdotal evidence he implies that gay men are disproportionately violence-prone. Never did Maginnis countenance that domestic violence occurs with at least equal frequency in heterosexual relationships. The religious right looks at human failings and sees them solely as gay failings. Antigay rhetoric never concedes that gays are like everyone else, only that they are worse than everyone else.

However mutually demeaning the two groups, gay activists do not go nearly as far as the leaders of the religious right in defaming an entire group of people and creating an atmosphere that contributes to harassment or worse. While both sides mischaracterize the other, the religious right goes beyond distortions to promulgating outright lies about gays and lesbians. And it may be unfair to compare focal figures on the religious right like Sheldon with fringe figures in the gay movement like the Lesbian Avengers. Nonetheless, gay activists, by displaying smugness and insensitivity, often give short shrift to the faith that drives religious conservatives and to the deep-seated economic and social uncertainties that motivate them. And they often fail to acknowledge the legitimate claims that religious conservatives make about the way they are presented in the media. Like gays and lesbians, fundamentalist, "born-again," evangelical, and Pentecostal Christians, who are often conflated by gay activists, feel that their lives and views are not reflected accurately in the media or in the larger culture. In just one example of anti-Christian bias, the popular Hollywood movie *Misery* features a deranged female character who feels compelled to kill because of her extreme biblical views. The media, by contrast, was more sensitive to complaints about the portrayal of a bisexual serial killer in *Basic Instinct.* That the media often takes the claims of defamation by gay activists more seriously than the religious right's only exacerbates religious conservatives' anger at what they consider the insensitivity of secular society.

At times, some gay activists, prone to creating their own dark fantasies about the religious right, have done more than underestimate people's faith—they mock it. For an article in the gay magazine *Out,* lesbian writer Donna Minkowitz donned a wig and a tacky dress to "infiltrate" a Christian Coalition meeting, thereby equating the group with secretive underground groups such as the Ku Klux Klan. But perhaps the most egregious example of mocking people's faith was a protest by the AIDS Coalition to Unleash Power that disrupted mass at St. Patrick's in 1989. Toting signs and stickers reading STOP THE CHURCH, ACT UP members invaded the mass, standing on pews to shout at parishioners. One activist threw a consecrated host to the floor. The protest betrayed the activists' inability to distinguish between positions taken by the Catholic Church hierarchy and by the parishioners in the pews, who often disagree with their leaders. Even within the Church leadership, there is hardly unanimity. Numerous clergy have actually endorsed nondiscrimination legislation for gays, and several bishops have been vocal in opposition to the repeal of such laws. And while gay activists were targeting the Catholic Church, far more fervently antigay conservative Christians were gaining political momentum beneath their radar. Like the Lesbian Avengers' 1994 stunt in Austin, the St. Patrick's protest, along with an equally disrespectful action at Hamilton Square Baptist Church in San Francisco in 1993, has been recited to a fare-thee-well by such leaders as Robertson and Sheldon, who would have supporters believe that such actions are a staple of the "gay agenda," when in fact many gays and lesbians find them of dubious use at best, and downright offensive at worst. Yet the religious right's exploitation of the insensitivity of some gay activists does not absolve the activists from responsibility for their lack of respect for religious diversity. Rather than recognize evangelicals' place in American politics and society, many gay activists would just as soon eliminate it.

The sense of victimhood that pervades both movements goes a long way toward helping both sides further their goals. To shore up support for their cause, gay organizations and religious right groups inveigh against the threat they are under. Like gay activists who throw the term *homophobia* around with reckless abandon, religious right leaders brand any disagreement with them as anti-Christian bias. In a typical response to criticism of the way religious conservatives have conducted themselves in the political debate, the Christian Coalition's newspaper, *Christian American,* ran a front-page banner headline in September 1994 that read, "Assault on Faith; Liberals Launch Campaign of Bigotry." The headline referred to, among other things, a B'nai B'rith Anti-Defamation League report alleging that several religious right-wing leaders, most notably Pat Robertson, regularly traffic in anti-Semitism. That the exaggerations help rake in millions of dollars from contributors only confirms the strategy's usefulness. According to Mel White, a former ghostwriter for evangelical leaders who has since come out as gay, Falwell once told him in an unguarded moment, "If homosexuals didn't exist, we'd have to invent them." In their own way, gay activists are almost as dependent upon Falwell and his allies.

~ The religious right's intentional misreading of homosexuality deprives the public of accurate information about the lives of gays and lesbians. If Americans were to take the religious right's depiction of homosexuals at face value, they would assume that gay life consists entirely of NAMBLA conventions, S-and-M orgies, and Queer Nation demonstrations. In reality, the gay community is at least as diverse as the evangelical community, and its "gay agenda" encompasses every imaginable ideology. Homosexuality and left-wing politics are not necessarily any more analogous than evangelism and political conservatism. Indeed, the genius of the modern gay rights movement is that it has translated homosexuality into gay identity, which has spawned a rich plethora of churches, businesses, political groups, sports associations, and publications across the country. Instead of furtive sex and clandestine relationships, gay identity offered a way for gays and lesbians to contribute to each other and to the larger community. The communal spirit of gays and lesbians, born to protect one another from the slings and arrows of a prejudiced society, has been exemplified by their response to AIDS. While the government dragged its feet in the early days of the epidemic, the gay community set up organizations to care for its sick and dying, launched massive HIV prevention campaigns, and sounded the alarm for other communities at risk. But because the gay cause has often been framed by left-wing activists in terms of individual freedom and sexual liberty, the familial and communal aspects of gay life in America—and its contribution to and integration within the larger society—have largely been lost on the general public.

The religious right's limited understanding and mischaracterization of gays and lesbians represents the ultimate victory of fear over fact. By its obsessive focus on sexual behavior, it overlooks the depth and complexity of gay lives. To some evangelical activists, gays and lesbians can never compensate for the intrinsic "immorality" of their sexual orientation. As a "sin," it negates every other virtue, no matter how considerable. In a 1992 interview with The Advocate, Jay Grimstead, who as a dominion theologian contends that Christians are entitled to complete rule over all political institutions, explained that even a monogamous lesbian couple who contributed mightily to the larger community by caring for the homeless should be imprisoned or possibly even executed for their sexual sins. Heterosexual Americans, Grimstead explained, could simply be recruited to fill their vacant charitable role.

The evangelical drumbeat against gays and lesbians takes a heavy toll. The heat of the rhetoric has a dehumanizing effect on individuals, making them and their lives seem worthless both to others and themselves. Gay and lesbian youths, who often lack a community to protect them, are particularly vulnerable, succumbing to suicide at an alarming rate. In this hostile environment, it's not surprising that some people take the antigay rhetoric as license to lash out against gay people physically. Statistics collected by groups that monitor hate-inspired violence are staggering. According to Klan Watch, an organization of the Southern Poverty Law Center, gays and lesbians were the victims in over half the hate-inspired physical attacks in 1994, and gay men are the group most likely to be murdered. For gays and lesbians who do not conceal their identity, the fear of being assaulted on even the most gay-friendly streets in America remains palpable. Leaders of the religious right who are garrulous in their condemnation of homosexuality have skirted the all-too-real problem of violence against gays and lesbians, except to deny that they are responsible for it.

Having witnessed the currency of the victim card in contemporary politics, the religious right has sought to deal itself into the game, sometimes without any standing whatsoever. In an effort to portray her group as tolerant, Carolyn Cosby, head of Concerned Maine Families, a group that promoted an unsuccessful statewide antigay referendum in 1995, launched a campaign against gay- and straight-bashing in local churches that supported her antigay efforts. In doing so, Cosby implied that the two types of attacks are committed with roughly equal intensity and frequency. They are not in fact, although Cosby maintains that antigay violence statistics are inflated, in order to garner sympathy for gays and lesbians. There must be easier ways. While Cosby scrambles to cite even one incident of mistreatment of antigay activists, she pays short shrift to one of the most notorious cases of antigay violence in the country, which occurred in her own backyard. When he was attacked by taunting gay-bashers in Bangor in 1984, Charlie Howard, a twenty-three-year-old gay man, pleaded for his life. Instead, the gang threw him from a bridge into a river, killing him.

More often religious conservatives elevate their experiences with a few crank calls and legitimate, if sometimes raucous, demonstrations against their antigay views with Roman-style Christian-bashing. D. James Kennedy, a leading antigay minister in Florida, has repeatedly insisted that he is the true victim of the gay rights battle because he has been subjected to death threats. In 1994, Scott Lively, an Oregon Citizens Alliance activist, sought to have angry phone calls from opponents of his antigay views classified as a hate crime. Sometimes gay rights supporters do include harassment or the threat of violence, the cowardly action of intolerant individuals. But the threats have almost always remained just that. They are not the same as the epidemic of random physical attacks—some of which culminate in murder—

against gays and lesbians. Evangelical Christians are not being attacked in the streets on a daily basis because of who they are. Nor do their institutions regularly face the prospect of vandalism and arson, which have proved all too real for gay bars, bookstores, and churches over the last thirty years.

In responding to charges of intolerance, leaders of the religious right regularly invoke their supposed love and compassion for gays and lesbians, but only by wishing their very identity out of existence. "Christians feel compassion for homosexuals and sincerely desire that they receive Jesus Christ as their Lord and Savior and experience liberation from their lifestyle," wrote religious right leaders Tim and Beverly LaHaye in their 1994 book, *A Nation Without a Conscience*. The strategy of offering to bring gays and lesbians to the Lord in exchange for their renunciation of their sexual identity allows the LaHayes and other antigay activists to portray themselves as compassionate and to deny the deleterious effects of their rhetoric. Responsibility for antigay discrimination and violence, they suggest, must lie with gays and lesbians themselves.

⟶ Given the dismal state of political discourse in America, it may be hoping for too much for the gay rights discussion, let alone a presidential campaign, to be polite. But at least it should be fair, reflecting a commitment to accuracy, and civilized. Both sides have joined a battle for the hearts and minds of Americans, which goes beyond votes. With cynicism toward political arguments running high, demonstrations of these qualities will go far in impressing people about the sheer urgency of taking a stand on gay rights and in encouraging them to make their judgments informed. Both sides should keep in mind that not just the futures of the gay rights movement and conservative Christianity in America are at stake, as important as these remain. At issue is the very integrity of the political process itself. The struggle, after all, involves not just the combatants.

The current debate casts into clear relief deep fissures in American culture and politics—between individual freedom, a classically liberal cornerstone of the nation's legal system, and absolute adherence to a strict Christian moral code, whose roots advocates claim date back to the country's founding. The contest between gays and the religious right has come to signify a test not only of the core principles of American democracy, but also the basic tenets of Christianity. Underlying the debate are not just conservative and liberal views on sex and religion, but competing theories of justice. The way America decides to treat its most unpopular members has a lot to say about what kind of society we live in and which direction American democracy is headed.

Ralph Reed Jr., the executive director of the Christian Coalition, has spoken eloquently about the need to break away from the stereotype of the poor, easily led, inflexible evangelical. He is right when he says that any public debate requires decency, honesty, and respect for the other side. No matter what one thinks of their positions, evangelicals have long felt outside the political process, and their participation in it should be welcomed. Gay activists should recognize this and give their opponents credit for learning how to make the party system work for them.

But standards cut both ways, and Reed has been silent on the religious right's use of the most vicious stereotypes against gays and lesbians. Many of Reed's most fervent supporters, most notably his boss, Pat Robertson, continue a campaign by canard against gays and lesbians. Rabidly antigay fund-raising letters go out under the Christian Coalition letterhead on a regular basis, raking in millions of dollars for the group. Gays and lesbians, a June 1995 fund-raising letter charged, are "undermining" the bond between parents and their children by teaching that "homosexual love relationships can be as fulfilling as heterosexual relationships." That brand of antigay marketing is precisely the reason Robertson dealt so gingerly with a March 1995 hunger strike by Mel White, a gay onetime ghostwriter for Robertson who demanded that his former employer publicly denounce antigay violence. For Robertson and Reed, the stakes were high. If White had succeeded in raising the issue of the Christian Coalition's verbal gay-bashing to the level of a national issue, and had the press taken sufficient notice, it could have rocked the foundation of the group's thriving fund-raising machine. Perpetuation of antigay intolerance has become such a lucrative business, generating such a following among the groups' membership pool, that they cannot afford to step away from their hostility, lest they alienate their base. (In exchange for White's agreement to end his twenty-two-day hunger strike, which garnered little press attention, Robertson released a tepid statement criticizing antigay violence, which he later read on *The 700 Club,* the cable-television talk show he hosts.)

Acknowledging the Jewish community's growing alarm at the ascendancy of the religious right and Robertson's history of anti-Semitism, in April 1995 Reed delivered a conciliatory speech to members of the Anti-Defamation League, claiming that "to be an object of fear rather than an agent of love and healing is contrary to all that we aspire to be as people." The reference made Reed's failure to extend an olive branch to gays and lesbians all the more glaring. Robertson is nothing if not an "object of fear" among gays and lesbians. Reed himself has said little about gays and lesbians. In his 1994 book, *Politically Incorrect: The Emerging Faith Factor in American Politics,* Reed scolded gay activists for taking on Eugene Lumpkin, the minister dismissed from the San Francisco Human Rights Commission. But what Reed doesn't say in his book is that Lumpkin had suggested that gays and lesbians should be stoned for their sins. Were the defamation redirected, and the safety of conservative Christians thus so badly threatened, Reed would have been first in line to demand Lumpkin's ouster.

In his Anti-Defamation League speech, Reed pledged to teach the history of the Holocaust—"however painful it may be"—to the Christian Coalition's membership in order to help "insure that Jews are never again the target of hatred and discrimination." But those sentiments were undercut by Robertson's support for a movement among a small group of religious conservatives to pin blame for the Holocaust on homosexuals. "When lawlessness is abroad in the land, the same thing will happen here that happened in Nazi Germany," Robertson said on the September 14, 1994, *700 Club.* "Many of those people involved with Adolf Hitler were satanists. Many of them were homosexuals. The two seem to go together." While among the first brownshirts there was a small cadre of homosexuals (who were violently purged early on), no reputable historian has ever suggested that the Holocaust had any connection to Germany's gay rights movement. Gays did not determine the direction of the Third Reich; in fact, gays were among the groups that Hitler targeted for extermination, sacking the offices of an early gay-rights advocacy group; ensnaring, arresting, and imprisoning homosexuals; and instituting the pink-triangle insignia, which latter-day gays would reclaim as a symbol of empowerment. The religious right's use of the Holocaust is an attempt to wrest control of the ultimate symbol of political repression away from gay activists, not legitimate historical inquiry.

Thus, some views promulgated by the religious right have no place in the political debate. The line of legitimacy is crossed when religious conservatives call for the "elimination" of homosexuality, as Reed has, as if gays and lesbians were not people, inextricably connected to every institution vital to the nation's survival, their families, churches, and each other, but simply a scourge. One wing of religious conservatives, with ties to a number of prominent leaders of the religious right, is particularly open in its contempt for constitutional democracy and hearty in its call for a theocratic rule in which gays and lesbians would cease to exist. Dominion theologists, or reconstructionists, seek to replace the American legal system with laws derived from the Old Testament. The father of that movement, the Reverend R. J. Rushdoony, advocates instituting the death penalty for "practicing homosexuals," a term one doubts could ever be applied to heterosexuals, as well as abortionists. Robertson has never gone that far. But he has mused openly about the idea. At a 1980 prayer meeting, he told his audience, "You've got a country filled with homosexuals, people who are living together outside of wedlock, who are engaged in drunkenness, fornication, drug addiction, crime, and violence. Now what are you going to do with these people? Are you going to kill them all? Are you going to put them in jail? How are you going to enforce righteousness on them?"

Not all members of the religious right would subscribe to a militant call for theocracy and an antigay pogrom. But they don't necessarily distance themselves from such proposals either.

Robertson, for example, has close ties to Rushdoony, raising questions about the televangelist's commitment to the fair and nonviolent discussion of politics that he claims to want. For all his claims of moderation, Reed's credibility is undercut by the connection to someone so openly theocratic in his leanings. As much disregard for the political process as gay activists occasionally display, they do not go so far as to advocate the overthrow of the democratic system of government, which includes the separation of church and state, or the elimination of antidiscrimination protections for their opponents, enshrined most notably in the same 1965 Civil Rights Act in which gays still seek inclusion.

Reconstructionism may be the most extreme example of the antidemocratic tendencies of the religious right, but it is not the only one. As much as the religious right trumpets the antigay ballot measures as triumphs of democracy, such initiatives are merely facades. True, the method allows issues to be brought directly before the voters. But the intent to harness majoritarian will is essentially antidemocratic, fencing out one group in particular from the political process forever and casting the durability of every minority's legal standing into doubt. Statewide measures are particularly repressive because they inhibit local political autonomy, where personal relationships between gays and the rest of the community, including evangelical churches, have the most potential for fomenting mutually agreeable resolutions on exactly how to protect gays and lesbians from discrimination, harassment, and violence. At any given point in the country's history, other minorities whose legal protections from discrimination would now never be subjected to such campaigns could just as readily have lost a direct vote aimed at them. This includes evangelicals, who, as Reed himself points out, have long suffered bigotry and discrimination. Evangelical activists would do well to consider how the vehicle they have commandeered against gays and lesbians could be applied against themselves.

Worse than the ballot measures are the arguments employed to promote them. The "special rights" slogan is as effective as it is dishonest. The shorthand term *gay rights* generally refers to ordinances that prohibit discrimination on the basis of sexual orientation in housing, employment, and public accommodations. In other words, you cannot be fired if your boss finds out you are gay (or, for that matter, straight). The laws uniformly provide broad exemptions for religious institutions, so that they do not have to obey a law that may run counter to their faith's traditions or beliefs. *Gay rights*, although a handy phrase, makes the legislation look far more sweeping than it actually is, and the religious right plays up that misapprehension. Because voters know little about the dry intricacies of the ordinances, the religious right can get away with raising the specter of quotas and conflating them with affirmative action policies and far more sweeping civil rights legislation. In fact, no reputable gay leader has ever advocated that affirmative action laws be extended to gays and lesbians. But gay groups have contributed to the problem. Every time an ordinance passes, gay leaders describe it as a huge victory for gay rights, when in fact it should be just one more step in the ongoing education of the public.

The media has failed in its responsibility to clear up these misunderstandings, much less elucidate the complexity of the debate and the possibility of common ground between the opposing forces. Newspapers from the *Colorado Springs Gazette-Telegraph* to the *New York Times* have failed to explain the elementary distinction between antidiscrimination protections and gay rights or special rights. Only a handful of reporters cover religious or gay issues on a regular basis, and few are well versed on the intersection of the two. Confronted by two worlds that are alien to them, journalists too often turn to the conventional wisdom about their subjects, which is pat and superficial, instead of delving below the surface to see what actually motivates the activists. Alternately cowed by the fear of offending either group and ignorant of the complexities of the topic, journalists rarely raise tough questions about the intemperate political tactics of each. Within the evangelical and gay press, the situation is not much better. Too much of the reporting and writing by both sides is intended to celebrate the cause rather than cast a cold eye on the players or strategies involved. Caught up in a culture war, each side is loath to show vulnerability by admitting mistakes, much less adopt a conciliatory tone to facilitate negotiations.

Ultimately, the religious right's antigay crusade boils down to reasserting the right not to associate with homosexuals in diverse areas of American life, from the military to the workplace, a right they do not apply nor dare advocate with regard to any other minority group. Such reckless arguments, going far beyond recognizing the right of religious people to make up their minds on matters of morality, improperly establish discrimination as a theological imperative, thus rendering gay activists' suspicion of religious arguments in public policy all the more well-founded and driving the wedge between the groups still deeper. Similarly, antidiscrimination protections, which have also come under attack from gay conservatives, embody, for the religious right, the federal government's propensity to force homosexuality on an unwilling citizenry. But the logical extension of that argument is that gays and lesbians should be denied a roof over their heads and the ability to earn a living. That position is not only cruel, but represents an abdication of the responsibility all Americans share to learn to live and work with one another. This responsibility, again, however, cuts both ways, as gays and lesbians also must learn to respect the sensibilities of their evangelical neighbors and coworkers, refusing to succumb to stereotypical Southern accents in lampooning antigay adherents just as those ignorant about gay people should not stoop to mimicking gays with a deliberate lisp.

Neither the religious right nor the gay movement has been fully able to acknowledge the challenge of those who question the standard left-right dichotomy of the debate or to recognize their constituencies' severely flagging interest in waging a culture war. As the conservative evangelical leader Tony Campolo has demonstrated, it is indeed possible to adhere to a strict interpretation of biblical dictates against sex outside of traditional, heterosexual marriage while granting that, as hardworking, tax-paying, God-fearing American citizens, gays and lesbians deserve an equal place in the military and in all aspects of American life. Campolo, who has nearly impeccable credentials among religious conservatives, believes that some religious-right activists find refuge for their reflexive prejudice in the Bible. "It is too easy for any of us out of intense emotion to use Scripture in inexact ways to affirm what we believe to be right or to condemn what we believe to be wrong," he wrote in *20 Hot Potatoes Christians Are Afraid to Touch,* which was published in 1988. "The fact that homosexuality has become such an overriding concern for many contemporary preachers may be more a reflection of the homophobia of the church than the result of the emphasis of Scripture." Campolo's measured stance, however, satisfies neither evangelicals, who consider it heretical, nor gay activists, who are offended that he continues to insist that homosexuality is a sin. After publicly advocating that the military ban on gay and lesbian service members be lifted, Campolo was inundated with criticism from conservative evangelicals, who seemed more concerned that he was calling into question the nearly unanimous opposition to equal rights for homosexuals on the religious right than about the merits of his argument. Gay activists who say they're only seeking "tolerance" while refusing to settle for anything less than "approval" risk precluding the possibility of finding common ground with the religious right for the sake of an admirable, but unobtainable, principle.

As the nation grapples with gay rights in the future, we hope that this book will have helped to explain the seemingly disparate pieces of the battle over "gay rights" and to show their interconnections. We hope to have shed some light on the unacknowledged complexities of the debate. If the religious right and the gay movement are ever to enjoy the mainstream political acceptance that they seek, they are going to have to put aside their more destructive urges and engage in the hard work of politics: educating the public about the merits of their positions. Otherwise we will only see more ugly skirmishes where the participants go at one another and forget everyone else. Even if one side should emerge victorious, its integrity will have been so besmirched by its behavior that its triumph will be hollow. There's no honor in winning a culture war but losing the hearts and minds of a nation.

Index